CAMBRIDGE SERIES ON
HUMAN-COMPUTER INTERACTION 8

The MUSE Method for Usability Engineering

Cambridge Series on Human-Computer Interaction

Managing Editor
Professor J. Long, Ergonomics Unit, University College, London.

Editorial Board
Dr. P. Barnard, Applied Psychology Unit, Cambridge
Professor T. Bosser, University of Münster
Professor W. Buxton, Xerox EuroPARC, Cambridge.
Dr. J. M. Carroll, University of Virginia
Dr. J. Grudin, University of California, Irvine
Dr. T. Landauer, University of Colorado
Professor T. W. Malone, Massachusetts Institute of Technology
Professor H. Thimbleby, University of Stirling
Professor T. Winograd, Stanford University

Titles in the Series

The MUSE Method for Usability Engineering

Kee Yong Lim
Nanyang Technological University, Singapore

John Long
University Collge, London

CAMBRIDGE
UNIVERSITY PRESS

CAMBRIDGE UNIVERSITY PRESS
Cambridge, New York, Melbourne, Madrid, Cape Town, Singapore, São Paulo, Delhi

Cambridge University Press
The Edinburgh Building, Cambridge CB2 8RU, UK

Published in the United States of America by Cambridge University Press, New York

www.cambridge.org
Information on this title: www.cambridge.org/9780521479998

First published 1994
This digitally printed version 2009

A catalogue record for this publication is available from the British Library

ISBN 978-0-521-47494-8 hardback
ISBN 978-0-521-47999-8 paperback

Contents

PART FOUR: THE INTEGRATION OF HUMAN FACTORS WITH STRUCTURED SOFTWARE ENGINEERING METHODS 213

Chapter 7: Pre-requisites and Examples of the Integration of Human Factors with Structured Software Engineering Methods 214

PART FIVE: SYNOPSIS 261

Chapter 8: Assessment and Future Development of MUSE and MUSE*/JSD 262

List of Figures

Preface

We (Ergonomists) borrow and invent techniques to serve our special needs.

A. Chapanis, 1990.

Current human factors input to system development is effected through methods, tools and guidelines. Although the input prompts the consideration of human factors concerns during system development, reports have highlighted inadequacies with respect to the scope, granularity, format and timing of the contributions (see Smith, 1986; Chapanis and Burdurka, 1990; Sutcliffe, 1989; etc.).

To improve the effectiveness of human factors input to system development, problems with existing approaches need to be examined. Such an examination would:

(1) highlight requirements pertaining to the role of human factors in system development; such as the concerns of the *'who', 'what', 'when'* and *'how'* of human factors input;
(2) support the enhancement of existing approaches for human factors input;
(3) facilitate the specification of new and more promising solutions to existing problems of human factors input.

This book argues that current problems of input to system development cannot be solved by early human factors involvement alone. Instead, it is emphasised that the problems would be solved only by ensuring early human factors involvement that is then continued throughout system development. To achieve this objective, human factors designers must also contribute actively to system specification as opposed to system evaluation only. In addition, the requirements and activities of human factors specification should be made explicit. Thus, both software engineering and human factors needs may be represented and accommodated appropriately by an overall system development agenda. Intersecting design concerns between the disciplines may also be identified and addressed more effectively in this way.

To support the derivation of an overall system development agenda, current conceptions of the design cycles of the two disciplines need to be examined. Since the conceptions are instantiated at a lower level as methods, an overall agenda may be expressed more specifically by integrating explicitly defined methods from the individual disciplines. Such an integration would facilitate the identification of important design inter-dependencies between the disciplines. Furthermore, complementary roles may be specified to co-ordinate better the scope, process and notation of software engineering and human factors design. Thus, design collaboration and communication (especially if a common notation could be used) between designers from the disciplines may be supported more effectively.

Methodological integration is facilitated if the design scope, process and notation of the methods are well defined. Such characteristics are found in a class of software engineering methods commonly referred to as structured analysis and design methods. Unfortunately, similar methods do not exist for human factors. In particular, its methods tend to be unstructured, and are generally focused only on later stages of system development.[1] Consequently, a pre-requisite for methodological integration is the development of a reasonably complete and structured human factors method. Since software engineering methods are already well established, it would be appropriate (for the purposes of methodological integration) to examine their requirements for human factors support. Such requirements should be accommodated by the structured human factors method to be developed. Thus, methodological integration entails the development, test and integration of a structured human factors method, followed by its integration with particular structured software engineering methods. This book describes such an undertaking, namely the development of **MUSE** (**M**ethod for **US**ability **E**ngineering) and its subsequent integration with the Jackson System Development method.

The preceding concerns are addressed in this book as follows:

Part One: The Need for a Structured Human Factors Method to Support System Development
This part describes problems of existing approaches for human factors input to system development. The potential of structured analysis and design methods as a solution to the problems is examined and compared with other approaches for human factors input. An appropriate solution is then proposed; namely the development and integration of a structured human factors method with a similar software engineering method.

---

[1] The imbalance in scope derives from the historically late recruitment of human factors to system development.

<u>Part Two: Development and Overview of MUSE – A Structured Human Factors Method</u>
General requirements entailed by the development of a structured human factors method are described. A scheme for method development is then presented. In accordance with the scheme, a survey of existing conceptions of human factors design is described. The report of the survey is followed by an account of the derivation of a more complete conception of human factors design. Using the conception, a structured human factors method may then be developed. MUSE, a product of such a development, is then introduced.

<u>Part Three: Detailed Account of MUSE – A Structured Human Factors Method</u>
The three chapters comprising this part of the book provide a detailed account of MUSE.

<u>Part Four: The Integration of Human Factors with Structured Software Engineering Methods</u>
General requirements and pre-requisites of methodological integration are set out in this part. MUSE*/JSD, an integration of MUSE with the Jackson System Development (JSD) method, is then presented. Design inter-dependencies between the methods are highlighted. Subsequently, the integration of human factors with other structured software engineering methods is reviewed and compared with MUSE*/JSD.

<u>Part Five: Synopsis</u>
Four concerns are addressed in this part of the book; namely how MUSE and MUSE*/JSD should be assessed, the results of assessments, the status of MUSE and MUSE*/JSD, and potential developments of the methods.

In summary, the book contributes to the design community in the following ways:

(a) Developers of human factors methods. The book describes how similar methods may be developed. Parts One, Two, Four and Five of this book would be directly relevant to this group of readers.
(b) Human factors designers. The book describes a structured human factors method, MUSE, that empowers designers to assume a more active role in the *specification* of human-computer systems. This group of readers would find Parts Two and Three of the book particularly helpful.
(c) Software engineers involved in inter-disciplinary design teams. Parts One to Four of the book review the main concerns of inter-disciplinary design, and provide an explicit insight to software engineers who may need to be more aware of human factors design activities. Similarly, software engineers involved with method development will also find the book of

interest. The integration of human factors with a number of established structured software engineering methods (Part Four), may be particularly relevant to this group of readers.[2]

Kee Yong Lim,
Nanyang Technological University, Singapore.
(previously at University College London, UK)

John Long,
University College London, UK.

Note:
Both authors of this book have been involved and committed to the method and its development from its inception. The ordering of authors' names reflects their relative effort and contribution to the work.

---

[2] Parts One to Three should still be read, since the context for methodological integration is established in the earlier chapters.

Acknowledgements

Our gratitude is extended to Nigel Silcock and Paul Walsh for their indirect contributions to parts of this work. Particular thanks are also due to Nigel for (unknowingly) being the first 'subject' in 'informal tests' on the learnability of MUSE.

We are grateful to Andy Whitefield and Andrew Life for their encouragement and effort in reviewing an early version of MUSE. Thanks are also due to Linda Herman for her meticulous proof-reading of the final manuscript, and to other members of the Ergonomics Unit (University College London) for providing such a stimulating and pleasant work environment.

We are happy to acknowledge the Procurement Executive (Ministry of Defence), for supporting our work on early versions of Parts Three and Four of this book.[3] Special acknowledgements are due to individual members of staff[4] at CA2 (Royal Armaments Research and Development Establishment, RARDE), for their contributions in priming work on those parts of the book.

Last but not least, we thank close friends whose encouragement and companionship made life during this period a balanced and enriching experience. Not forgetting our families also, since without their love and support, the fruition of this work would remain a dream.

---

[3] It should be noted that views expressed in this book are those of the authors, and should not be attributed to the Ministry of Defence.

[4] Regulations of the Ministry of Defence do not permit citation of their names.

*This book is dedicated to Gan Sok Lan. Her
endless sacrifice, patience and love as a mother
made this book possible.*

PART ONE:

THE NEED FOR A STRUCTURED HUMAN FACTORS METHOD TO SUPPORT SYSTEM DEVELOPMENT

1
On Human Factors Contributions to the Development of Interactive Systems

.......in the design domain we can never know enough.

Rosson, 1985

If at first you know where you are, and whither you are tending, you will better know what to do and how to do it.

Abraham Lincoln, 1809–1865

The primary objective of this chapter is to characterise the problem addressed by MUSE,[1] a structured human factors Method for USability Engineering. To this end, existing problems of human factors contributions to system development are reviewed; namely, existing contributions are poorly timed and contextualised to the support required at different stages of the system[2] design cycle. As a result, the relevance, format and granularity of human factors contributions are not optimal for effective uptake during design. By establishing the nature of the problems, promising solutions may then be assessed. Arguments supporting a structured analysis and design method, such as MUSE, are thus exposed.

1.1. General Problems of Human Factors Contribution to System Development

Recent developments in computer technology (e.g. the availability and affordability of personal computers and the rapid diversification in computer applications) have resulted in

---

[1] MUSE: to reflect and ponder *(about Human Factors);* a goddess that inspires (design) creativity; a Greek goddess that protects a specific science *(Human Factors).*

[2] The term 'system' implies a user-computer system that carries out tasks in a particular environment to perform work. In this context, human factors is concerned with user behaviours as they interact with computers, while software engineering is concerned with computer behaviours as they interact with users. A system may comprise one or more sub-systems which execute tasks that bring about desired changes in state of real world objects in the domain of application (Dowell and Long, 1989).

a shift from mainframes to personal computers. Today, such interactive computers have made significant inroads into both the workplace and the home. Consequently, the user base of computers has widened considerably.

The extended user base, together with market forces, highlighted the importance of designing computer applications that are appropriate in *both* functionality and usability. The success of Macintosh computers is an example (see also Shackel, 1985 and 1986b; CCTA (Draft) Report, 1988, Annex 1; Shuttleworth, 1987). In addition, it was recognised that poor usability may result in:

(a) greater training requirements. This problem is particularly serious since the information technology work force is highly mobile;
(b) incomplete utilisation of the software application (Hirschheim, 1985; Stevens, 1983);
(c) failure of the system to achieve its intended purpose (Underwood, 1987; Lucas, 1975);
(d) slower than anticipated uptake of information technology in the workplace (Fähnrich et al. 1984; Eason and Cullen, 1988).

In short, poorly designed systems do not compete well in the market. The importance of user testing, and hence human factors, was thus recognised. This recognition established the recruitment of human factors for usability *evaluation* (Rosson, 1987). As a result, human factors techniques focused on the later stages of system development. This emphasis on human factors evaluation of specific designs prevailed until Software Engineering design conceptions became more established. The latter developments were prompted by the following events:

(a) the advent of more powerful computers led to the development of larger and more complex systems. Such developments required longer term projects with multiple designers (i.e. an emphasis on design teams as opposed to individual designers or even hackers), and multiple design deliverables, with a greater propensity to over-run project deadlines;
(b) the penetration of software applications into novel domains (which were ill defined) as opposed to a direct computerisation of manual systems (Benyon and Skidmore, 1987; Galliers, 1984);
(c) the emergence of expert systems and artificial intelligence.

These events prompted the following requirements for system development:

(i) to facilitate the 'correct' conduct of system development. In particular, the development process should encourage systematic analysis and specification to support better and more effective design management. For instance, intermediate design modifications and post-delivery maintenance might thus be supported more efficiently;

(ii) to ensure the development of a valid or 'correct' system. Thus, the development process should include a reliable means for the capture and confirmation of user requirements, and for the continuous verification of design specifications;

(iii) to support greater design consistency and throughput. Thus, the development process should facilitate the development of computer-based tools to reduce system delivery times and the employment of greater human power to handle large scale projects.

In turn, these requirements prompted the development of specific Software Engineering solutions, namely:

(a) explicit design principles and techniques, e.g. delaying design commitment, incremental design, rapid prototyping, software re-usability;

(b) executable specifications and high level languages, e.g. new generation languages (Fourth and Fifth Generation Languages);

(c) formal notations and methods, e.g. Z, Communicating Sequential Processes (CSP), Calculus of Communicating Systems (CSP), Vienna Development Method (VDM);

(d) structured analysis and design methods, e.g. Structured Systems Analysis and Design Method (SSADM), Jackson System Development (JSD) method;

(e) computer-based tools, e.g. Computer Aided Software Engineering (CASE), Integrated Project Support Environment (IPSE).

These solutions support software engineers in a number of ways. For instance, more reliable specification may accrue through the proveability afforded by formal methods; more efficient and effective utilisation of design resources may accrue by using directly executable notations and computer-based tools (such as code generators and consistency checkers); better design management and more systematic analysis may accrue by using structured analysis and design methods; etc.

The above developments in Software Engineering also established more explicit conceptions of the system design process. Specifically, the design concerns of each stage of system development were defined more explicitly. Despite significant design contributions from human factors during this period, it became apparent that its involvement only at the evaluation stage was inadequately effective in supporting an efficient development of a valid system. In particular, late involvement often results in poor realisation of human factors contributions, since inputs may become unacceptably difficult to incorporate at later stages of system development. This problem may be referred to generally as the *'too-little-too-late'* problem of human factors input to system development. An account of the problem follows.

Contributions may be *'too late'* because human factors activities do not presently constitute a basic component of design specification. The lateness of human factors involvement makes it more difficult to formulate contributions, since information on decisions made during conceptual design (e.g. rationale) are often documented poorly. As a result, human factors recommendations may be incorporated into the design ineffectively. In the worst case, the recommendations may not be acted upon (Rosson, 1987) because the desired modifications might be too extensive[3] and hence too difficult and expensive to implement. Figure 1-1 shows this proportional relationship between the cost of design modifications and the stages of system development at which they are undertaken (Böhm, 1981). The end result of these difficulties is that the possibilities for design modification may become restricted due to inter-locking dependencies (Grudin et al. 1987; Bury, 1984). In other words, developed designs become 'frozen' and are thus more resistant to change. Consequently, late human factors involvement may also result in contributions that comprise little more than advice, i.e. *'too little'*.The overall result is often an inefficient design cycle skewed disproportionately towards design maintenance. For instance, up to

Figure 1-1: Cost of Fixing Design Errors Relative to the System Design Cycle

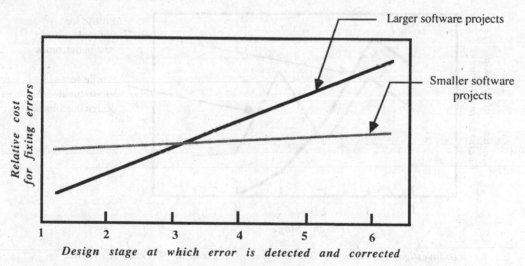

Design stage at which error is detected and corrected

1: Requirements;   2: Design;   3: Code;   4: Development Test;   5: Acceptance Test;   6: Operation

---

[3] This situation may be a direct result of early errors becoming magnified through successive design stages, i.e. system specifications may be degraded progressively (Alvey MMI Workshop Report, 1984).

70% of project resources have been reported to be consumed by design maintenance[4] alone (Böhm, 1976 and 1981; Multi-User Computing, 1989, pg. 20). In addition, large software projects cost, on average, twice as much as their initial budgets. Thus, despite frequent reports on the potential of human factors for reducing maintenance costs (e.g. Norman, 1986; Rubinstein and Hersh, 1984), its impact has yet to be realised in full. Other accounts report that large software projects are usually completed a year late; and a quarter of them are never completed at all (Multi-User Computing, 1989, p. 22).

One reason for such non-optimal design outcomes may be inferred from Figure 1-2, which shows that, for an approximately equivalent amount of effort (represented by the area under each curve), adequate human factors input at early stages of system development is more effective at ensuring a desirable design outcome. In addition, the figure indicates that an unfavourable design outcome may not be avoided by investing greater human factors efforts (for design modifications) at later stages of system development. Although minor problems may be fixed readily at these stages, it may not be possible to accommodate major and more wide ranging or extensive design problems.

Figure 1-2: Relating Design Outcomes to the Duration of Human Factors Involvement at Various Stages of System Development (after Lundell and Notess, 1991)

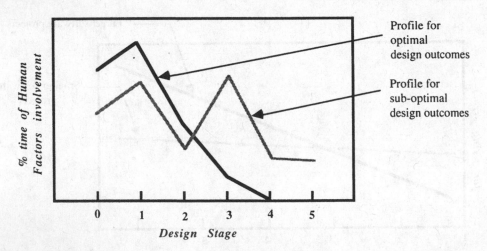

0: Investigate; 1: Design; 2: Prototype; 3: Implement; 4: Test; 5: Release.

---

[4] Design maintenance, by definition, includes corrective actions resulting from design errors, and modifications, and/or enhancements arising from changes in initial design requirements (Fitzgerald, 1988).

Thus, the 'too-little-too-late' problem prompted a growing awareness that *early* and *continued* design involvement throughout the system design cycle is a necessity if effective human factors contributions are to be ensured (Alvey Human Interface Committee Report, 1987; Eason and Cullen, 1988). Early design involvement ensures more effective human factors input because human issues predominate at early stages of system design (see Figure 1-3). By defining these issues earlier, user requirements may be defined appropriately to constrain later design stages that largely concern the device (Alvey MMI Workshop Report, 1984, p. 20). Continuous involvement then ensures a correct translation and timely incorporation of human factors inputs into the design. It also ensures that the inputs are contextually relevant to the design concerns addressed at each stage of system development.

In other words, to achieve appropriate system usability and functionality, human factors should be involved in design *specification* as opposed to only design *evaluation*. For instance, human factors involvement at design specification would ensure that design concerns that pertain to user goals, tasks and abilities are represented and addressed appropriately during functional design. Human factors design contributions should therefore include the analysis, specification, implementation and evaluation of systems; i.e. its contributions should permeate the entire system design cycle (see Alvey Human Interface Committee Report[5] 1987, p. 32; Alvey MMI Workshop Report 1984, pp. 37 and 39; Buxton et al. 1983). In this way, human factors inputs may be made at a stage where their impact is greatest (see Figures 1-3 and 1-4). A better uptake of contributions may thus accrue.

Unfortunately, these positive developments could not be supported directly because human factors being a relatively young discipline, was led by Software Engineering requirements. Thus, there was a time lag between the demand for more extensive human factors support for system development and the required extensions of its design support capabilities (see also Underwood 1987; CCTA (Draft) Report 1988, Annex 1; Galliers, 1984). Specifically, to improve the effectiveness of existing human factors contributions, the following developments and extensions would be required:

(i) the means of human factors design input (e.g. standards, methods, etc.) should be configured more specifically to support each stage of system development. For instance, existing human factors techniques could be made more explicit and complete to support the development of computer-based tools;

---

[5] This report went even further to emphasise that unless human factors is incorporated in all phases of the system design cycle, its impact would be insignificant.

Figure 1-3: Ideal Effort Ratios for Human and Machine Design Relative to the System Design Cycle (Adapted from Alvey MMI Workshop Report, 1984, p. 20)

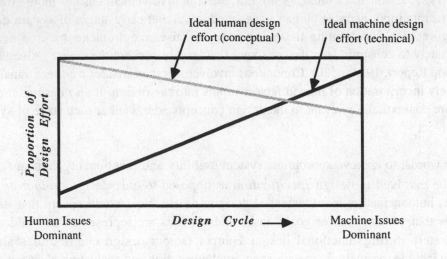

Figure 1-4: Relating the Impact of Human Factors to Various Phases of System Development (after Moraal and Kragt, 1990)

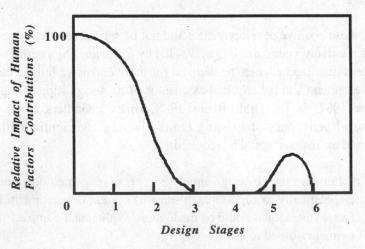

1: Conceptual Phase; 2: Prototype; 3: Detailed Version;
4: Production; 5: Evaluation; 6: Operation.

(ii) human factors design processes should be made more explicit to elevate its practice from craft towards engineering (Long and Dowell, 1989). For instance, current human factors inputs tend to focus on what should be done, but how design requirements could be met, however, is often left implicit or under-specified (Sutcliffe, 1989). Thus, Klein and Newman (1987) reported human factors to be 'lacking in methodology';

(iii) human factors descriptions should be more specific to rectify existing problems in their translation into design specifications. For instance, existing human factors notations are insufficiently developed to accommodate more complex task descriptions (Lim and Long, 1993a and b). In addition, the format of existing human factors inputs does not support inter-disciplinary design communication (Mantei and Teorey, 1988). Thus, effective design collaboration between human factors designers and software engineers may be thwarted. Consequently, appropriate notations should be developed for human factors specification to ensure that the content, format and granularity of its inputs are pertinent to the system development context;

(iv) the scope of human factors contribution to system development should be extended to rectify the historically narrow coverage of the system design cycle (ALV/MMI/PRJ/143, 1988, pg. 3). In particular, Sutcliffe (1989) reported that existing human factors techniques rarely address system specification from user requirements to display screen design. For instance, task analysis techniques for design evaluation are well established, but techniques for design specification remain largely undeveloped. To address these problems, the conception of human factors contribution to system development needs to be more complete and comprehensive;

(v) mismatches between Software Engineering and Human Factors design approaches and activities should be reconciled, e.g. system design approaches engendered by machine-centered versus user-centered perspectives. The mismatches arose largely because previous solutions for supporting system development were formulated independently by the two disciplines. For instance, Grudin et al. (1987) observed that human factors is either represented inadequately or omitted from the Software Engineering literature. Human factors has also been 'perceived as irrelevant to system development' (Klein and Newman, 1987). Thus, to facilitate wider human factors design involvement, its solutions for improving system development should be intersected *explicitly* with existing Software Engineering solutions. Human Computer Interaction, as a discipline, is compatible with this perspective (see Long and Dowell, 1989; [6] Carroll and Campbell, 1986[7]).

---

[6] Human Computer Interaction is conceptualised as comprising Human Factors and Software Engineering sub-disciplines (Long and Dowell, 1989).

[7] Carroll and Campbell's (1986) conception of Human Computer Interaction comprises Computer Science and Psychology. The difference may be attributed to the scope assumed for the component disciplines.

The above considerations were summarised aptly by Carroll and Campbell (1986) as follows:

> *Human-computer interaction.......will favour inter-disciplinary co-operation between psychology and computer science......will not sustain approaches that are too low level, too limited in scope, too late, and too difficult to apply in real design..............*

Having characterised general problems of human factors input to system development, existing means for its input should be assessed more specifically to determine *what* enhancements may be necessary to improve their effectiveness. To this end, three complementary means of human factors input are reviewed, namely:

(a) principles, guidelines and standards. These provide mainly declarative[8] human factors input;
(b) computer-based tools which provide either procedural[9] or declarative human factors input;
(c) techniques and methods. These provide mainly procedural human factors input.

Following the review, greater emphasis will be placed on human factors design contributions delivered via techniques and methods. The latter emphasis is chosen because a member of its class (namely structured analysis and design methods) could provide a system design framework that supports the development and recruitment of declarative means of human factors input and computer-based tools. In particular, the desired framework may be inferred from the explicitly defined design scope, process and representation of structured analysis and design methods. Thus, requirements for human factors support at various stages of system development may be established. On this basis, individual means of human factors input could be enhanced and set appropriately against specific system development contexts. Similarly, complementary means of input could be organised and recruited more effectively. By maximising their symbiosis, the weaknesses of individual means of design input may be compensated appropriately, while strengths are exploited jointly. For instance, complementary means for procedural and declarative human factors input may be defined at specific stages of the system design cycle.

Following these considerations, a case may then be made for the development of a

---

[8] This form of human factors input is explained in greater detail in Sub-section 1.2.

[9] See Footnote 8.

structured analysis and design method to support human factors specification. In addition, the potential benefits of integrating Human Factors and Software Engineering methods are discussed. An account of these concerns is provided in Chapters Two and Seven.

In summary, the remaining sub-sections of this chapter are concerned with the following:

(i) to review existing means of human factors input;
(ii) to highlight typical problems of the individual means of input reviewed;
(iii) to indicate how existing input means could be extended/modified to address the problems that have been highlighted;
(iv) to examine the integration of Human Factors and Software Engineering methods as a solution to the problems that have been highlighted. A comparison is then made between methodological integration and the solutions proposed in (iii).

1.2.   Existing Means of Human Factors Contribution to System Development

Existing means of human factors input may be characterised and assessed in terms of their scope (subject matter) and process (delivery) (see Figure 1-5). A brief account of these characteristics follows:

(a) Scope (subject matter) – declarative-procedural dimension. If the subject matter of human factors inputs is concerned directly with attributes of the artefact to be designed, its support is termed declarative (or substantive). Generally, the requirements of declarative design input comprise the provision of information that is:

• correct and relevant to the design concerns at hand, i.e. the accuracy and scope of the information provided should match the context applicable at each stage of system design;

• presented in a format that is easily accessible and concise, i.e. the information provided should be presented appropriately using suitable notations and documentation schemes;

• expressed at a level of description appropriate to the design concerns at hand, i.e. the granularity of the information provided should not be pitched at too high or too low a level of description.

Alternatively, human factors input may comprise procedural (or methodological) guidance on how the design of an artefact should be developed. For instance, to support problem analysis and design specification, a set of intermediate design representations and transformations may be prescribed. Generally, the requirements of procedural design input are as follows:

• they should be compatible with established design practices;
• they should cover the system design cycle adequately;
• they should be expressed appropriately to support design reasoning and the management of design complexity. Prescriptions pitched at too low a level of expression may impose undesirable constraints on designers (e.g. methods have been criticised for hampering designer creativity), and limit their applicability across different design scenarios. Conversely, prescriptions pitched at too high a level of expression may result in inadequate design guidance, e.g. some methods are no more than checklists.

Figure 1-5:   Basic Characteristics of Existing Means for Effecting Human Factors Design Contributions

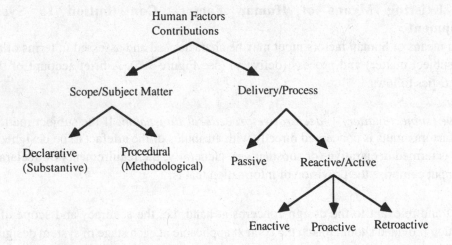

It should be noted that declarative support is invariably required in some form, since procedural support is not a substitute for substantive human factors knowledge.

(b) Process (delivery) – passive-active dimension. This dimension describes how and when human factors contributions could be delivered during system development, e.g. handbooks are passive in their delivery, while computers and consultants would be active or interactive to various degrees. Active input can influence system development in three ways, namely:

• retroactively (or 'after-the-fact' intervention), e.g. human factors audit;

- proactively (or 'before-the-fact' intervention or feed-forward prescription), e.g. design handbooks;
- enactively (or 'during-the-fact' intervention), e.g. participative design.

Ideally, a means of human factors input should support design actively to ensure the timeliness, relevance and granularity of human factors contributions, with respect to design support needs at specific stages of system development. In other words, there is a need to consider:

(1) *what* human factors inputs would be required to specify and satisfy requirements of end-users of the target system, i.e. the need to specify a (reasonably) complete and explicit *scope* of human factors contribution to interactive system development;
(2) *how* and *when* human factors design products should be derived and incorporated during system development; i.e. to support software engineers as users of human factors design inputs, the *processes* and *timing* for incorporating the inputs should be defined explicitly. Furthermore, by contextualising human factors inputs to existing Software Engineering conceptions of the process of system development, better understanding and conceptual cohesion may result. Thus, the uptake of human factors contributions (and their eventual realisation in the design artefact) may be expected to improve.

Since the *process* (how and when) and *product* (form and content) of human factors input are equally important concerns for improving uptake of its design contributions, attention should be directed both at incrementing human factors design knowledge (i.e. to extend its scope), and at improving its delivery and presentation.

Bearing in mind the preceding considerations, specific means of human factors input will now be assessed.

First, the means of input comprising design guidelines, principles and standards, provides predominantly declarative human factors support (see Williams 1989; Smith and Mosier 1984). The declarative content supported by this means of design input is wide ranging, since its objective is to provide substantive knowledge to cover the entire system design cycle. Individual classes within this means of design input may be distinguished by specific traits. For instance, design guidelines in general tend to be detailed and lengthy. Their focus can, however, be either vague or specific. In contrast, design principles tend to be simple, compact and general (McKenzie, 1988; Norman, 1988). Both of these classes of design inputs may be delivered informally as advice, and/or implemented explicitly as local house-styles. Alternatively, they may be legislated into national and/or international standards.

Although this means of delivering design inputs has supported significantly human factors contributions to system design, a number of problems have been reported. The problems may be summarised as follows:

(a) Poor scope and format of human factors contributions. The contributions tend to be presented at either too high or too low a level of description. As a result, the design recommendations become respectively too vague to provide effective guidance, or too rigid and specific for application across different design scenarios (Smith 1986; Chapanis and Budurka 1990; Hirsch 1984). In both cases, extensive interpretation, adaptation and extrapolation would be required to apply the human factors recommendations presented via this means of design input (Klein and Brezovic 1986). To aggravate matters, Smith (1986) reported that designers who are not adequately competent in human factors may not even recognise the need to adapt the declarative content of these inputs. These problems highlight important limitations in this means of design input.

(b) Conflicting human factors advice may be offered. As the declarative content of this means of input become more comprehensive and detailed, contradictory human factors advice may arise (Maguire 1982; Alexander 1987). In general, guidance on how such contradictions may be resolved is not included with this means of human factors input (Marshall 1984). In addition, such contradictions may not be discovered if the reference manual has been collated and compiled incrementally over a period of time.

(c) Poor accessibility of human factors information. This means of human factors input is difficult to use (Rogers and Pegden 1977; Eason and Cullen 1988). In particular, the reference manual quickly becomes voluminous and daunting (Norman 1988). For example, Smith and Mosier (1984) identified more than 600 guidelines for user interface design alone. Thus, the reference manual tends to become part of the back-drop of design, and the human factors inputs overlooked (McClelland 1990).

(d) Questionable validity of human factors recommendations. The validity of human factors standards may be doubtful, since existing knowledge may not be adequate to support wide ranging imposition (Smith 1986). Furthermore, existing human factors standards are not testable (Chapanis and Budurka 1990). Effective enforcement may thus be contentious.

(e) Poor mapping of human factors inputs to the system design context. Recent reports have indicated that system developers frequently fail to make relevant human factors considerations at appropriate stages of system development (McKenzie 1988; Smith 1986). In response to the problem, a common exhortation is that human factors advice should be sought earlier in the system design cycle. However, in the absence of an explicitly structured framework of human factors design, judgements on what constitutes appropriate and early human factors input remain subjective. It may be noted presently that, at the highest level, a structured design framework may specify a human factors design life-cycle; while at the lowest level, a structured analysis and design method may be defined to support human factors design.

(f) The declarative emphasis of this means of input may encourage a narrow view of human factors recruitment. For instance, human factors designers may be recruited as 'auditing' consultants as opposed to active participants in design specification. Thus, an effective and efficient address of human factors concerns may not be possible due to late design input.

(g) Project resources allocated may not be adequate to accommodate comprehensive consideration and implementation of human factors inputs. In other words, insufficient managerial commitment to human factors, and/or the exclusion of human factors from the system design agenda, may result in the imposition of unrealistically tight schedules that preclude a comprehensive address of relevant guidelines, principles and standards.

For these reasons, this means of human factors input may be considered restrictive. For instance, designers have been reported to view such inputs as mere formalities at best, and a hindrance at worst (Smith, 1986).

To summarise, this means of human factors contribution fails to address adequately the *process* and *product* requirements of design input. Specifically, the *when* and the *how* requirements for the delivery of design inputs (process); and the *what* requirements of design inputs to be recruited for specific system development contexts (product), have not been defined explicitly. To improve the effectiveness of this means of human factors input, the following requirements would have to be satisfied:

• The configuration and declarative content of design inputs should be contextualised appropriately to the human factors support required at each stage of system development. In other words, an explicit structured human factors design framework should be specified to support a matching of the content and format of existing human factors guidelines, principles and standards, to the system design cycle. Such work was reported by Esgate, Whitefield and Life (1990);

• A more effective means of data access should be developed to manage the rapidly increasing pool of declarative human factors knowledge. In particular, passive delivery to designers through handbooks and reference manuals may no longer be adequate. Smith's (1986) suggestion of conducting an initial review to identify a reduced set of relevant design guidelines would only provide a short term solution. Although such a review may be helpful, it remains a daunting task in view of the ever increasing size of the database, and the limited availability of project resources for human factors design (see (c) and (g) above). A more promising enhancement of this means of human factors input is to develop computer-based tools to support database management and access. Such tools are discussed later.

In conclusion, guidelines, principles and standards as a means of human factors input, relies heavily on appropriate consultation during system development. In addition, a structured framework of human factors design is required to address the following pitfalls:

(a) The perception of human factors designers as 'auditors' as opposed to active participants in the specification of a system design.
(b) Human factors design as a craft practice (see Long and Dowell, 1989). By establishing a structured design framework, the processes of human factors design may then be specified in greater detail. A systematic and explicit human factors method may then be derived.
(c) Inadequate or non-allocation of project resources for human factors design. By specifying the human factors design process explicitly, its resource requirements may then be represented and accommodated more appropriately at the project planning stage.

The second means of human factors input comprises computer-based tools. As with guidelines, principles and standards, computer-based tools should not be developed in a 'vacuum'. Specifically, the functions provided by computer-based tools should address adequately the human factors design support required at each stage of system development. In this respect, computer-based tools may be configured to provide both procedural and declarative design support.

The procedural support provided by computer-based tools may include the following:

• project planning, e.g. scheduling of design deliverables, tracking of project progress;
• design specification and documentation, e.g. text and graphics editing, consistency checking of notational rules;
• design evaluation, e.g. simulation, prototyping, animation;
• design implementation, e.g. compiling, linking.

To provide a *'total systems solution'* or *'design cycle support'*, the above design tasks should be accommodated comprehensively by computer-based tools (Hewett and Durham, 1987). Tools that provide such procedural support have already been developed (see later).

In contrast, computer-based tools that provide declarative design support have only been developed recently. Specifically, tools that support the management, access and appropriate application of the declarative knowledge base are emerging. For instance, Perlman (1987) reported the development of a tool to support the recruitment of human factors guidelines.

Generally, computer-based tools suffer from the same limitations as guidelines, principles and standards. For instance, Hartson and Hix (1989) reported that the scope of system development covered by computer-based tools is too narrow. Aside from such problems, an excessively long time lag separates the recognition of computer support requirements from their satisfaction by the development of a computer-based tool. Also, from experiences reported for Software Engineering, CASE and IPSE tools could not be developed until computer support requirements for system development became better defined by structured analysis and design methods (Hewett and Durham, 1987). Consequently, it may be expected that comprehensive computer-based tool support for human factors design would not be forthcoming unless conceptions of its design cycle are defined explicitly. The development of comprehensive computer-based tools to support human factors design would therefore be a longer term objective.[10]

The final means of human factors input describes the class of design techniques and methods, e.g. task analysis. Further examples of the class may be found in Meister (1984) and Kloster and Tischer (1984). Although these reports indicated a wealth of human factors techniques and methods, the (procedural) support they provide suffers generally from the following limitations:

(a) Too narrow a coverage of the system design cycle. In particular, existing human factors techniques and methods tend to focus on later stages of system development.
(b) The scope and format of their outputs are contextualised poorly to the design support required at each stage of system development.
(c) They are difficult to use (Wilson et al. 1986), and are expensive and time consuming to apply, e.g. rigorous experiments. In addition, the validity of the results derived may be doubtful. For instance, the results of experiments may not be applicable to real world tasks if they have been derived under controlled laboratory conditions.

In conclusion, to achieve maximum effectiveness, all means of human factors input should be configured with respect to an explicitly defined human factors design cycle. Thus, the scope of existing human factors methods and techniques may be extended to cover the system design cycle more completely. Since comprehensive computer-based tools to support human factors design are generally unavailable at present, design tasks defined by

---

[10] Computer-based support for human factors design is in the early stages of development. The support provided by existing computer-based tools tends to be limited, e.g. HUFIT tools (ESPRIT 385, 1989 and 1990) comprise primarily checklists and form-fill schemes.

the extended methods and techniques could facilitate their development. Specifically, design support requirements to be satisfied by the computer-based tool may be inferred from explicitly defined characteristics of methods and techniques (see also CCTA (Draft) Report 1988, p. 20; Alvey Human Interface Committee Report 1987, pp. 18 and 32).

Consistent with preceding observations on other means of human factors input, a prerequisite for enhancing existing human factors methods and techniques is the definition of a *structured* framework of human factors design. Such a framework is characterised by design stages whose *scope, process* and *notation* are reasonably *explicit* and *complete* with respect to the *system design cycle*. To specify a structured design framework for human factors, the following questions need to be answered:

• What human factors conceptions of the system design cycle presently exist? In addition, well developed Software Engineering conceptions of the system design cycle should be examined.
• Which conception would best support the explicit identification and location of specific human factors contributions to each stage of system development? A structured framework of human factors design is thus defined.
• What research is entailed by the derivation of such a design framework?

Concerns that relate to the research question are addressed in Chapters Two and Seven. Questions concerning conceptions of the system design cycle and the location of human factors contributions will be discussed here. To this end, two prominent but contrasting Software Engineering conceptions of the system design cycle are reviewed, namely those entailed by rapid prototyping and by structured analysis and design methods. The objective of the review is to assess the strengths and weaknesses of the conceptions with respect to their support for the development of a structured framework of human factors design.

1.3.   Alternative Conceptions of the System Design Cycle: Rapid Prototyping versus Structured Analysis and Design Methods

Rapid prototyping essentially involves 'fast-building' a preliminary prototype followed by iterative cycles of testing and prototyping. Prototyping may be undertaken in a number of ways, namely step-wise or incremental prototyping, evolutionary prototyping and throw-away prototyping (Hekmatpour and Ince, 1987).

Rapid prototyping is frequently equated with prototyping (e.g. Wilson and Rosenberg, 1988). Consequently, the benefits of *prototyping* have been cited frequently to support arguments in favour of *rapid* prototyping. Such a perspective is misleading since the benefits of *prototyping* may be accrued *without* incurring the costs that are unique to *rapid* prototyping. In particular, to speed up prototype construction, a *rapid* prototyping approach typically minimises the time spent on design analysis and specification. Thus, *rapid* prototyping may be distinguished from *prototyping*,[11] since it assumes (implicitly or otherwise) that an intensive phase of design analysis and specification may be substituted adequately by iterations of prototype construction and test. It cannot be over-emphasised that such an assumption is false since prototyping a design is *not* the same as designing a prototype. Specifically, the former activity may involve little design analysis and specification. The time saved by economising on such a design phase may subsequently incur heavy costs for maintenance, updates and bug fixing (Shuttleworth 1987). Alternatively, an uneconomic number of prototypes may have to be developed and tested before a satisfactory design solution is derived (Long and Neale 1989; Keller 1987). Since *rapid* prototyping frequently involves entering a design directly into a computer, the design documentation is usually inadequate. Poor documentation aggravates further the earlier problems, since decisions on the necessary prototype tests and resulting modifications would not be supported appropriately.

To facilitate later comparisons of the system design process implied by *rapid* prototyping and structured analysis and design methods, some of the advantages and disadvantages of a *rapid* prototyping approach are summarised in Figures 1-6 and 1-7 respectively.

Structured analysis and design methods,[12] as a class of Software Engineering methods, are defined by the following characteristics:

• the procedural support they provide is reasonably complete with respect to the system design cycle;
• system development is advanced in stages that are defined explicitly with respect to their design scope, process and notation. Thus, system development involves a series of intermediate design products;
• independent system design concerns are addressed separately. Thus, design analysis is undertaken before design specification and implementation.

---

[11] In contrast with rapid prototyping, prototyping is usually undertaken *following* comprehensive design analysis. Further differences will be highlighted later when rapid prototyping is compared with structured analysis and design methods.

[12] Although formal methods have made significant contributions to system development, they are excluded from the review since they do not generally cover the system design cycle sufficiently. For instance, requirements capture is usually omitted by formal methods (Norris 1985).

Figure 1-6:   Advantages of a Rapid Prototyping Approach to System Development

(a) earlier and better visualisation of the design problem is supported by demonstrating the prototype. Since it facilitates the elicitation of user feedback, user requirements may be identified more accurately. Thus, more complete functional specifications may be expected. Consequently, it is more likely that expected system performance would be achieved;

(b) it reduces the duration of system development and encourages wider investigation and testing of different design solutions;

(c) it provides a tangible artefact for problem analysis and discussion among design team members;

(d) it provides a means of testing specific system design concerns.

Figure 1-7:   Disadvantages of a Rapid Prototyping Approach to System Development

(a) its emphasis on design analysis and problem formulation tends to be inadequate. Thus, two unsatisfactory outcomes may occur; namely: an inappropriate prototype may be constructed; and incorrect test criteria may be applied to the prototype leading to erroneous interpretations of test results. Thus, the design rationale used to construct subsequent prototypes may be flawed. As a result, successive iterations may not enable efficient convergence to a design solution;

(b) inappropriate prototypes may cause end-users to be committed prematurely to a specific design solution. As a result, inadequate problem analysis and poor design solutions may be exposed too late during system development (Long and Neale 1989). Thus, Thimbleby (1987) pointed out that rapid prototyping violates the principle of delaying design commitment;

(c) there may be resistance to discarding prototypes especially if the time and effort expended in their creation is not insignificant. Thus, non-optimal designs may be carried forward. In the worst case, prototypes may be passed off as the final design product (Boar 1984; Fox 1982);

(d) audits cannot be conducted properly as the design documentation is frequently inadequate. Rapid prototyping may also propagate design communication problems similar to those associated with program 'hacking'. In particular, inadequate documentation implies poor support for subsequent design modification and maintenance;

(e) an excessively heavy reliance on computer-based tools to support the rapid generation of prototypes can lead to over-design (Mantei 1986). In addition, by encouraging direct entry of design knowledge into the computer-based prototype, rapid prototyping engenders an ad hoc or 'magic box' strategy. Such a strategy would not adequately support projects with ill defined domains. Furthermore, for large system development projects, work collaboration between design teams would not be supported adequately by a rapid prototyping approach (Long and Neale 1989);

(f) inappropriate deferment of design decisions may be encouraged, since rapid prototyping engenders an excessive reliance on their resolution by prototype construction and test (Grudin et al. 1987);

(g) limitations and constraints that apply to the final design artefact may be ignored during prototyping;

(h) a prototype can be oversold, creating unrealistic expectations in the final design artefact;

(i) the prototyping process may be difficult to manage and control.

Having defined the main characteristics of structured analysis and design methods, existing misconceptions of the methods may now be rectified, namely:

(1) Structured analysis and design methods, as a class, emphasises 'getting-it-right-the-first-time' (Gould and Lewis 1983). Such a view has been interpreted erroneously to imply that the methods do not involve iterative design. A more appropriate characterisation of the emphasis of the methods is 'getting-it-right-to-begin-with' (Grudin et al. 1987) or 'getting-the-first-best-guess-solution'.

(2) Structured analysis and design methods prescribe top-down design exclusively. This generalisation cannot be true for two reasons, namely:

• design is seldom confined to top-down processes only, i.e. design methods rarely prescribe a purely 'top-down' or 'bottom-up' design approach;

• some structured analysis and design methods have explicitly 'disowned' a top-down design approach, e.g. the Jackson System Development method emphasises a 'middle-out' approach to design.

Thus, criticisms against top-down design should not be applied unquestioningly to structured analysis and design methods. Unfortunately, such criticisms have continued. For instance, it has been claimed recently that structured analysis and design methods can only be applied in well defined domains.

(3) Structured analysis and design methods do not encourage prototyping. This misconception is addressed later when the methods are compared with rapid prototyping. It suffices to say here that the opposite is true, since the well defined stage-by-stage design descriptions prescribed by the methods would provide better support for prototyping.

To facilitate later comparison with rapid prototyping, the advantages and disadvantages of structured analysis and design methods are summarised respectively in Figures 1-8 and 1-9.

A comparison between rapid prototyping and structured analysis and design methods follows. It is argued that the explicit characteristics of the methods would support better the specification of a complementary human factors design cycle. Following such a specification, a structured analysis and design method may be developed for human factors, and later integrated with similarly structured Software Engineering methods. Thus, human factors inputs may be incorporated more effectively throughout the system design cycle. Arguments in favour of structured analysis and design methods may be advanced further on two grounds. First, it may be shown that the benefits of adopting a methodological approach would match at least those achieved by rapid prototyping. To this end, the following arguments would be pertinent:

(1) Design discussions and the elicitation of user feedback (i.e. advantages (a) and (c) of rapid prototyping, Figure 1-6) are also facilitated by the explicitly defined and documented stage-wise design products prescribed by structured analysis and design methods. Prototyping is similarly facilitated by this characteristic of the methods (Long and Neale 1989; Essink 1988; Keller 1987). Thus, by encouraging prototyping and the use of

Figure 1-8:   Advantages of Structured Analysis and Design Methods

(a) better quality assurance. The well-defined stage-wise scope and process of these methods support more systematic design analysis and decisions. Thus, complete logical analysis is encouraged before physical design (Hares 1987);
(b) efficient management of design complexities. In particular, independent design concerns are separated, and related concerns are grouped appropriately;
(c) better design communication. The graphical notations of these methods are developed sufficiently to support a range of intermediate design descriptions. Thus, communications between system developers, between developers and managers, and between developers and users are facilitated (Hares 1987);
(d) effective design audits. The methods emphasise heavily on comprehensive design documentation. Thus, a more complete review of design decisions and rationale is facilitated;
(e) continuous verification and validation of design specifications. Since the methods require the stage-wise generation of design products, testing, prototyping and design iteration are encouraged throughout the system design cycle;
(f) accurate and detailed project planning. Since the range of intermediate design products are defined and documented explicitly by these methods, data on previous projects may be collated to support future project planning, e.g. in estimating design resource requirements and in setting project milestones;
(g) efficient recruitment of inter-disciplinary design knowledge. The explicit structure of these methods provides a well-developed framework for locating relevant inter-disciplinary knowledge.

Figure 1-9:   Disadvantages of Structured Analysis and Design Methods

(a) they do not address user requirements adequately;
(b) they do not address user interface design explicitly;
(c) their notation may not adequately convey the actual workings of the system to the user (Mantei and Teorey 1988). However, it should be noted that positive reports on these notations have also been published, e.g. Hares (1987);
(d) their emphasis on comprehensive design documentation exacts heavy demands on resources that are not available to smaller system development projects;
(e) their application may be cumbersome unless supported by computer-based tools.

graphical notations for design description, the elicitation of user feedback would be supported appropriately (see also Fitter and Green 1979). As a counter argument against rapid prototyping, it should also be noted that the latter may not be viable in novel design scenarios (Thimbleby 1987). Specifically, an adequate start-point is required before a design can be prototyped. Thus, in such cases, an extended period of design analysis and specification would be required contrary to the basic premise of a rapid prototyping approach. Such a requirement is already accommodated by structured analysis and design methods.

(2) Reduction in system development time (i.e. advantage (b) of rapid prototyping, Figure 1-6) may not accrue due to the following:

• poor formulation and documentation of the system design problem (i.e. disadvantages (a) and (d) of rapid prototyping, Figure 1-7);
• design management problems inherent in rapid prototyping (i.e. disadvantage (i) of rapid prototyping, Figure 1-7. See also Crinnion (1989) for case-study examples);
• difficulties in integrating final design specifications (Böhm 1984; Morrison 1988).

Such failures of rapid prototyping in realising faster system development have been reported. For instance, Grønbák (1989) reported that in nine projects undertaken using rapid prototyping, deadlines for design completion were all exceeded considerably. As a result, there was no difference in overall system development time between rapid prototyping and other system design approaches.

The second argument in favour of structured analysis and design methods comprises an examination of human factors reservations concerning rapid prototyping. Specifically, a rapid prototyping approach may conflict with human factors objectives as follows:

(1) Rapid prototyping may be seen as *replacing* rather than *supplementing* earlier human factors involvement in system development (Grudin et al 1987; Clark and Howard 1988). In particular, it may restrict human factors involvement to prototype evaluation as opposed to active participation in design specification. This problem is serious since rapid prototyping is not a substitute for adequate system analysis and design (see disadvantages (a), (b) and (f) of rapid prototyping, Figure 1-7).

(2) Rapid prototyping engenders a false impression that human factors is contributing actively and effectively to system development. In most cases, human factors is only recruited at the prototype evaluation stage. Although such a recruitment would remove some design problems, the 'too-little-too-late' problem of human factors input would remain unaddressed. In the worst case, resistance against discarding an expensive

prototype may result in non-implementation of human factors recommendations (i.e. disadvantages (a), (c) and (f) of rapid prototyping, Figure 1-7).
(3) Rapid prototyping engenders a false impression that end-users are invariably involved in prototype testing and modification. A survey of reports indicated that prototype evaluation and modification undertaken exclusively by expert reviewers is a common practice, e.g. 'expert walkthrough' (Long and Neale 1989).

From the above arguments, it may be concluded that a number of critical human factors problems remain unaddressed by a rapid prototyping approach to system development. Particularly serious concerns comprise the absence of direct human factors contribution to design analysis and specification, and the frequently inadequate documentation of design decisions and rationale. The importance of adequate design documentation is highlighted by the emergence in Software Engineering of design recovery, reverse engineering and re-documentation methods (see Chikofsky and Cross II 1990). Although design inadequacies may be rectified by such methods, high project costs in terms of both human and financial resources are exacted. Consequently, structured analysis and design methods are increasingly applied in system development.

On the basis of the preceding observations, it may also be concluded that structured analysis and design methods, as a class, would provide a better framework for structuring human factors input to system development.[13] To complete the argument in favour of these methods, their capability of providing more specific system development contexts for locating human factors inputs should be assessed. These concerns are addressed next.

1.4. Structured Analysis and Design Methods: Enhancement of Human Factors Contribution to System Development

Having argued in favour of using the framework of structured analysis and design methods as the basis for organising human factors inputs, a further question needs to be answered; namely: should human factors methods be similarly structured? Alternatively, should human factors recruit from structured analysis and design methods only their conception of the system design process? These questions indicate two possible solutions to the existing

---

[13] A choice must be made between the two approaches to system development because rapid prototyping (*not* prototyping) and structured analysis and design methods are incompatible. In particular, the methods emphasise extensive design analysis, specification and documentation, rather than the direct and rapid construction of a prototype. The different design perspectives dictate the emphasis, and time and effort spent on design specification.

problems of human factors input to system development:

(a) Using the system development framework defined explicitly by structured analysis and design methods, human factors concerns may be identified and intersected appropriately with software engineering concerns. On this basis, existing means of human factors input may be 'clustered' as 'toolkits' around specific stages of structured analysis and design methods. Such a clustering of human factors 'toolkits' was proposed by Grandjean (1984); Berns (1984); Rubinstein and Hersh (1984); Gould (1988); McClelland (1990); Meister (1984); and Eason (1987).
(b) Using the well defined methodological characteristics of structured analysis and design methods (i.e. their stage-wise design scope, process and notation), a similar method for human factors design may be developed. To this end, a structured framework of human factors design is first derived. On the basis of the framework, existing human factors techniques may be recruited, integrated and extended to generate a structured analysis and design method *for human factors*. Since both software engineering and human factors design contributions are made explicit by their methods, integration of their design stages, processes, products and notations (if possible) is facilitated. Inter-disciplinary design collaboration may thus be optimised by a structured integration of their individual methods.

In summary, to ensure appropriate scope and timing of human factors inputs, its design concerns have to be related to the system development context. This requirement was addressed in both solutions using structured analysis and design methods. An assessment of the strengths and weaknesses of the solutions follows.

To satisfy a requirement of locating human factors against specific system design concerns, Olson (1991) suggested a simple solution similar to (a) above; i.e. discrete clustering of existing means of human factors input against the system development context. The solution scheme involves characterising existing human factors techniques with respect to the following:

(1) The ability to 'illuminate' a set of design issues, e.g. ease of learning, errors, etc. The results of such an attempt are shown in Figure 1-10 (left part).
(2) The design support provided, e.g. techniques for discovering the task, for generating a 'first-cut' design, etc. The results of such an attempt are shown in Figure 1-10 (right part).

To select a suitable technique for application, a designer would have to specify the human factors design issue(s) of interest, and the system development activity undertaken. For instance, if a designer is interested in discovering *What Knowledge to Do the Task,*

Figure 1-10:   Design Concerns Addressed and Supported by Existing Human Factors Techniques (Olson, 1991)

Design Issues Illuminated by Human Factors Techniques

Design Support Provided by Human Factors Techniques

Existing Human Factors Techniques

Existing Human Factors Techniques	What Knowledge to Do the Task	Vocabulary for Objects and Actions	Relationship between Objects	Task Flow	Ease of Learning	Perceptibility	Clues about How to Do Task	Working Memory Load and Feedback	Motor Movement Difficulty	Time and User Delays	Errors	Discovering the Task	Generating First Cut Design	General Analysis of Proposed Design	Specific Analysis of Proposed Design
Observe Users on Old or Alternative System	*	*								*	*	*			
Operator Function Model	*	*	*	*								*			
Decision Tree Interviews	*	*										*			
Semantic Net Interviews		*	*									*			
Participatory Prototyping					*		*						*		
Checklists/Guidelines	*	*		*	*	*	*	*	*					*	
Hallway/Storefront Methodology	*		*	*	*	*		*		*				*	
Walkthrough	*		*	*	*	*					*			*	
Component Analysis						*	*	*						*	
Visual Display Analysis						*									*
Metaphor Analysis		*	*		*								*	*	
Object/Action Analysis		*	*		*								*	*	
Generalised Transition Network				*	*		*							*	
Grammar Analysis	*	*			*						*				*
GOMS/CCT/MHP	*			*	*					*	*				*
Cognitive Walkthrough					*		*				*				*
Claims Analysis					*		*				*				*
Prototype with Role Playing	*			*	*	*	*	*	*					*	
Usability Test				*	*	*	*	*	*	*	*			*	
Interactive Transaction System	*	*	*	*								*			

Key to Acronyms – GOMS: Goals, Operators, Methods and Selection;   CCT: Cognitive Complexity Theory;   MHP: Model of Human Processor suitable techniques may be identified by locating rows with asterisks indicated in column 1 of the left part of Figure 1-10. Thus, *Observe Users on Old or Alternative System*, together with nine other human factors techniques, would be suitable. If the designer is concerned only with the initial system development activity of *Discovering the Task*, the set of suitable techniques would then be reduced to three, i.e. those indicated in rows 1 to 3. These techniques are identified by locating rows with asterisks in column 1 of *both* the right and left parts of Figure 1-10. By cross-referencing both parts of Figure 1-10, human factors techniques may thus be assigned more appropriately against specific needs of system development. The system design cycle used in this solution comprises: *Discover the Task → Generate First Cut Design →* etc. (see Figure 1-10, right part). Another example may be useful to clarify the proposed solution scheme. Figure 1-10 (left part) is consulted first to identify existing techniques that would address specific design issues of interest, say *Vocabulary for Objects and Actions*. Thus, *Object/Action Analysis* and *Grammar Analysis* may be identified as suitable techniques. Figure 1-10 (right part) may then be consulted for a more specific assignment of the techniques to the particular system design context. In this way, it may be inferred that *Object/Action Analysis* is more suited for application when *Generating First Cut Design*, while *Grammar Analysis* is more appropriate for *Specific Analysis of Proposed Design*. Thus, a more appropriate recruitment of human factors techniques is supported.

While the figure undoubtedly provides some guidance for identifying appropriate human factors techniques for recruitment, a number of problems remain. Specifically, the set of design issues used to characterise existing techniques needs to be more complete and representative (see Figure 1-10, left part). However, in view of the wide range of human factors concerns in system development, it is unclear which design issues could conceivably constitute such a set. Thus, the utility of Figure 1-10 (left part) is limited to the identification of a design issue that is both of interest to the specific design context and a member of the tabulated set. In addition, since design considerations for some of the issues in Figure 1-10 (left part) would pervade the entire system design cycle at some level of description (e.g. *Task Flow* issues), it may be difficult to locate specific points for recruiting applicable human factors techniques. The result may be a failure to address human factors issues at the earliest possible stage of design specification. Thus, human factors contributions would be incorporated less effectively. Another outcome that may result from the categorisation of techniques against such pervasive issues is that the techniques would be distinguished poorly with respect to their suitability for a particular design context; e.g. which one of the ten *Task Flow* techniques is most appropriate for variant design (see Figure 1-10, left part)? In addition, uncertainties may arise on whether the whole or a part of a technique should be applied in particular system development contexts.

Another shortcoming of the solution scheme is that the designer is required to infer the intersection between the scope of a particular design stage and the system design activities identified in Figure 1-10 (right part). For instance, the designer would be required to determine the system design stages concerned with *Generating First Cut Design*. To solve the problem, the design activities and *sets* of human factors issues addressed (as opposed to *single* issues), should be intersected explicitly with each stage of system development. In this way, the design support provided by particular human factors techniques may be characterised more specifically. Such enhancements are discussed further in sub-sections 2.5 and 2.6. It suffices to say here that Olson's (1991) solution may be improved by ensuring:

• a more detailed, complete and specific characterisation of existing human factors techniques (i.e. improvements to the left part of Figure 1-10);
• a more explicit definition of the scope of human factors contributions at each stage of system development. In particular, the simple system design cycle assumed in Figure 1-10 (right part) needs to be replaced by a structured framework for human factors design. Thus, existing techniques may be matched against better defined requirements at each stage of system development.

Although Olson's solution (and solutions in general that involve discrete clustering of existing means of human factors input) may be enhanced to alleviate the 'too-little-too-late' problem of human factors input to system development, some problems remain unaddressed, namely:

(a) The encroachment and inadequate allocation of project resources for human factors design. Such problems have been reported widely (e.g. Meister 1984; Chapanis and Budurka 1990; Pikaar et al. 1990), and have been attributed to the absence of a well defined conception of human factors design. Although the problem may be alleviated by including a human factors engineer at the project planning stage, accurate prediction of resource requirements (e.g. system development time and effort) would still be difficult without comprehensive records of previous projects. In this respect, O'Niel (1980) reported that records gathered according to a structured conception of system development are vital for good project planning. The alternative solution scheme of developing a structured analysis and design method for human factors is consistent with this objective. Such a development could facilitate an explicit representation of human factors in the overall system design agenda. Resource requirements for human factors design may then be accommodated appropriately and resource encroachment avoided.

(b) The difficult integration of design descriptions derived by applying individual human factors techniques. In particular, the format and notation used to describe the outputs of individual techniques may be very different. Again, the alternative solution scheme of developing a structured analysis and design method for human factors would solve the problem.

(c) Poor communicability of existing human factors descriptions due to their inadequately developed notations. This problem may be solved by recruiting the notations of existing structured analysis and design methods.

(d) The inefficient utilisation of project resources. Following the identification of suitable human factors techniques, care must be taken to avoid unnecessary repetitions in their application. Thus, activities of individual techniques that address overlapping design concerns have to be identified and concatenated appropriately. Information requirements also need to be reconciled across the design stages of different techniques. Consequently, in the absence of a structured analysis and design method for human factors, valuable project time would have to be spent on:

• assessing the suitability of individual human factors techniques;

• tailoring relevant techniques into a coherent set, e.g. to ensure that the outputs of a preceding technique comprise suitable inputs to a succeeding technique;

• extending the scope of the techniques to ensure adequate coverage of the system design cycle. Individual human factors techniques may also need to be developed further to define more explicitly their stage-wise product, process and notation. For instance, it has been reported that existing human factors techniques tend to indicate only what should be designed, but not how. In particular, prescriptive advice on how design decisions may be formulated following initial analysis is omitted frequently (Sutcliffe 1989; Chapanis and Budurka 1990).

To perform all the above tasks, a human factors designer would have to be very well informed.[14]

In summary, six requirements for improving human factors input to system development have been highlighted by the assessment:

(1) Human factors coverage of the system design cycle needs to be sufficiently complete.

---

[14] Such an undertaking may not be trivial in view of the increasingly large number of human factors techniques. For instance, a recent survey indicated 96 techniques for task analysis alone. Thus, a requirement to process design techniques in this way would result in poor utilisation of project resources.

In addition, human factors design contributions need to be defined more explicitly.

(2) Individual means of human factors input needs to be integrated coherently. In addition, the means of input needs to be contextually appropriate to each stage of system development.

(3) Resource requirements for human factors design need to be accommodated explicitly by the overall system design agenda.

(4) Inter-dependencies between human factors and software engineering design need to be defined explicitly. In this way, human factors contributions may be located optimally throughout the system design cycle.

(5) Prototyping (with user tests) needs to be adopted in the interim to compensate for areas of incomplete human factors knowledge, i.e. to derive empirically design information that cannot be approximated or prescribed analytically. In the longer term, analytic prescription may be developed further by accumulating pertinent human factors design knowledge.

(6) Human factors solutions need to be developed to complement existing means of software engineering input to system development,[15] since the latter are better developed. For instance, existing software engineering design notations, techniques, methods and tools need to be accommodated appropriately.

From the preceding arguments, it has been shown that the above requirements would be satisfied by an integration of structured human factors and software engineering design methods. The motivation for such a solution is discussed briefly below.

Since their introduction in the seventies and eighties, structured analysis and design methods have made rapid inroads into system development. For instance, the Structured Systems Analysis and Design Method (SSADM) has been adopted as a CCTA standard (Hewett and Durham, 1987). Such events necessitate a re-appraisal of existing means for human factors involvement in system development. In particular, the following possibilities should be considered:

(a) The impact of structured analysis and design methods on the effectiveness of existing means of human factors input. For instance, are existing human factors techniques compatible with structured analysis and design methods? These concerns are addressed later when the integration of human factors and software engineering methods is discussed.

(b) Exploitation of structured analysis and design methods to improve the effectiveness of

---

[15] This requirement is also consistent with the typical configuration of system design teams, i.e. development is led by software engineers with human factors designers providing collaborative support.

human factors input, for instance:

• The design framework of the methods provides an explicit and well defined context for configuring human factors input to system development. In particular, by defining the design support requirements of each stage of system development, human factors inputs may be made more timely and appropriate in granularity and format.

• The desirable characteristics of the methods may be emulated by human factors techniques (namely explicit and well-formed stage-wise design scope, process and notation; and reasonably complete coverage of the system design cycle). Since existing human factors techniques (in general) address the system design cycle only partially, a comparison with the design conception of structured analysis and design methods could highlight incomplete areas of design support. Existing human factors techniques may then be developed further to widen their coverage of the system design cycle. With greater efforts, a structured analysis and design method for human factors may also be developed.

• Human factors and software engineering design concerns may be integrated by intersecting their structured methods. Such an integration is facilitated by the explicit characteristics of structured analysis and design methods.

Further arguments for the integration of human factors and software engineering contributions via structured analysis and design methods follow:

(1) The well-developed notations of structured analysis and design methods may be recruited to support more specific human factors descriptions of a system design. Furthermore, the use of a common notation may facilitate the communication of human factors specifications to software engineers. The potential of a common notation is realisable, since existing structured analysis and design methods frequently include well-developed notations that are also appropriate for describing human factors specifications (see Carver and Cameron 1987; Carver 1988).

(2) The emphasis of structured analysis and design methods on comprehensive design documentation encourages the capture of design rationale. In particular, antecedents and consequents of design decisions are documented explicitly. Comprehensive documentation is essential for quality assurance, since it provides an effective means for detecting and correcting design errors. Thus, design audits by human factors designers and end-users are supported better (see Long and Neale 1989; Butler et al. 1989; Akscyn and McCracken 1984; Alvey Human Interface Committee Report 1987, p. 34). Consideration should also be given to the recruitment of the documentation schemes of structured analysis and design methods, because comprehensive design records are frequently included as contractual obligations.

(3) The well-defined characteristics of structured analysis and design methods support more specific location and intersection of software engineering and human factors design concerns. Appropriate human factors techniques may thus be matched against specific design support requirements at each stage of system development. The set of techniques identified may then be developed into a structured human factors method. Such a method could benefit human factors design in three ways:

• It provides an appropriate basis for further developments of existing means of human factors input. First, deficient areas of declarative human factors knowledge may be identified for further research. In the interim, a structured method could highlight particular user test requirements for prototype designs, to compensate for deficient areas of declarative human factors knowledge. Second, computer-based tools comparable to existing software engineering tools may be developed to support human factors design, e.g. Computer Aided Software Engineering (CASE)-type and Integrated Project Support Environments (IPSEs)-type tools. Since such software engineering tools were developed on the basis of structured analysis and design methods (Hewett and Durham 1987; Bott 1988), it follows that similar tools may also be developed for human factors design if its methods are sufficiently structured. Specifically, a structured method would support the identification of appropriate computer functions, since its design stages and tasks are defined explicitly.

• The recruitment of appropriate declarative human factors knowledge is facilitated. Specifically, the identification of relevant declarative knowledge is facilitated by the explicitly defined stage-wise design concerns of a structured method.

• By integrating structured human factors and software engineering methods, inter-disciplinary design dependencies may be identified explicitly and accommodated. Methodological integration would improve inter-disciplinary design collaboration and promote greater awareness and understanding of mutual design needs. In particular, the integration would establish familiar reference points to support the assimilation of human factors inputs by software engineers, who are already familiar with their own structured methods (and vice versa). A greater uptake of design contributions may thus be expected.

(4) An integration of structured human factors and software engineering methods would generate a more complete conception of the system design cycle. Such a conception would facilitate an explicit allocation of resources for human factors design. Appropriate

accommodation of resource requirements may then be achieved[16] as follows:

• By ensuring that human factors is represented explicitly on the system design agenda. In this way, design resources may be allocated specifically to support human factors design. Explicit allocation is important because encroachments on human factors resources have been reported frequently. For instance, unrealistic time schedules may be imposed on human factors design (often considered a lower priority), if technical difficulties and delays in system launch were to arise (Eason and Cullen 1988; Meister 1984). By including human factors deliverables explicitly in the overall system design agenda, potential encroachments on its resources may be prevented.

• By improving project planning and estimates of resource requirements. To enable more accurate projections, timescales and resources expended in previous system development projects should be recorded with respect to the design stages of the structured methods. In this way, it would be more likely that the resources allocated would be adequate to support human factors design.

For these reasons, this book focuses on the development of a structured human factors method (named MUSE, Method for USability Engineering), followed by its integration with a particular structured software engineering method. These concerns are addressed in the book as follows:

(a) The general requirements and research activities for developing a structured human factors method (henceforth referred to directly as MUSE) are described in Chapter Two.

(b) An overview followed by a detailed account of MUSE is provided in Chapters Three to Six.

(c) A review of previous research on the integration of structured human factors and software engineering methods is presented in Chapter Seven. The integration of MUSE with the Jackson System Development (JSD) method is then introduced and compared with its predecessors. The method derived from the integration of MUSE and JSD is termed MUSE*/JSD.

(d) An assessment of the current state of development of MUSE and MUSE*/JSD, and their potential developments are described in Chapter Eight.

---

[16] These measures would also encourage greater managerial commitment to human factors. An explicit commitment is vital to prevent later encroachment on resources allocated to human factors design.

PART TWO:

DEVELOPMENT AND OVERVIEW OF MUSE – A STRUCTURED HUMAN FACTORS METHOD

2
The Development of MUSE

All things exist in time. They are not unchanging, and they cannot be designed
without regard for the way they operate and are used over time.

Charles Owen, 1986, **Design Processes Newsletter**

To every Form of being is assigned', Thus calmly spoke
the venerable Sage, 'An active principle.

William Wordsworth, 1814, **The Excursion**

In Chapter One, the 'too-little-too-late' problem of human factors contribution was identified. The problem highlights the importance of earlier and wider human factors involvement in system development. Although additional areas of human factors contribution have been identified, the problem could not be simply or directly rectified, since the contributions map poorly onto the design support requirements of each stage of system development. In particular, existing human factors design processes were observed to be largely implicit, and its design techniques provide only a narrow coverage of the system design cycle.

To solve this problem, a more explicit and complete conception of human factors design with respect to system development, is required. Such a conception would facilitate the identification of more specific requirements for human factors support. On the basis of the requirements, existing means of human factors contribution may then be recruited and extended as appropriate. It was also asserted that a *structured* human factors method should be developed because:

(a) its methodological framework could support the development and recruitment of other means of human factors contributions, namely declarative inputs such as design guidelines and standards, and computer-based tools;
(b) its explicit methodological characteristics are appropriate for integration with existing structured software engineering methods. In particular, methodological integration is facilitated by the well-defined design product, process and notation of such methods. Thus,

the inter-disciplinary concerns of system design may be intersected and co-ordinated appropriately in terms of their timing, scope, format and granularity. The structured human factors method and its subsequent integration with a similarly structured software engineering method are addressed in Chapters Three to Seven.

Since existing human factors techniques in general do not cover the system design cycle adequately, a structured human factors method does not exist. Thus, the development of such a method, namely MUSE, is described in this chapter. To this end, the objectives of the chapter comprise the following:

(a) Specification of a (reasonably) complete and explicit *scope* of human factors contribution to system development, i.e. *what* human factors design products would be required to specify *user* requirements and to satisfy them in the design of a system?

(b) Definition of explicit *processes* and *timing* for incorporating human factors into system development, i.e. *how* and *when* (or at which stage of system development) human factors design products should be derived and incorporated?

(c) Development of a structured human factors method named MUSE. The account includes a description of how existing human factors techniques have been recruited and incorporated into the structured human factors method.

These objectives suggest a requirement for 'tighter' specification of the conceptual scope, methodological definition and application context of existing human factors techniques. The required enhancements are described next followed by an account of how they may be satisfied.

2.1. Required Enhancements of the Design Coverage of Existing Human Factors Techniques

The conceptual scope of existing human factors techniques needs to be extended to include design specification (as opposed to focusing solely on design evaluation). To this end, particular emphasis should be placed on the following inter-related concerns:

(1) The specification of conceptual level tasks as opposed to focusing solely and/or prematurely on interaction level tasks. Thus, task design may be related more appropriately to the work goals to be achieved. In this way, premature commitment to 'secondary or house-keeping' tasks may be avoided, e.g. interactions required solely for device operation. To support the shift in emphasis, basic terms in human factors need to be defined more explicitly.

Examples of possible definitions are given in Figures 2-1 and 2-2. Figure 2-1 provides a graphical summary of task classes and relationships, while simple hierarchical relationships among the terms 'task', 'work', 'operations', etc., are shown in Figure 2-2. These definitions are adapted from a number of reports, in particular those of Johnson et al. (1988); Waddington and Johnson (1989); Blyth and Hakiel (1989); Sutcliffe (1988a); and Dowell and Long (1989). For a detailed account of particular terms, the reader should refer to the figures and the Glossary (at the end of the book).

(2) The specification of domain semantics in addition to task control and operationalisation. The latter concerns may then be set against an appropriate context. Useful examples of semantic descriptions may be found in the knowledge elicitation and engineering literature (e.g. Ragoczei and Hirst 1990).

(3) The specification of error recovery and user support, device and user interface design, and training programme development. These specifications should be derived on the basis of conceptual level tasks and domain semantics.

Figure 2-1: A Simple Taxonomy of Task Classes and Relationships for a Human-Computer System

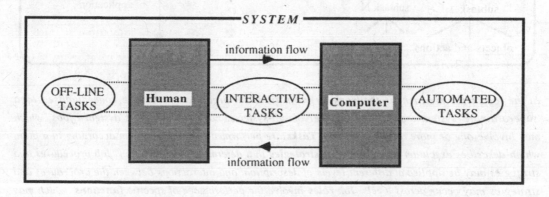

On-line tasks = Interactive tasks + Automated (or Device) tasks
System tasks = Off-line tasks + On-line tasks

On-line tasks involve human and computer components, while off-line tasks are unsupported by the computer. On-line task components may also be assigned entirely to the computer, i.e. automated tasks.

2.2. Required Enhancements of the Methodological Characteristics of Existing Human Factors Techniques

The products, procedures and notations of existing human factors techniques need to be defined explicitly to support effective application during system development. In particular:

(1) The nature, format and granularity of intermediate human factors *products* should be

Figure 2-2:   A Simple Conception of Task Hierarchies

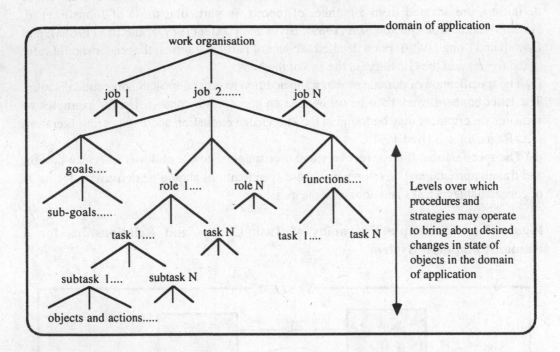

At the top of the hierarchy is the **work organisation.** An organisation may be conceptualised as a 'superordinate' system comprising a number of sub-systems. Each sub-system is assigned **jobs**, which may involve one or more **roles** (and tasks). **Tasks** are performed by the sub-system according to a plan, which describes execution **procedures** and **strategies** that determine their selection. Job procedures and strategies may be applied at different levels of description, and interactions between the procedures and strategies may occur across levels. Job **roles** involve the performance of specific **functions**, which may be considered as (non-trivial) units of behaviour (human or device) required to accomplish the system 'mission' (Drury 1983). Thus, a function may be allocated to a human or device, and may include tasks that do not result directly in work. **Work** may be defined as the achievement of desired changes in states of a set of real world objects. Thus, work **goals** and **sub-goals** may be described in terms of the desired initial-to-final state transformations to be effected by the system. In this context, a **system** comprises human and computer components working together in a specific environment. A distinction is thus made between the work to be accomplished by the system, and the tasks to be performed by human and computer components. Since work and tasks may not share a one-to-one relationship, tasks may either produce work directly or facilitate its eventual attainment.

The hierarchy may be decomposed into three branches that describe complementary design perspectives. The role (or object and action) branch supports specific task description, while the goal and function branches address the logic underlying particular characteristics of task performance.

defined appropriately to support design advancement between stages of system development. For instance, task analysis should not be confined solely to final task description or initial task analysis. Instead, task 'analysis' products should support different design perspectives, such as initial description of current system tasks; derivation of intermediate design descriptions; and synthesis of new system tasks. Relevant declarative human factors knowledge (e.g. design guidelines) may then be identified at appropriate stages, and incorporated appropriately into the design. In addition, to support better uptake of human factors contribution, the format and granularity of task 'analysis' products should be appropriate to the design context of each stage of system development.

(2) The design procedures of human factors techniques should be sufficiently explicit to support effective transformation of intermediate design descriptions. The range of transformations supported should span initial task analysis to the specification of screen displays. In other words, existing human factors techniques should be developed further to enhance their procedural and generative support for system design. This requirement is particularly important, since existing human factors techniques tend to be product-oriented. For instance, task analysis is focused predominantly on the description of tasks using particular notation and documentation schemes. Human factors design processes tend to be left implicit, resulting in a need for craft-oriented design practices. To develop a structured human factors method, such implicit design processes should be formulated into explicit design procedures. To this end, basic human factors design processes need to be defined. Definitions for some of the processes, adapted from a number of reports (in particular those of Johnson et al. 1988; and Waddington and Johnson 1989), are described below:

• *Abstraction.* This process is generally applied to derive a particular perspective of the design requirements. For instance, the tasks required to achieve work system goals may be conceptualised in terms of user operations with a device, or the performance of high-level sub-task units. Here, abstraction is used primarily to expose the conceptual rather than specific requirements of user task performance.

• *Generification.* This process is generally applied to facilitate the identification of common elements across discrete objects so that a basis may be established for design comparison. To this end, common elements across the original objects are collated to define a super-ordinate or 'generic' class. As an example, consider objects A, B and C whose attributes are represented respectively by the sets $\{1, 2, 3, 4\}$, $\{1, 2, 3, 6, 7\}$ and $\{1, 2, 3, 8, 9\}$. For the purposes of a particular design context, a generic class G comprising the intersection of their attributes (i.e. $G = \{1, 2, 3\}$), may be defined to characterise objects A, B and C as set. On this basis, generification may be used to support the following:

(a) The identification and selection of extant systems for analysis. In this case, the set G would describe key characteristics of the system to be designed, while A to C would characterise extant systems selected for analysis. By selecting particular subsets of G, a wider range of extant systems may also be identified for analysis (if appropriate).

(b) The derivation of a single task description from information elicited from various sources. Taking the above example further, A, B and C may correspond to task accounts offered by different performers. A generic task description, considered by the performers to be equivalent to their original account, may be derived to facilitate system design. Such a description may be characterised by H = {1, 2, ??}, where ?? was considered by different task performers to be equivalent to operations {4}, {6, 7} and {8, 9}.

Four other design contexts for applying generification are described in Figure 2-3 below. A brief account of these contexts follows. First, generification *across sub-tasks* may be applied to *a* task description elicited from *a* task performer. In this case, generification is applied to remove inconsistent descriptions. To this end, a generic set of attributes, actions and objects is established to support the derivation of a consistent sub-task description.

Figure 2-3:   Design Contexts for Applying Generification[1]

Design Context	Generification Type
Single task performer and single task	Across objects, actions and attributes
Many task performers and single task	Across task performers
Single task performer and many related tasks	Across tasks
Many task performers and many related tasks	Across task performers and/or tasks

Second, generification *across tasks* may be applied when *a* task performer describes *many related* tasks that share a common underlying 'logic'. Depending on the design context, it may be useful to derive a generic description of common aspects across the tasks.

Third, generification *across task performers* may be applied when *a* task is described by *many* task performers. In such cases, the descriptions of task objects and their manipulations may vary across performers. The variations may be removed by generification if they are due to inconsistent description, rather than a result of different task performance strategies. A single task description may thus be derived to support design.

Fourth, generification *across task performers and/or tasks* may be applied when *various*

---

[1] Note that generification across sub-tasks is assumed to be applicable to all design contexts.

related tasks are described by *different groups* of task performers. Such an application of generification was reported by Johnson, Diaper and Long (1984), for the specification of training syllabi to support different task performance requirements of distinct groups of students. In applying generification, Johnson et al. strove to achieve the following:

(i) establishment of a *common* training module to support task requirements that are *generic* across the student groups;
(ii) definition of *distinct* training modules to support task requirements that are *unique* to each student group.

To this end, a generic description was derived to characterise the tasks of each group of students. The descriptions were then compared to identify common and unique knowledge requirements of each student group. Appropriate training modules were thus developed for the students in accordance with their task requirements.

In conclusion, it should be noted that the type of generification selected for application is determined largely by the purpose of the analysis and the prevailing system design context.

• *Decomposition.* The process of decomposition is concerned with the successive breakdown of design descriptions to a level that would adequately support decisions required at particular stages of system development. For instance, task decomposition may be used to describe extant system tasks and to generate detailed specifications from a conceptual design.
• *Synthesis.* This process addresses the appropriate composition and extension of design descriptions so that system goals are achieved at acceptable cost. At particular stages of system development, design synthesis may involve the identification and recruitment of appropriate features of extant systems. Thus, synthesis should be undertaken only after a common underlying logic has been established (using abstraction and generification) between the extant system and the system to be designed. For instance, the synthesis of new system tasks may involve the selection, extrapolation and incorporation of appropriate extant system tasks.

(3) the design notations should be developed sufficiently to support the description of human factors concerns, e.g. organisational hierarchies, conceptual level tasks, domain semantics, performance requirements and human-computer interaction. Specifically, a notation should satisfy the following requirements:

• *Description specificity and range.* Notations for human factors description should be versatile enough to support the documentation of a comprehensive range of intermediate design products (see Figure 2-4). In addition, they should be specific enough to accommodate the requirements for tighter specifications in the development of complex human-computer systems. For instance, task specifications of safety critical systems should be detailed enough to support design simulation, workload assessment and probabilistic human reliability assessments. In particular, notational constructs for specifying task control should include the following:

(i) hierarchy, sequence, selection, iteration, posit and quit constructs to specify **intra**-task

Figure 2-4: Structured Notations to Support Human Factors Specification

Level of design specification	Human factors system design specifications	Notation that support human factors specifications
Organisational (super-ordinate system) level	Structure of formal (and informal) work relationships between sub-systems	Semantic net
	Execution control of information flows between sub-systems	Network diagrams
	Semantics of overall work domain	Semantic net
	Performance requirements of each sub-system	Function flow diagrams
Task (sub-system) level	Structural relationships between tasks	Structured diagrams
	Allocation of functions between user and computer	Annotated structured diagrams
	Control of computer presentation of task support functions in response to user task executions	Annotated structured diagrams
	Control of user task executions	Structured diagrams
	Semantics of task domain	Semantic net
	Performance requirements of user and computer	Tables, function flow diagrams
Interaction (input-output) level	Structural relationships between interaction objects	Semantic net
	Semantics of interaction objects and actions	Text tables
	Representation of interaction objects	Pictures
	Execution control of user inputs	Structured diagrams
	Behaviour of interaction objects in response to user/computer actions	Annotated structured diagrams
	Composition (form and content) of display screens (including messages)	Pictures and text
	Presentation control of display screens in response to user/computer actions	Structured diagrams

control (including error recovery specifications);
(ii) multiplicity, concurrency and inter-leaving constructs to specify **inter**-task control.

These notational constructs are required for the description of more complex tasks such as:

(a) Inter-leaved tasks. These are discrete tasks whose operations are interwoven. In other words, the user is required to execute a *current* task and monitor a *background* task. At a pre-specified point(s) of task execution, the status of the tasks would be reversed.
(b) Concurrent tasks. These are discrete tasks that are performed at the same time, e.g. data input while monitoring displays.
(c) Multiple tasks. These are multiple units of the same task that are performed at the same time.

• *Description communicability*. Notations for human factors description should facilitate discussions between designers and users, and between different groups of designers. Generally, discussions with users would be supported better by graphical notations (as opposed to formal or algebraic notations), since they are communicated more easily (Finkelstein and Potts 1985; Fitter and Green 1979; Hares 1987). In this way, user feedback elicitation and design validation may be supported better throughout system development. As for discussions between different groups of designers, the potential of a common notation should be exploited to support closer design collaboration between human factors designers and software engineers (see Carver 1988; Sutcliffe 1988b).
• *Description maintainability*. The characteristics of a notation should facilitate the generation and maintenance of design documentation, i.e. to support design specification and modification respectively. In particular, a notation that is amenable to computer support would be more desirable.

2.3. Required Enhancements of the Context for Applying Existing Human Factors Techniques
To improve the recruitment of human factors techniques during system development, the following related pre-requisites need to be satisfied:

(i) Human factors techniques should be matched appropriately against specific design contexts throughout system development. In other words, particular techniques should be located against specific stages of the system design cycle. The identification and recruitment of appropriate human factors techniques may thus be facilitated. Better management of method recruitment is particularly important, since the proliferation of human factors techniques is expected to continue.
(ii) The scope and design support capabilities of human factors techniques should be

extended to cover the entire system design cycle. By making human factors an active participant in design specification, the 'too-little-too-late' problem of human factors contribution may thus be avoided. To this end, existing craft practices of human factors design should be formulated into methods with explicit products and processes. A more explicit and complete conception of human factors contribution to system development may thus be derived. On the basis of such a conception, a suitable set of existing human factors techniques (part or whole) may be identified and integrated. To facilitate integration, further development of existing techniques may be necessary to defined more explicitly their stage-wise design product, process and notation. A structured human factors method may thus be developed, and integrated later with similarly structured software engineering methods. Since the scope, process and notation of such methods are explicit and (reasonably) complete with respect to the system design cycle, appropriate intersections between software engineering and human factors design concerns would be easier to identify. Explicit dependencies between inter-disciplinary design concerns may thus be established, and more timely and relevant human factors contributions are ensured throughout the system design cycle.

(iii) Computer-based tools should be developed to support the structured human factors method derived in (ii) above. Computer support requirements may be specified by examining the design tasks entailed by an application of the method. In particular, computer functions may be specified to support the application of method procedures and notations, and the generation of prescribed design products. Computer-based tools may also be specified to 'enforce' adherence to the design dependencies described above.[2]

In summary, by satisfying the above requirements, human factors contributions may be configured more appropriately to support each stage of system development. The development of a structured human factors method[3] will now be reported as follows:

(a) Sub-section 2.4 reviews how an explicit conception of human factors design was derived.

(b) Sub-section 2.5 describes how the conception was instantiated as a structured design framework. To illustrate how the framework could facilitate the recruitment of human factors techniques, the existing techniques listed in Figure 1-10 will be used as examples.

(c) Sub-section 2.6 describes how a structured human factors method may then be

---

[2] The specifics for developing computer-based tools will not be discussed here. Interested readers should refer to Lim and Long (1992b) for a review of how tool development may be supported by a structured human factors method.

[3] For a detailed account of the development of a structured human factors method, the reader is referred to Lim et al (1990a and b) and Lim (1992).

developed.

2.4. A Conception of Human Factors Support for System Development

An explicit conception of human factors design may be derived as follows:

(1) Review existing conceptions of human factors design, and formulate a *'consensus'* conception.

(2) Construct an *analytic* conception of human factors design to support appropriate interpretation and extension of existing design conceptions. An analytic conception may be derived by decomposing basic human factors design premises in terms of stage-wise manipulations of its design primitives; namely task, human, device and environment.

(3) Derive an explicit conception of human factors design by extending and integrating the *analytic* and *'consensus'* conceptions derived above.

An account of the above activities follows.

To support the derivation of a *'consensus'* conception of human factors design, a survey of relevant reports by human factors researchers and practitioners was conducted. Since the survey was extensive (totalling about a hundred reports), a comprehensive account cannot be provided here. Instead, the conception proposed by Shackel (1986a) is reviewed briefly to illustrate the concerns of the survey.

Figure 2-5 shows Shackel's (1986a) conception of human factors contributions to system development. The conception proposed is basically Jones' (1973) conception extended to provide a more comprehensive account of human factors design. Shackel grouped system development activities into three sets; namely machine factors, human factors and inter-disciplinary design factors. Although Shackel's conception is clearly an advance over its predecessor, the rationale for some of the proposed extensions remain unclear. In particular:

• The rationale for substituting *man-machine interface design* with *man-machine workstation design* is unclear. The substitution could be misleading since workstation design is currently understood as comprising largely anthropometric design. It is thus unclear where user-computer interface design would be addressed, since Shackel's conception excludes human factors involvement in software and hardware design (these concerns were designated as machine factors).

• The reason for separating task description, analysis and synthesis is unclear. Although a case may be made for distinguishing between task analysis and synthesis,[4] it is unclear why task description would not be a sub-activity of both activities.

• The purpose of the *relate to* arrow exiting from the *Other systems* circle is unspecified. The intention of the arrow may be to highlight the need to examine existing systems to account for transfer of learning effects. However, this interpretation may be inconsistent with other parts of Shackel's conception. In particular, the location of extant systems analysis *before* task analysis seems to imply that the former is unsupported by the latter. This implication is illogical since the strongest contribution from task analysis is the analysis of extant systems. Furthermore, the location of task analysis in parallel with

Figure 2-5:   Shackel's (1986a) Conception of Human Factors Design Contributions

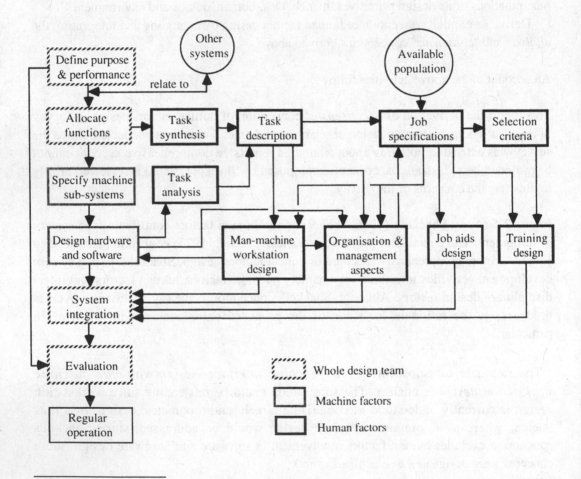

---

[4] It has been argued that task analysis cannot be applied in the absence of an extant or reasonably developed system. Thus, to contribute to design *specification* (as opposed to design *evaluation*), task analysis needs to be supported by an additional step to address task synthesis.

function allocation and task synthesis also seems to indicate (erroneously) that the latter design concerns are not supported by task analysis (see Figure 2-5);

• the purpose of the *regular operation* box is unspecified. Its inclusion is misleading since it may be inferred erroneously that abnormal or emergency operations are excluded from the scope of human factors design;

• the designation of some of the boxes as solely 'machine factors' is debatable, e.g. software and hardware design.

Such ambiguities were typically found during the survey of existing conceptions of human factors design. In particular, the survey uncovered the following problems:

(a) The scope and taxonomy of existing human factors design concerns are defined poorly. As a result, the location of human factors concerns relative to the system design cycle was found to be inconsistent across reports. For instance, Shackel (1986a) located task analysis after function allocation, while Grudin et al. (1987), Haubner (1990) and Pikaar et al. (1990) reported the reverse order.

(b) The scope, process, product and notation of the design stages were usually undefined. Similarly, relationships between inter-connected design stages were not specified explicitly.

Thus, it remains unclear how human factors design should be advanced. Such problems had to be addressed during the derivation of a *consensus* conception of human factors design. For this purpose, a simple two-step procedure was applied to process the information collated.

First, a list of human factors design concerns was collated from all the reports reviewed.[5] The number of items in the list was then reduced by grouping similar concerns under one generic category. For instance, reported concerns of human factors design such as *user analysis* and *user characterisation* were grouped together under the latter category name. Similarly, subsets were grouped into a super-ordinate set where appropriate, e.g. *task description* was subsumed by *task analysis*. Peripheral human factors design concerns were excluded, e.g. *late customisation* and *product survey*. To reduce further the categories of human factors concerns, a basic or minimum set was selected from the collated list by imposing an acceptance threshold. Specifically, only design concerns

---

[5] To support more specific interpretations of reported human factors design concerns, relevant low-level details were also noted. The identification and sequencing of equivalent design concerns with respect to the system design cycle were thus facilitated. Some discrepancies in the reported locations of task analysis were reconciled in this way.

mentioned in more than fifty percent of the reports were selected. Nine categories of human factors design concerns were thus derived; namely system performance definition, task analysis, job design, function allocation, user interface design, user characterisation, training design, evaluation and environment design. These concerns comprise the basic building blocks for constructing a *consensus* conception of human factors design. The reported human factors design conceptions were then re-described in terms of the basic categories of design concerns.

Second, the sequence of design concerns was ranked numerically for each reported conception of human factors design. Since the total number of design concerns identified varies between reports, the ranking was normalised to the maximum number of categories of human factors design concerns, i.e. to base 9. The modal and adjacent rankings of the normalised set were then used to specify a *consensus* sequence for addressing human factors design concerns. To support more specific interpretations of reported human factors design concerns, pertinent low-level details noted during the literature review were then taken into account. More specific human factors design concerns (e.g. task synthesis), were thus introduced into initial versions of the *consensus* conception. It should be emphasised that the sequence of design concerns derived is approximate. The conception may be updated following further research on existing human factors design practices.

Figure 2-6 shows the *consensus* conception of human factors design that was derived. Although the conception seems reasonably complete with respect to the system design cycle, the underlying premises for advancing human factors design remain implicit. Further insight in this respect may be derived by constructing an analytic conception of human factors design. In an analytic conception, human factors design is described in terms of manipulations of a set of basic design primitives; namely task, user, environment and device. The derivation of an analytic conception is described next.

Grandjean's (1988) concept of human-centered design may be used as the basis for constructing an analytic conception of human factors support for interactive system development. In the context of Grandjean's concept, the primary objective of human factors design is viewed broadly as *'fitting <x> to the human'*, where *x* is some intersection of the desirable properties of the task, device and environment. The perspective may be interpreted to imply the following design stages of system development:

(1) identification of the target user population;
(2) definition of performance requirements for the human-computer system;
(3) definition of user requirements in respect of the task, environment and computer (both hardware and software);

(4) specification of the conceptual and interaction level tasks, environment, user interface and workstation design, so that user and system performance requirements are satisfied. Any 'shortfall' in the design specifications that cannot be rectified (e.g. due to technological limitations), may then be 'compensated' by intensive user training and selection. In other words, an acceptable level of *fitting the human to <x>'* may precede and/or follow *'fitting <x> to the human'.* This design perspective is consistent with the human factors objective of achieving satisfactory system performance at acceptable costs. In the context of human-computer systems, satisfactory performance is attained if work goals are achieved at acceptable human and computer costs (Dowell and Long 1989).

Figure 2-6: A 'Consensus' Conception of Human Factors Design

Level of Design Consideration	Design Stage	Human Factors Design Concerns Addressed
System level	1	System performance definition and user characterisation (requirements specification)
	2	High-level function allocation, extant task analysis, task synthesis, environmental design and training projection
Sub-system level	3	User characterisation, low-level function allocation
	4	Job design, training design
	5	Task analysis, high-level user interface design
	6	Environmental design
	7	Low-level user interface design and training design
	8	Late evaluation

To summarise then, human factors design involves manipulating the attributes of its design primitives (namely user, task, device and environment) to satisfy system performance requirements. The performance of the system is thus a function of the design attributes of human factors primitives. This relationship may be represented informally as follows:

$$\text{System performance} = f \{\text{environment, task, device, user}\}$$

or $$P_{system} = f\{E, T, D, U\}$$

Human factors manipulations of these design primitives will now be examined in greater detail. To begin with, the development of a new system may be motivated by:

• Required improvements of the existing level of system performance.

• Incidental modification of the attributes of the system or sub-systems (e.g. a re-distribution of sub-system functions) to maintain or increase overall system performance.

At the overall system level, human factors design is concerned primarily with defining system and sub-system configurations to satisfy specific performance requirements. To this end, socio-technical implications of particular distributions of sub-system functions are assessed (e.g. potential disruption of established work relationships). The high-level allocation of functions between human and device components is also considered for each sub-system. The objective at this stage is to define the purpose and performance requirements of the target or new system. A design basis is thus established to support a modular development of the sub-systems followed by their integration. Such an approach to system development has been reported widely, e.g. Eason (1987); Gillett and Northam (1990); Shackel (1986a); Jones (1973); and Pikaar et al. (1990).

During the specification of sub-systems, a human factors designer may apply the following strategies:

• Attributes of central and critical primitives are manipulated *first*, since design constraints are less severe at earlier stages of design. This assertion is true since the number of design constraints would increase (and hence the degrees of freedom would decrease) as the system becomes more developed. The strategy is thus to ensure that incrementally difficult constraints are accommodated by design primitives that are more amenable to manipulation. For instance, users' jobs and tasks should be addressed before device design. Attributes of the latter may then be designed to accommodate the constraints imposed by the former.
• Attributes of *stable* design primitives are specified next. Interactions between design primitives may thus be managed more effectively. This assertion is true because attributes of stable primitives specified at earlier design stages, would remain largely unaffected by later design decisions. A more rapid convergence to the desired design solution may thus accrue.

Sub-system level design is initiated by a more specific definition of user groups and their needs. Specifically, key user characteristics are identified and documented as design constraints.[6] Potential implications of the new task should also be noted to highlight possible transfer of learning effects. In addition, high-level assumptions pertaining to key attributes of the task, environment and device should also be noted. Using the set of constraints as a design basis, attributes of individual design primitives may then be

---

[6] Such constraints, however, do not obviate the need for user testing, since they are rarely if ever complete or known to be so.

manipulated so that the performance requirements of the sub-system are satisfied. The design is thus advanced to lower levels of description. Since the design primitives are mutually interacting, it should be noted that a change in the design basis at this stage would imply wider design iterations.

Next, the design of the user's *task* is addressed. Task design involves decomposing sub-system functions (comprising human and device elements) so that on-line and off-line task components are detailed sufficiently to support job and training design. On-line and off-line tasks correspond to computer-supported and manual tasks respectively. At this design stage, on-line tasks may also be decomposed further into interactive and automated task components (see Figures 2-1 and 2-2 for an account of these types of tasks). To support the design activities, participatory design approaches and task analysis techniques may be recruited.

The preceding manipulations of human factors design may be represented informally as follows:

$U \longrightarrow U$ *(i.e. user attributes are defined and carried forward to constrain task design)*

$T \longrightarrow T'$ *(i.e. the existing task T is transformed into task T'. In other words, attributes of task T are modified)*

Since $T = \{T_{off\text{-}line}, T_{device}, T_{interaction}\}$:

$$\{T_{off\text{-}line}, T_{device}, T_{interaction}\} \longrightarrow \{T'_{off\text{-}line}, T'_{device}, T'_{interaction}\}$$

      (i.e. new device tasks (T'_{device}), interactive tasks ($T'_{interaction}$) and off-line tasks ($T'_{off\text{-}line}$), are specified)

Following task design, system level assumptions of the social and physical *environment* may be specified at a lower level of description. In particular, socio-technical implications are defined explicitly; and the design of the physical environment is addressed. The design concerns addressed may comprise one or more of the following:

(1) the macro-environment may be tempered to a range that is acceptable to the target or new system, e.g. air conditioners may be used to reduce the ambient temperature;
(2) a micro-environment may be created via an ancillary device, e.g. protective clothing to shield the user from adverse atmospheric conditions;
(3) the machine is designed to withstand the physical conditions, and the user is trained

physiologically to tolerate work periods in the environment, e.g. fighter pilots are trained to tolerate higher than normal gravitational forces.

An appropriate design solution is thus derived by considering the implications of psychological and physiological stressor(s), and the technological constraints. The preceding manipulations of human factors design may be represented informally as follows:

$$U \longrightarrow U$$
$$\{T_{off\text{-}line}, T_{device}, T_{interaction}\} \longrightarrow \{T'_{off\text{-}line}, T'_{device}, T'_{interaction}\}$$
(i.e. attributes of these primitives are carried forward to constrain environmental design (E))

$$E \longrightarrow E'$$
(i.e. the attributes of the existing environment (E) are transformed (E'))

At this juncture, ***device*** design (comprising software, hardware and workstation design) may be undertaken. To this end, functional design is pursued via iterative decomposition of the device and interactive components of the on-line task, i.e. T'_{device} and $T'_{interaction}$ respectively. The decompositions derived should be consistent with earlier design decisions and constraints. In addition, the inputs and outputs of T'_{device} and $T'_{interaction}$ should complement each other. On the basis of the inputs and outputs of $T'_{interaction}$ and the requirements of the in-house style (if any), a user interface design may then be specified. Since all design extensions leading to the interactive task and user interface design are constrained by the adopted user-task model, a closer match between the designer's and user's model of the system may be expected. Better device usability and functionality may thus accrue. The preceding manipulations of human factors design may be summarised informally as follows:

$$U \longrightarrow U$$
$$E \longrightarrow \{E', E\}$$
$$\{T_{off\text{-}line}, T_{device}, T_{interaction}\} \longrightarrow \{T'_{off\text{-}line}, T'_{device}, T'_{interaction}\}$$
(i.e. attributes of these primitives are carried forward to constrain device design (D))

$$T'_{interaction} \longrightarrow \{sub\text{-}tasks, procedures, object\text{-}action pairs\}$$
(i.e. the interactive task is decomposed to derive a device level description)

$T'_{device} \longrightarrow \{device\ programs\}$

$D \longrightarrow D'$

$T_{on\text{-}line}, D \longrightarrow T'_{on\text{-}line}, D' \qquad$ or $\qquad \{T'_{device}, T'_{interaction}\}, D'$

      (i.e. a new device is designed to replace the old, and a new set of on-line tasks is defined).

Other design contexts may be summarised similarly as follows.

(i) Re-design of an existing user interface

In this case, the off-line and device tasks would remain largely unchanged. Thus, the manipulations of human factors design may be described informally as follows:

$T_{on\text{-}line}, D \longrightarrow T'_{on\text{-}line}, D' \qquad$ or $\qquad \{T_{device}, T'_{interaction}\}, D'$

      (i.e. the device task is unchanged while interactive tasks are re-designed)

$T'_{interaction} \longrightarrow \{sub\text{-}tasks,\ procedures,\ object\text{-}action\ pairs\}$

      (i.e. the new interactive task is decomposed to derive a device level description)

$T_{device} \longrightarrow \{device\ programs\}$

$D \longrightarrow D'$

      (i.e. the core application remains unchanged but a new user interface is designed to

      replace the old user interface)

(ii) Re-design of an off-line task without changing on-line support from the device

Such a design context may be undesirable, since greater demands from the off-line task could imply a higher user workload. In particular, the re-design may be instigated by inadequate on-line support, i.e. the user is compelled to take on further off-line tasks to compensate for inadequacies in the support of the on-line task. In other words, user costs are increased to satisfy performance requirements, while device costs remain unchanged. The above manipulations of human factors design may be summarised informally as follows:

$T \longrightarrow T'$

$T' = \{T_{on\text{-}line}, T'_{off\text{-}line}\}$

$T, D \longrightarrow T', D \qquad$ or $\qquad \{T_{on\text{-}line}, T'_{off\text{-}line}\}, D$

      (i.e. the on-line task and device design are unchanged while the off-line task is re-designed)

(iii) Re-design of manual tasks

In this case, on-line tasks do not exist. Thus, the manipulations of human factors design may be summarised informally as follows:

$$T = T_{off-line} \quad \text{or} \quad T_{manual}$$
$$T \longrightarrow T' \quad \text{or} \quad T_{manual} \longrightarrow T'_{manual}$$

(iv) Automation of manual tasks

The introduction of a device to support existing tasks essentially involves function allocation and the specification of new on-line tasks. Thus, the manipulations of human factors design may be summarised informally as follows:

$$T_{manual} \longrightarrow \{T'_{on-line}, T'_{off-line}\}$$
$$\textit{(i.e. function allocation)}$$

$$T'_{on-line} = \{T'_{device}, T'_{interaction}\}$$
$$T'_{interaction} \longrightarrow \{\text{sub-tasks, procedures, object-action pairs}\}$$
$$T'_{device} \longrightarrow \{\text{device programs}\}$$
$$T_{manual} \longrightarrow \{T'_{off-line}, T'_{device}, T'_{interaction}\}$$
$$\textit{(i.e. the manual task is replaced by a new task comprising off-line, interactive and}$$
$$\textit{device task components)}$$

(v) Extension and automation of an existing set of manual tasks

This scenario is a variant of (iv) above since the existing task is extended with the additional provision of device support. The manipulations of human factors design may be summarised informally as follows (transformations of the on-line task are not shown – please refer to (iv) above):

$$T = T_{off-line} \quad \text{or} \quad T_{manual}$$
$$T_{off-line} \longrightarrow T'_{off-line} \quad \text{or} \quad T'_{manual}$$
$$\textit{(i.e. the existing manual task is extended)}$$

$$T'_{manual} \longrightarrow \{T''_{on-line}, T''_{off-line}\}$$
$$\textit{(i.e. function allocation of the extended set of manual tasks)}$$

Finally, *user* selection and training may be considered if the desired level of sub-system performance cannot be achieved economically through further design iterations. The manipulations of human factors design may be summarised informally as follows:

$$T \longrightarrow \{T'_{on\text{-}line}, T'_{off\text{-}line}\}$$
$$T'_{on\text{-}line} = \{T'_{device}, T'_{interaction}\}$$
$$E \longrightarrow E'$$
$$T'_{interaction} \longrightarrow \{sub\text{-}tasks, procedures, object\text{-}action\ pairs\}$$
$$T'_{device} \longrightarrow \{device\ programs\}$$
$$D \longrightarrow D'$$

(i.e. training requirements and user selection criteria are defined, based on the attributes of the above primitives).

$$U \longrightarrow U'$$

(i.e. user attributes presumed at design outset are modified by training and selection)

Although the preceding account is a simplified description of human factors design (e.g. stage-wise design iterations and evaluation have been omitted), its focus on the manipulation of design primitives supports a more specific interpretation of the *consensus* conception. In particular, it highlights the following:

• the need for task synthesis at different levels of description; for instance, task synthesis is addressed at the system level to support functional allocation, and again at the sub-system level to support the design of human-machine interactions;
• the relationship between design primitives.

By comparing the *consensus* and *analytic* conceptions derived, a more explicit conception of human factors design was inferred (see Figure 2-7). The explicit conception essentially comprises three sets of human factors design activities; namely system level design (top part of Figure 2-7), sub-system level design (middle part of Figure 2-7), and sub-system integration and overall system evaluation (lower part of Figure 2-7).The figure shows that, following system level design, an iteration of sub-system level design activities is undertaken (comprising all design activities within the square envelope – middle part of Figure 2-7). Note that wider design iterations are not shown in this simple representation. The reader may refer to Lim (1992) for a more detailed account of the explicit conception.

On the basis of the explicit conception, a structured framework of human factors design may be defined (see Figure 2-8). Complementary sets of human factors techniques may

Figure 2-7:   A More Explicit Conception of Human Factors Design

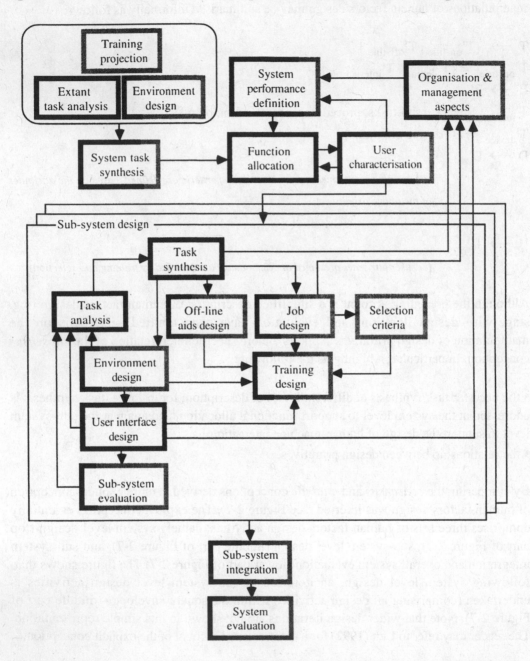

Bold outlined boxes indicate human factors design concerns addressed by the structured human factors method, named MUSE. Incomplete address by the method is similarly indicated by partially outlined boxes.

then be identified and located against the framework. Subsequently, the techniques may be extended and integrated to satisfy the following requirements of a structured method; namely:

• the scope of design support provided by the integrated techniques should cover reasonably completely the system design cycle;
• the products, processes and notations of all design stages of the integrated techniques should be defined explicitly (see Lim et al. 1990a and b).

The development of a structured human factors method is described next.

Figure 2-8: A Structured Framework for Human Factors Design

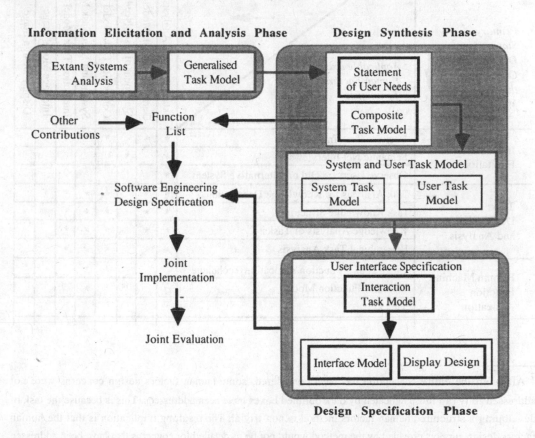

Design Specification Phase

2.5. Structuring Human Factors Support Throughout System Development
Figure 2-8 shows how the explicit conception has been instantiated as a structured

framework for human factors design.[7] On the basis of the framework, a structured human factors method may be developed. Presently, the framework is reviewed. An indication of where existing human factors techniques may be located within its design stages, is also included in the review (see Figures 2-9 and 2-10). A more detailed account of the framework may be found in Chapters Three to Six, where MUSE is described.

Figure 2-9: Locating Existing Human Factors Techniques against Design Concerns of the Structured Framework

Primary Stage-wise Design Concerns of the Structured Method	Applicable Existing Human Factors Techniques	Extant Systems Analysis Stage	Generalised Task Model Stage	Statement of User Needs Stage	Composite Task Model Stage	System and User Task Model Stage	Interaction Task Model Stage	Interface Model Stage	Display Design Stage
Information Elicitation	Decision Tree Interviews	*	*		*	*	*		
	Semantic Net Interviews	*		*					
	Observe Users on Old or Alternative System	*							
Task Description and Analysis	Task Analysis for Knowledge Description	*	*		*	*	*		
	Task Knowledge Structures	*	*		*	*	*		
	Knowledge Analysis of Tasks	*	*		*	*	*		
	Hierarchical Task Analysis	*	*		*	*	*		
Human Machine Function Allocation	Clegg et al.'s Function Allocation Technique					*	*		
	Operator Function Model					*	*		
	etc.......								

Design Stages of the Structured Method →

---

[7] Although the entire conception has been considered, some human factors design concerns were not addressed fully (all those indicated by dark outlined boxes have been addressed). This is because the task of developing a structured human factors method is non-trivial. The resulting implication is that the human factors design support provided by the method would not be as detailed for concerns that have been addressed partially. Nevertheless, the design support provided by the method would still be an advance over existing human factors techniques. Later versions of the structured method could be developed to address incrementally the remaining concerns.

Generally, the structured design framework comprises two streams of inter-disciplinary design activities, namely the software engineering design stream (including other design contributors) and the human factors design stream. To define human factors design contributions more explicitly, its design stream is decomposed in greater detail to show how its design stages are operationalised. The design stages of the stream are also grouped into three design phases, namely the Information Elicitation and Analysis Phase; the Design Synthesis Phase; and the Design Specification Phase (see Figure 2-8). An account of individual design stages follows.

(i) Extant Systems Analysis Stage. The scope of this stage comprises the elicitation and analysis of extant system[8] information, e.g. user needs and problems; existing task characteristics, design features and rationale, etc. In addition, extant designs are assessed to determine their potential for recruitment to the design of the target or new system. A wide range of human factors techniques may be recruited at this stage. First, the elicitation of extant system information may be supported by 'off-the-shelf' techniques such as structured, decision tree and semantic net interviews; unobtrusive user observations; etc. (i.e. column 3 rows 1 to 3, Figure 2-9). Second, the derivation of appropriate task descriptions may be guided by techniques for task decomposition, abstraction and generification (i.e. column 3 rows 4 to 6, Figure 2-9). Third, assessments of extant design features may be supported by general evaluation techniques such as component and artefact analysis techniques, etc. (see column 2, Figure 2-10).

(ii) Generalised Task Model Stage. The concerns of this stage comprise the generation of device-independent descriptions to facilitate analytic mapping between relevant design features of an extant system(s) and target or new system requirements. In particular, a *generalised extant task model* is derived to support the recruitment of extant system features. A *generalised target task model* is also derived at this stage to expose the conceptual support required by newly introduced target system tasks. The objectives of these models are to inform conceptual design and to support early assessments of potential transfer of learning effects and training requirements. Existing techniques for task analysis such as Task Analysis for Knowledge Based Descriptions (or TAKD, Johnson et al. 1984. See also column 4 rows 4 to 6, Figure 2-9), may be recruited to support the derivation of both generalised task models.

(iii) Statement of User Needs Stage. This stage summarizes the conclusions of extant systems analysis (e.g. the rationale for recruiting particular design features of an extant system(s) to the target system), and defines more specific user requirements, performance

---

[8] The term *extant* systems refers generally to both the *current* system (i.e. the system (computerised or not) currently in use in the client organization) and *related* systems (i.e. similar systems in use in other organizations).

Figure 2-10: Location of Some Existing Human Factors Techniques against Specific Stages of the Structured Design Framework

Design Stages of a Structured Human Factors Design Method →

↓ Existing Hman Factors Techniques

	Extant Systems Analysis Stage	Generalised Task Model Stage	Statement of User Needs Stage	Composite Task Model Stage	System and User Task Model Stage	Interaction Task Model Stage	Interface Model Stage	Display Design Stage
Observe Users on Old or Alternative System	*							
Operator Function Model	*			*	*			
Decision Tree Interviews	*	*		*	*			*
Semantic Net Interviews	*		*					
Participatory Prototyping				*	*	*	*	*
Checklists/Guidelines	*		*		*		*	*
Hallway/Storefront Methodology	*		*	*	*	*	*	*
Walkthrough	*	*		*	*	*	*	*
Component Analysis	*						*	*
Visual Display Analysis	*						*	*
Metaphor Analysis		*	*	*			*	
Object/Action Analysis	*	*		*	*	*	*	
Generalised Transition Network		*		*			*	
Grammar Analysis	*		*			*		*
GOMS/CCT/MHP							*	*
Cognitive Walkthrough	*						*	*
Claims Analysis	*						*	*
Prototype with Role Playing	*			*	*	*		*
Usability Test			*	*	*	*	*	*
Interactive Transaction System (ITS)	*		*	*	*	*		

Design stages of the structured method may be supported by the following human factors techniques:

Extant Systems Analysis Stage
General elicitation, evaluation and task analysis techniques.

Generalised Task Model Stage
General evaluation and task analysis techniques.

Statement of User Needs Stage
General evaluation, task analysis and performance specification techniques (e.g. scenario analysis).

Composite Task Model Stage
General evaluation, task analysis, paper based prototyping, simulation and function allocation techniques.

System and User Task Model Stage
General evaluation, task analysis, paper based prototyping, simulation, function allocation and job design techniques (e.g. workload analysis).

Interaction Task Model, Interface Model and Display Design Stages
General evaluation, task analysis, mock-ups, and more advanced prototyping and simulation techniques.

Key to Acronyms – GOMS: Goals, Operators, Methods and Selection;   CCT: Cognitive Complexity Theory;   MHP: Model of Human Processor

criteria and domain semantics for the target or new system. Techniques for performance specification and semantic analysis may thus be recruited at this stage of design, e.g. scenario analysis (Malin et al. 1991) and metaphor analysis respectively (see column 4, Figure 2-10).

(iv) Composite Task Model Stage. This stage is involved with the generation of a conceptual design of the target system task. To this end, appropriate parts of both generalised task models (derived earlier) are extended and synthesised to derive a *composite task model* that supports function allocation between the human and computer. Existing human factors techniques that could support the design stage include techniques for task design and function allocation (column 6, Figure 2-9. See also Clegg et al. 1989; Price 1985), and for basic prototyping and simulation (see column 5, Figure 2-10).

(v) System and User Task Model Stage. The scope of this stage comprises the detailed design of target or new system functions, and job design. The design entails further decomposition of the *composite task model* to establish information flows between the user and computer. In addition, the on-line and off-line task descriptions generated could support time-line assessments of the acceptability of intended user tasks. To support task decomposition, existing techniques recruited at the preceding stage may also be applied (see column 7, Figure 2-9 and column 6, Figure 2-10).

(vi) Interaction Task Model Stage. This stage is involved with device level specification of the tasks to be performed by the user. The task model derived is termed an *interaction task model*. Low level task actions may then be grouped into coherent units of interaction to constrain the specification of error recovery schemes, feedback messages and screen displays. Since user feedback is very important at this stage, more advanced prototyping, simulation and evaluation techniques may be recruited to support design demonstration and assessment (see column 8, Figure 2-9 and column 7, Figure 2-10).

(vii) Interface Model Stage. The scope of this stage comprises the detailed specification of screen objects, e.g. object behaviour and appearance changes. Thus, object modelling, command syntax and icon design are addressed at this stage. Techniques that could be recruited to support the stage include object and action analysis, visual display analysis, metaphor analysis, usability test, etc. (see column 8, Figure 2-10).

(viii) Display Design Stage. This stage is concerned with the following: specification of screen contents and layouts; compilation of a glossary of screen objects; definition of contexts for triggering error and feedback messages and for presenting computer functions to support the user's task. Techniques recruited at the Interaction Task Model Stage may also be applied at this stage (see column 9, Figure 2-10).

In the preceding review, appropriate locations for recruiting some of the techniques listed in Figure 1-10 have been indicated in the structured framework. For completeness, Figure 2-10 summarises the locations for the complete set. It should be noted that the locations were determined approximately by intersecting the concerns and needs of system development (defined explicitly by design stages of the structured framework) against the design support capabilities of the techniques. To confirm the appropriateness and hence the 'accuracy' of the locations, a more detailed examination of individual techniques would be required. Specifically, the techniques should be examined further to determine whether the information required for application can be met at a particular design stage; and whether the outputs of the techniques would address adequately the design concerns of that stage. In addition, the resources required for technique application need to be assessed against the design priorities of a particular stage.

2.6. Development of a Structured Human Factors Method

Although Figures 2-9 and 2-10 support a more specific recruitment of existing human factors techniques, the projection and allocation of resources required for their application remain unaddressed. Thus, complete application of appropriately recruited techniques may be thwarted by inadequate resourcing and the imposition of unrealistic time frames for project deliverables. Alternatively, non-allocation or encroachment[9] of resources for human factors design may also arise (see Eason and Cullen 1988; Grudin 1991; Meister 1984).

To support better accommodation of design resource requirements, an appropriate set of human factors techniques should be identified, extended and integrated into a structured method. In particular, the well-defined stage-wise design scope and process of such a method would facilitate explicit representation of human factors requirements in the system design agenda. More detailed arguments for the development of a structured method were presented in Chapter One, e.g. it provides a sound basis for developing computer-based tools to support human factors design.

For a comprehensive account of what is entailed by the development of a structured human factors method (and of MUSE in particular), the reader may wish to refer to Lim et al. (1990a and b). Such an account would be relevant to readers who are interested in method development. For the purposes of this book (namely to disseminate the method and support its application), it suffices to say that the procedures of method development comprises the following steps:

(1) Examine existing human factors techniques (whole or part) that have been assigned to individual stages of the structured design framework (see Figures 2-9 and 2-10). Select a

---

[9] Encroachment of resources for human factors design has been attributed to inadequate accommodation by the design agenda, and/or to insufficient managerial commitment to human factors.

set of techniques that are promising, e.g. techniques that are well developed and established. Follow procedure 2a and/or 2b.

(2a) Identify a comprehensive set of *general* techniques that may be recruited across design stages of the structured method. Go to procedure 3.

(2b) Identify *alternative* combinations of more *specific* techniques that may be recruited across design stages of the structured method. For instance, the method might have three design stages {X,Y and Z} that are supported by techniques {X1 to X3}, {Y1 to Y3} and {Z1 to Z3} respectively. Depending on the compatibility of techniques assigned to successive design stages, the structured method may offer various combinations of techniques that may be recruited in different design contexts. For instance, a combination of techniques {X1, Y3, Z1} that emphasizes extant design analysis may be selected in a variant design context; while combination {X3, Y2, Z3}, which includes more rigorous design validation techniques, may be selected on another occasion to support novel design. Go to procedure 3.

(3) Extend individual techniques (as necessary) on the basis of the structured design framework. The objective is to ensure that the design support provided by the structured method is sufficiently explicit and comprehensive with respect to the system design cycle. For instance, a technique applied at a design stage may be extended to ensure that the information it generates satisfies input requirements of another technique assigned to a succeeding stage.

(4) Concatenate individual techniques (as necessary) on the basis of the structured design framework. The objective is to ensure that overlaps in the design scope of techniques assigned to successive design stages are eliminated.

(5) Iterate procedures 3 and 4 until the selected techniques have been integrated coherently.

Following the development of a structured method, the above procedures could be invoked periodically to incorporate further techniques. During incorporation, the characteristics of newly recruited techniques should be assessed to ensure compatibility with the techniques already incorporated in the method.

2.7. Summary

It is asserted in this chapter that, for effective recruitment of human factors techniques, the following requirements need to be satisfied:

• The scope, product and process of human factors techniques should be made explicit. Human factors design concerns may then be represented explicitly and accommodated by the system design agenda. Design resources that are appropriate to support method application may then be allocated.

• The notations of human factors techniques should be developed to support more specific design descriptions.

• Human factors techniques should be located explicitly against a structured design framework. Two reasons motivate this requirement. First, the well-defined stage-wise design scope of the structured framework could support a closer matching of existing techniques with system design needs and contexts. Relevant human factors techniques may thus be identified for recruitment at appropriate stages of system development. Second, existing human factors techniques assigned against a structured design framework could be extended and integrated to derive a structured human factors method. Such a method could support system development comprehensively, and also facilitate the identification of intersecting human factors and software engineering design concerns. The product, process and notation of human factors design contributions may then be positioned and timed more appropriately to the stages of system development.

• Computer-based tools should be developed following the specification of a reasonably complete structured human factors method. In particular, computer support should be provided to facilitate the generation, documentation and delivery of design descriptions as prescribed by the structured human factors method.

A structured human factors method (namely MUSE, **M**ethod for **US**ability **E**ngineering) that satisfies the above requirements has been developed following seven person-years of research. Case-study tests applied during the research have indicated the method to be promising for facilitating human factors contribution to system development.[10] In addition, MUSE has been integrated with a particular structured software engineering method to facilitate the co-ordination and timing of inter-disciplinary design activities (see Lim et al. (1992) for a detailed account). Since human factors and software engineering design stages and activities are intersected explicitly in an integration of their methods, greater awareness and understanding of inter-disciplinary design concerns and needs may be expected. In other words, by establishing familiar reference points (corresponding to specific stages of the structured software engineering method), the integrated method supports better assimilation by software engineers of human factors design contributions (and vice versa). Consequently, a greater and more effective uptake of human factors inputs may be expected.

An account of the structured human factors method, namely MUSE, is presented in the next four chapters. Following the description of MUSE, various integrations of human factors with structured software engineering methods are reviewed. The review sets the context for exposing a similar integration of MUSE with the Jackson System Development (JSD) method (a structured software engineering method).

---

[10] The reader may wish to refer to Lim et al. (1990a and b) and Lim (1992), for detailed accounts of case-study tests conducted during the development of MUSE.

3
An Overview of MUSE

> *In the land of the blind, the one-eyed man is king.*
> *Bottom-line argument for the method?*   **John Long, 1990**

> *Good order is the foundation of all good things.*
> **Edmund Burke, 1790**

The objective of the present overview is to establish a conceptual foundation for a detailed stage-wise account of the method in Chapters Four to Six.

3.1. General Characteristics of the Human Factors Method

The primary focus of the method is on design specification because a literature survey indicated that current human factors contributions are well established at later stages of system development, e.g. human factors evaluation after design implementation. In contrast, human factors contributions to design specification are generally inadequate and implicit. Since the recruitment of human factors contributions is traditionally late, the discovery of design errors is also delayed. As a result, the required modifications are costly and difficult to implement (see Chapter One). Thus, greater emphasis is placed on ensuring human factors contributions to design specification. In this context, a participative followed by consultative design role for human factors contribution is envisaged at system specification and implementation respectively. During the latter stage, existing techniques for human factors evaluation may be recruited to support the method. An overview of the method follows.

The method is structured into three phases, each of which comprises a number of design stages (Figure 2-8 is reproduced overleaf for reference). The scope of the design phases is as follows:

(i) The Information Elicitation and Analysis Phase is concerned with user requirements capture and task analysis. Its design stages comprise the Extant Systems System Analysis and Generalised Task Model Stages.

Figure 2-8: A Structured Framework for Human Factors Design

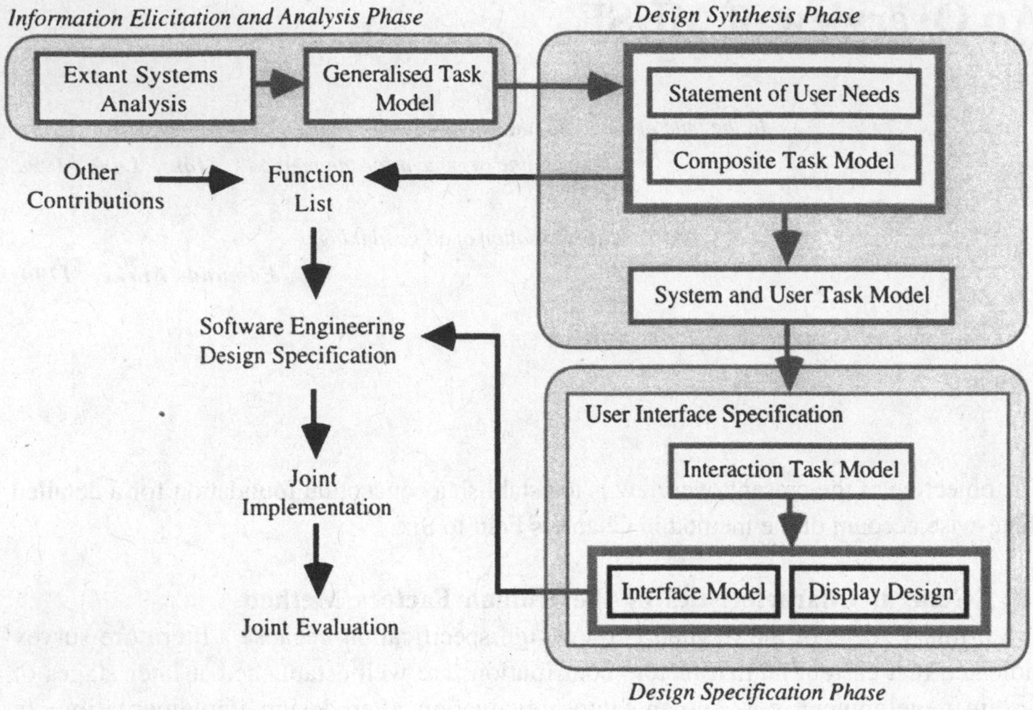

Information Elicitation and Analysis Phase   *Design Synthesis Phase*

```
┌─────────────────┐     ┌─────────────────┐        ┌──────────────────────────────┐
│ Extant Systems  │ ──→ │ Generalised Task│ ──→    │  Statement of User Needs     │
│ Analysis        │     │ Model           │        │                              │
└─────────────────┘     └─────────────────┘        │  Composite Task Model        │
                                                    └──────────────────────────────┘

    Other      ──→   Function  ←──
 Contributions         List                         │  System and User Task Model  │

                        │
                        ↓
              Software Engineering  ←──
              Design Specification

                        ↓                           User Interface Specification
                     Joint                              Interaction Task Model
                  Implementation
                                                        Interface Model    Display Design
                        ↓
                 Joint Evaluation
```

Design Specification Phase

(ii) The Design Synthesis Phase addresses the derivation of a conceptual design of the target system. Its design stages comprise the Statement of User Needs, Composite Task Model and System and User Task Model Stages.

(iii) The Design Specification Phase is focused on functional definition and user-interface design. Its design stages comprise the Interaction Task Model, Interface Model and Display Design Stages.

A detailed account of these stages of the method is presented in the next chapter. It suffices to say here that salient characteristics of the method include the following:

(1) Its stages correspond to coherent groupings of design processes that transform inputs to desired outputs. In most cases, the design output(s) of a stage constitute input(s) to a succeeding stage. Extended relationships, however, may also apply across a number of stages, e.g. design output(s) of one stage may feed into several succeeding stages. Such instances are identified as appropriate.

(2) The design scope, process and notation of each of its stages are defined explicitly. Thus, each stage is characterised respectively by a set of design products, procedures and

documentation schemes (see Sub-section 3.2).

(3) It encourages the use of prototyping as a means of making good the current incompleteness of human factors knowledge (see also (4) and (5) below). To this end, all design products of the method are defined explicitly to support prototype construction at each stage of system development. Thus, proposed designs may be exemplified to facilitate early and continuous human factors evaluation vis-à-vis the system design cycle. However, it should be noted that the design approach entailed by the method may be incompatible with that of rapid prototyping (as is the case with any structured method). In particular, structured methods emphasise a design analysis and documentation phase prior to the specification of a 'first-best-guess' solution (which may then be prototyped). Such a design phase may be precluded by the very rapidness required by a rapid prototyping approach.

(4) Its methodological structure supports the implementation of accepted design principles such as:

(i) the delaying of design commitments (Thimbleby, 1990), e.g. by ensuring that detailed design is preceded by appropriate design analysis and conceptual definition.

(ii) the conduct of early design evaluation, either analytically by the designer or empirically via a prototype.

(iii) the conduct of iterative design.

(iv) the conduct of incremental or modular design development. Specifically, detailed design may be pursued modularly following the specification of a conceptual design.

(5) Its well defined stage-wise scope, process and notation, i.e. its characteristic methodological features provide a basis for configuring and recruiting alternative means of human factors contribution, e.g. design guidelines, computer-based tools and prototyping. Firstly, its explicitly defined stage-wise design scope facilitates the recruitment of guidelines appropriate to each stage of system development. Secondly, its explicitly defined stage-wise scope, process and notation facilitate the identification of computer-support requirements. On this basis, computer-based tools may then be developed to support design specification. Thirdly, prototyping is encouraged at each stage of the method, since its design products are defined explicitly (see (3) above).

(6) Part of its notation is recruited from existing Software Engineering structured analysis and design methods (see Sub-section 3.3). The objective of recruiting such notations is two-fold; namely they facilitate communications between human factors designers and software engineers, and they support more specific human factors descriptions that are easily conveyed to end-users (Finkelstein and Potts, 1985; Hares, 1987). Existing notations were recruited following a series of assessments concerned with their suitability for particular human factors descriptions (Walsh, 1987a; Lim, 1988e; Carver, 1988).

(7) The level of description of its procedures is targeted at a human factors designer.

Specifically, the method does not (at present) provide comprehensive support for declarative human factors knowledge. In other words, the support provided by the method is predominantly procedural, i.e. its application facilitates the specification of a human factors solution and not the 'automatic' generation of a design solution.

(8) Its approach to design specification may be characterised as a 'user-task oriented' approach. The approach implies that a user model may be accommodated by particular task execution and performance characteristics of the system design.

(9) Its focus is primarily on design specification rather than on design implementation and evaluation. The bias is intended to redress the current imbalance in human factors contributions to system development.

(10) Its coverage of the system design cycle is sufficiently general to support directly 'base-line' integrations with a number of existing Software Engineering structured analysis and design methods. Subsequently, the integrated method may be enhanced further by tailoring MUSE (as necessary) to the design support needs of the specific Software Engineering method, e.g. particular areas of human factors support may be emphasised. In addition, explicit design dependencies should be defined to:

(i) co-ordinate inter-disciplinary contributions to system development.

(ii) support assimilation of MUSE by software engineers, e.g. familiar reference points corresponding to design stages of the Software Engineering method may be highlighted. A positive transfer of knowledge may thus be supported. It should be noted that a particular design team composition need not follow the inter-disciplinary streams of an integrated method. The only requirement of such a method is that Human Factors, Software Engineering and domain expertise should be represented. Thus, later references to design teams working in respective streams of an integrated method (Chapter Seven) are for expository purposes only. While design teams may be the case for most projects, complete application of the integrated method by a single designer should not be precluded.

3.2. Structure of the Human Factors Method

At the highest level of description, the method may be conceptualised in terms of a number of design stages. These stages define coherent groups of human factors design concerns to be addressed at each stage of system development. As an example, the human factors design concerns addressed at the extant systems analysis stage are shown in Figure 3-1, i.e. information elicitation, description and analysis of extant system(s).

At a lower level of description, the scope, process and notational components of each stage of MUSE are specified explicitly to support a systematic address of the design concerns of the stage (see Figure 3-1). These components are further decomposed to define a set of design products, procedures and documentation schemes. Included in the latter set are appropriate existing human factors techniques (part or whole) that have been modified, extended and incorporated into the method (see Chapter Two), e.g. existing techniques for user interviews and task analysis. A detailed account of the set of design products, procedures and documentation schemes of the method, is presented in the next three chapters.

Figure 3-1: Internal Structure of Each Stage of the Method

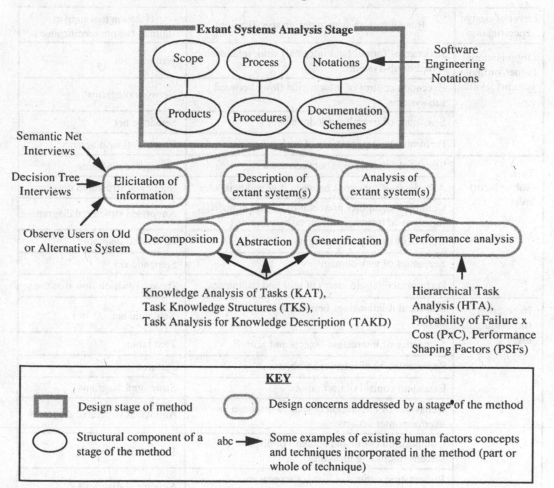

3.3. Design Notations and Documentation Schemes of the Human Factors Method

Generally, human factors design involve specifications at the organisational level (or super-ordinate system level); task level (or sub-system level); and interaction level (or input/output level). An account of the notations used for human factors specification at these design levels follows. Simple examples are used to illustrate the notations indicated in Chapter Two (Figure 2-4 is reproduced below for reference).

Figure 2-4: Structured Notations to Support Human Factors Specifications

Level of design specification	Human factors system design specifications	Notation that support human factors specifications
Organisational (super-ordinate system) level	Structure of formal (and informal) work relationships between sub-systems	Semantic net
	Execution control of information flows between sub-systems	Network diagrams
	Semantics of overall work domain	Semantic net
	Performance requirements of each sub-system	Function flow diagrams
Task (sub-system) level	Structural relationships between tasks	Structured diagrams
	Allocation of functions between user and computer	Annotated structured diagrams
	Control of computer presentation of task support functions in response to user task executions	Annotated structured diagrams
	Control of user task executions	Structured diagrams
	Semantics of task domain	Semantic net
	Performance requirements of user and computer	Tables, function flow diagrams
Interaction (input-output) level	Structural relationships between interaction objects	Semantic net
	Semantics of interaction objects and actions	Text tables
	Representation of interaction objects	Pictures
	Execution control of user inputs	Structured diagrams
	Behaviour of interaction objects in response to user/computer actions	Annotated structured diagrams
	Composition (form and content) of display screens (including messages)	Pictures and text
	Presentation control of display screens in response to user/computer actions	Structured diagrams

The reader should refer to Chapters Four to Six for more detailed illustrations involving a case-study.

At the organisation level, the following notations of the method may be applied:

(i) Semantic nets. This notation may be used for two types of specifications, namely to define organisational structure (e.g. organisation job chart); and to specify relations between entities, concepts, events and processes associated with the domain of the system. Semantic nets are essentially tree diagrams comprising nodes and numerically indexed inter-node relations (see Figure 3-2). A detailed illustration of a semantic net description is presented in Chapter Five. Rules of thumb that support the construction of a semantic net are as follows: its contents should adequately cover the scope of the system; its nodes should exclude device-specific information; and its inter-node relations should include taxonomic and composite relationships.

Figure 3-2: A Semantic Net Description of the System Domain

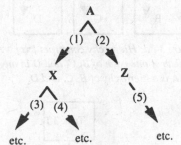

Node	Description	No.	Relation
A	Description of node A	(1)	Description of relation (1)
		(2)	Description of relation (2)
X	etc.	etc.	etc.

(ii) Other notations. To support discussions on conceptual design options, two other notations, namely network and function flow diagrams, may be used. Since these notations are still being developed, they will not be described here. Instead, the reader is referred to Annex B, for a description and illustration of the notations.

At the sub-system or task level, the following notations of the method may be applied:

(i) Structured diagrams. This notation may be used to specify the structure and control relationships between operations; sub-tasks; discrete and related tasks; and user and computer functions. For instance, structured diagrams may be used to specify when computer support functions should be presented to the user, i.e. to contextualise these presentations to the user's execution of the task. Simple illustrations of structured diagram specifications will be addressed when Figures 3-3 to 3-10 are described. The reader should refer to Chapters Four to Six for more detailed illustrations involving a case-study.

Notational constructs that may be applied in structured diagram specifications comprise the following set: sequence, selection, iteration, hierarchy, posit and quit. With the exception of the sequence construct (no symbol), each of these constructs is represented by a box with a symbol at either the top right- or left-hand corner (see Figure 3-3 for simple examples on the use of these constructs). Condition statements are indexed numerically below the boxes (see Figure 3-3c for an example of conditions for particular selections and termination of iterations).

Figure 3-3:   Notational Constructs for Structured Diagram Specification

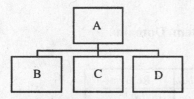

Figure 3-3a: Sequence construct [no symbol] – A consists of one each of B, C and D in the given order. A is a sequence of B, C and D.

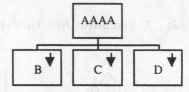

Figure 3-3d: Hierarchy construct [↓] – AAAA consists of one each of B, C, and D in any order. AAAA is a hierarchy of B, C, and D.

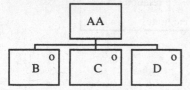

Figure 3-3b : Selection construct [o] – AA consists of either one B, or C, or D. AA is a selection of B, C, or D.

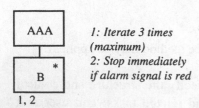

1: Iterate 3 times (maximum)
2: Stop immediately if alarm signal is red

Figure 3-3c: Iteration construct [*] – AAA consists of zero or more Bs. AAA is an iteration of B.

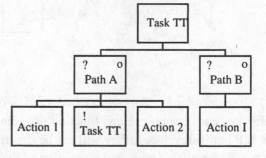

Figure 3-3e: Posit [?] and Quit [!] constructs – Task TT involves either Path A or B depending on situational conditions. Path A is first 'posited'. If unacceptable conditions are detected, e.g. after Action 1, then Path A is abandoned (quit/recover to 'Task TT') and Path B is 'admitted'. If unacceptable conditions are not detected, Path A is completed. In other words, the posit and quit constructs are used together to describe uncertain events, i.e. events which may involve recovery steps to rectify erroneous assumptions.

Generally, a structured diagram description is read from top to bottom and from left to right (in that order). When creating a structured diagram description, two simple rules should be followed, namely:

(1) The leaves of the diagram (i.e. boxes at the bottom of the diagram) should comprise actions (except 'quit' boxes, which indicate the sub-node box to which control is to be returned).

(2) Boxes at the *same* horizontal level in the diagram should have the *same* construct, e.g. all 'selection' boxes.

Individual boxes in a structured diagram description may also be differentiated to indicate functions allocated to the user and the computer (see Figure 3-4).

Figure 3-4:   Structured Diagram Specification of Functions Allocated to the User and Computer

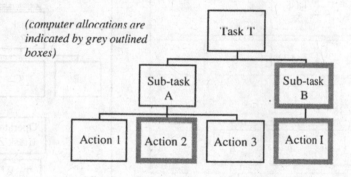

Apart from indicating function allocation, additional representation rules of the structured diagram notation are included to support the specification of task inter-leaving, concurrency and multiplicity (see Figure 3-5a to c). An account of these task concepts and notational rules follows:

(a) Inter-leaved tasks are discrete tasks whose operations are inter-woven. Thus, the user is required to execute a *current* task and monitor a *background* task. At a pre-specified point of task execution, the status of the tasks is reversed. To describe such tasks, separate structured diagrams with common actions are constructed and aligned vertically (see Figure 3-5a). Task inter-links are established by specifying common actions *across* the structured diagrams. Note that common actions are denoted by boxes assigned with the same identifier, e.g. actions {2, 4, 6} of Tasks X and Y in Figure 3-5a.

(b) Concurrent tasks are discrete tasks that are performed at the same time, e.g. data input while monitoring displays. To describe such tasks, *separate* structured diagrams are constructed and aligned horizontally (see Figure 3-5b). In addition, the root node (top box) of each diagram is assigned a common root identifier, e.g. Operator 1(data input) and Operator 1(display monitoring).

(c) Multiple tasks describe many units of the same task being performed at the same time. To describe such tasks, the root node (top box) is layered and the number of units is indicated, e.g. $n = 4 +$ (action 'C')/hour. The latter indicates that more than four units of the same task may be performed in the specified period, and the last unit is terminated at action 'C' (see Figure 3-5c).

Figure 3-5: Structured Diagram Specification of Inter-leaved, Concurrent and Multiple Tasks

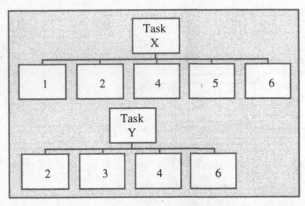

Figure 3-5a: Structured diagram specification of inter-leaved tasks X and Y. The common actions are {2, 4, 6}.

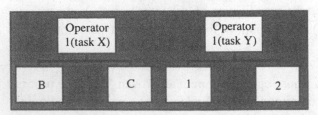

Figure 3-5b: Structured diagram specification of Operator 1's ability to perform task X and Y concurrently.

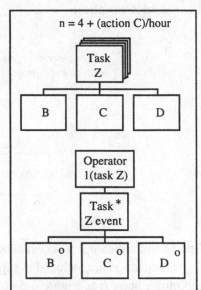

Figure 3-5c: Structured diagram specification of Operator 1's performance of multiple units of task Z without first having to complete each task unit. More than four units may be performed per hour, and the task terminates on action C at the fifth unit.

(ii) Semantic net and function flow diagrams. These notations may be used for human factors specifications at the sub-system level in the same manner as was illustrated for organisational level specifications (see earlier account and Annex B).

(iii) Performance tables may be constructed to specify tests and metrics to be applied on proposed design solutions. Generally, the tabular formats suggested by Whiteside et al. (1985) and Blyth and Hakiel (1989) would be suitable for the following specifications:

(1) *who* should be tested, e.g. a particular user group;

(2) *what* tasks test subjects should be required to perform, e.g. particular benchmark tasks;

(3) *how* tests should be conducted, e.g. laboratory simulation of the work environment;

(4) *what* test metrics should be used, e.g. task speed and accuracy (objective assessment); and attitude questionnaire (subjective assessment);

(5) *what* performance levels should be expected, e.g. worst and best levels for a particular prototype.

These performance specifications establish the basis for human factors design at the interaction level, and define the prescribed tests to which proposed solutions should be subjected to.

At the interaction level, the semantic net and structured diagram notations may be applied in the same manner as described for organisational and sub-system levels. Thus, these notations are not discussed further. Instead, a case-study is used to illustrate how the notations supplemented by screen diagrams (pictures), may be used to describe interactive behaviours between the user and computer; e.g. how computer functions and messages are actuated relative to the user's execution of the task. A simplified illustration involving a digital network security management system follows.

Figures 3-6 to 3-10 show a partial set of human factors specifications for a user interface design. The design specifications address the following human factors concerns:

(a) Interactive task and potential user errors. Figure 3-6 shows part of the network manager's inputs required to achieve on-line task goals of the (case-study) system. The relationship between specific display screens and inputs made by the network manager is also defined, e.g. the selection of a 'show user list' button and the consequent removal of Screen 4B (S4B) (see Figure 3-6 – the circle and arrow indicate the part of the diagram that has been enlarged). In other words, the structured diagram specification (termed an interaction task model), provides a *user-centered* perspective of the task of the interactive worksystem; i.e. the focus of the description is on user inputs. Note that grey bubbles in the figure indicate the point at which specified screens are removed or 'consumed', followed by an immediate presentation of the next screen. For instance, following input of the 'show user list' selection, Screen 4B (S4B) is 'consumed' and either Screen 5B-1 (S5B-1) or Screen E1-em3 (SE1-em3) is triggered (see Figure 3-6). The screen that is actually triggered depends on whether the required inputs have been made correctly (see (b) below).

Figure 3-6:   Part of an Interaction Task Model for Network Security Management

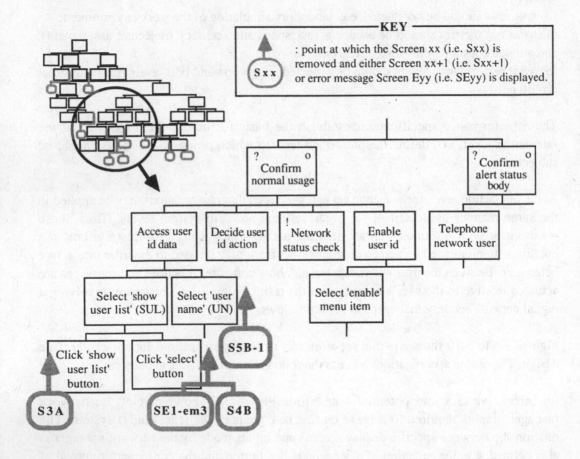

(b) Context and timing for presenting computer functions to support the user's task (including error handling). Figure 3-7 is a structured diagram (the circle and arrow indicate the part of the diagram that has been enlarged) that augments the human factors specifications shown in Figure 3-6. Specifically, it defines how screen actuations (e.g.

Screen E1-em3, Screen 4B) map onto particular actions of the network manager, from a *computer-centered* perspective (i.e. the focus is on computer actuations). For instance, the streams of network manager actions and screen actuations are linked as follows:

Manager Actions: 'show user list' ⟶ 'select user name'

Screen Actuations 1:   Screen 4B ⟶ ⟶ ⟶ ⟶ ⟶ ⟶ ⟶ ⟶ ⟶ ⟶ Screen 5B-1

Screen Actuations 2:   Screen 4B ⟶ Screen E1-em3 ⟶ Screen 4B ⟶ Screen 5B-1

Together, Figures 3-6 and 3-7 specify that *Screen Actuations 1* is applicable if all inputs required to select the 'show user list' have been made correctly, while *Screen Actuations 2* is applicable if an input error has occurred, i.e. an additional error screen (namely, Screen E1-em3 or SE1-em3) is triggered.

Figure 3-7:   Part of a Screen Actuation Specification for Network Security Management

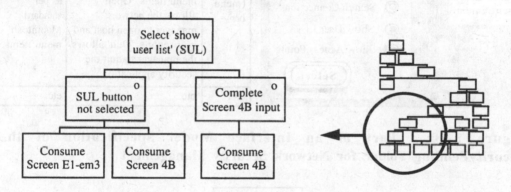

(c) Error, feedback and help messages. Figure 3-8 augments the specifications in Figures 3-6 and 3-7, with a tabular index of screen messages, e.g. error messages. As an illustration, consider Screen E1-em3 referred to earlier. The screen annotation indicates the display of a screen of pictorial design E1 (not shown) with an error message identified as number 3 (em3). The contents of this message are specified in Figure 3-8.

(d) Screen design and behaviour of screen objects. Figure 3-9 also augments the specifications in Figures 3-6 and 3-7 with pictorial specifications of display screens. The pictures may either be drawn on paper (to-scale or dimensioned), or prototyped using a computer-based tool. Additional information on the screen contents is provided in an accompanying table, and the behaviours of individual screen objects are described using structured diagrams (see Figure 3-10).

Figure 3-8:   Part of an Error Message Index for Network Security Management

Message Number	Message Content
em1	Sorry, your log-on inputs are incorrect. Your session will be terminated.
em2	Please indicate a host and/or user report action by selecting either the 'Delete' or 'Pending' radio.........etc.
etc.	

Figure 3-9:   Pictorial Screen Layout Specification of Screen 4B for Network Security Management

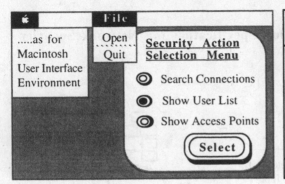

Screen Object	Description	Design Attributes
File (menu bar)	Offers 'Open' and 'Quit' menu items. 'Open' allows the network manager to open host and user reports. 'Quit' allows the manager to quit the security application.	Behaviour as per standard Macintosh menu items.
etc.	etc.	etc.

Figure 3-10:   Part of an Interface Model Specification of the SecurityPending Folder for Network Security Management

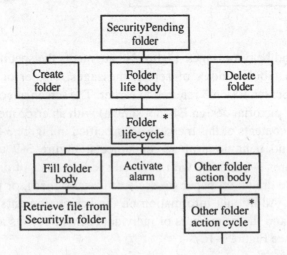

Using these notations and documentation schemes, task scenarios for a design are thus specified comprehensively at various stages of system development. Thus, more effective human factors contributions may be expected. The above account completes an overview of the notations and documentation schemes of the method. A detailed case-study illustration of the method is presented in Chapters Four to Six.

3.4. System, Sub-System and Interaction Design Levels of the Human Factors Method

Large human-computer systems usually involve a co-ordinated network of interactive sub-systems, e.g. tactical planning and control modules of defence systems of an aircraft carrier. In such cases, the method should be applied in two sequential steps as follows:

(i) An organisation level design is defined conceptually using the first two phases of the method, i.e. the Information Elicitation and Analysis, and Design Synthesis Phases. Having established the purpose of the super-ordinate work system, the requirements of individual human-machine sub-systems are then defined. To this end, 'official' or explicit socio-technical interactions among the sub-systems (e.g. work relationships and information exchanges) may be described using network diagrams (see Annex B). Human factors descriptions derived at these phases of the method complement the information derived by software engineers.

(ii) Conceptual and functional designs are then specified for each sub-system. To this end, the first two phases of the method are repeated to define each sub-system more specifically. Design specifications for the sub-system are then derived by a complete application of the method. This process is repeated until interaction level specifications are derived for all sub-systems.

Since organisation level design activities are repeated at the sub-system level, the method would be described completely by an exemplification of sub-system level design. Such an account is presented in Chapters Four to Six. Presently, the background information required to support a detailed account of the method is described.

3.5. Description Format of the Human Factors Method

In accordance with the definition of a structured method, the description of MUSE would include an explicit account of its stage-wise design scope, process and notation. In particular:

(i) The scope of each of its stages is specified in terms of the design products to be derived. To illustrate the products, examples are selected from one of the case-studies undertaken during method development, namely a Digital Data Network Management System.

(ii) Its design process is specified at two levels of description, namely at inter-stage and intra-stage levels. The former is addressed by a stage-by-stage description of the method, while the latter involved the definition of sub-processes and procedures for each design stage. Intra-stage level processes and procedures are described respectively using a block diagram (see Figure 3-11) and text. Rules of thumb (i.e. semi-formal notes) that support method application are also included in the procedures where appropriate.

(iii) The notations and documentation schemes that support the description of human factors products are specified for each design stage. As in (i) above, examples from the Network Management case-study will be used to illustrate the description schemes.

To facilitate further the assimilation of the method, the description of each design stage is structured as follows:

(a) an overview of the stage is first provided for readers who are generally interested in the method;
(b) the overview is followed by a detailed account of the design stage to support deeper understanding by readers who are interested in method application. To this end, design products, procedures and notations of the stage are described and illustrated using case-study examples.

Thus, the format of description allows the reader to peruse Chapters Four to Six selectively, for the desired level of exposure to the method.

Figure 3-11:   Block Diagram Summary of Each Design Stage of MUSE

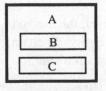
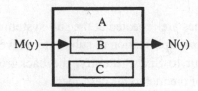
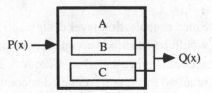

Stage A comprises sub-processes B and C.

Input Product M (of system Y) feeds into sub-process B only. The application of sub-process B results in Output Product N (of system Y).

Input Product P (of system X) feeds into all sub-processes of Stage A. The application of both sub-processes B and C results in Output Product Q (of system X).

3.6. Choice and Scope of the Case-Study Illustration of the Human Factors Method

During method development, many case-studies were undertaken to address specific methodological and system design concerns. Since a complete review of these case-studies is inappropriate,[1] a suitable case-study has to be chosen to exemplify the method. In particular, a suitable case-study should satisfy the following requirements:

(a) It should adequately illustrate the stage-wise design scope and notation of the method. This requirement involves a comprehensive illustration of the products and documentation schemes of each design stage.
(b) It should adequately exemplify design transformations between stages of the method. This requirement involves a comprehensive, coherent and traceable illustration of a design thread taken across the stages of the method.
(c) It should not introduce unfamiliar or complicated domain concepts that might interfere with the reader's assimilation of the method (and thus defeat the purpose of the illustration).

On the basis of these requirements, the Digital Network Management case-study is selected. Generally, the Network Management System is responsible for the following:

(a) network security, e.g. effecting real-time responses to illegal network access;
(b) network installation and planning, e.g. cost accounting and co-ordination of new lines;
(c) network support, e.g. performance monitoring and trouble-shooting;
(d) user support, e.g. addressing user problems with the network.

Since the scope of the case-study is large, a subset of the design descriptions derived for network security (i.e. (a) above), is used to illustrate Chapters Four to Six.

It should be noted that the objective of the case-study is to expose the procedural human factors design knowledge embedded within MUSE. Since the recruitment and application of declarative human factors knowledge fall outside the current scope of the method, they are generally excluded from the illustration. However, specific instances of such recruitment and application are highlighted in the illustrations when appropriate.

The above account completes an overview of the method. A detailed description of the method follows.

---

[1] Such a review is outside the scope of this book. In addition, some of the case-studies would not support a comprehensive exemplification of the method.

3.7. Exercise and Sample Solution

(This is a simple exercise to familiarise readers with the basic constructs of the structured diagram notation described in Sub-section 3.3. More extensive exercises may be found in Chapters Four to Six).

A hypothetical task involves booking one or more recreation facilities using a computer-supported booking system. To book a facility, the user must first enter a personal identity number to access the system. The user may then decide between two recreation facilities to book – squash or snooker. Following the decision, the user is shown booking sessions that are available for the selected recreation facility. A maximum of three sessions may then be booked. Describe the interactive task using a structured diagram and consider human factors implications for your task specification. (Note that there are more than one solutions to the exercise. One possible solution is given overleaf.)

<u>Solution to Exercise</u>

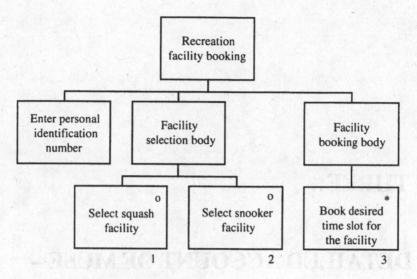

1: User determined selection criteria
2: User determined selection criteria
3: Maximum of three bookings

There are many solutions to this exercise. The suggested solution assumes that the desired time slot is always available, and that a single facility may be booked for each cycle of the interactive task. In other words, the system requires the user to enter his/her identification number again to book a different recreation facility. This exercise illustrates how a structured diagram description may prompt an earlier discovery of unacceptably cumbersome designs.

PART THREE:

DETAILED ACCOUNT OF MUSE –
A STRUCTURED HUMAN FACTORS METHOD

4
The Elicitation and Analysis Phase of MUSE

Really we create nothing. We merely plagiarise nature.

Jean Baitaillon

*Engineering attempts to fully constrain its outputs.....Engineering investigates
successful designs and adopts those 'means' that it finds generalisable.*

Jim Carter

This chapter describes in detail the Information Elicitation and Analysis Phase of the
method. The phase comprises two design stages, namely the Extant Systems Analysis
Stage and the Generalised Task Model Stage. The stages, described in the order of their
application (see Figure 4-1), are concerned with the generation and analysis of background
information to support subsequent derivation of a system design.

As indicated in Chapter Three, intermediate design processes, products and documentation
schemes for each stage of the method are described as follows:

(a) an overview of the stage is provided prior to a detailed description;
(b) a block diagram summary of the stage is provided to highlight the sub-processes
involved in transforming stage input(s) into one or more intermediate product(s);
(c) case-study illustrations of the products, processes and documentation schemes of the
stage are provided where appropriate.

4.1. The Extant Systems Analysis (ESA) Stage

The main objective of the ESA Stage is to generate background information to assist the
design of the target system at later stages of the method (see Figure 4-1 – the ESA Stage is
highlighted by a box outlined in bold). To this end, extant systems are analysed to
characterise current user needs and problems; existing function allocation between the user
and device; the design features and rationale of existing user interfaces; etc. The
information derived is processed into a number of ESA Stage products to highlight various
perspectives on the target design problem, e.g. task design, user interface design, etc. (see

later).

Figure 4-1:   A Simple Representation of the Structured Human Factors Method (with the Extant Systems Analysis Stage Highlighted)

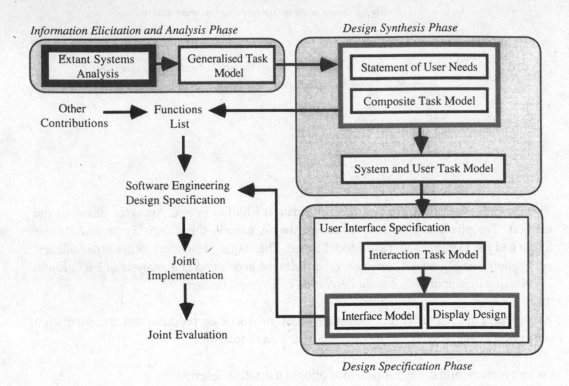

In performing extant systems analysis, three rules should be noted. Firstly, *extant* systems should be interpreted broadly to include both the *current* system (the system currently used by the client) and *related* systems (similar systems used elsewhere). The objective of analysing related systems (as opposed to studying only the current system) is to avoid the pitfalls of 'tunnel vision' at an early stage of system design. In practice, extant systems analysis entails an extensive analysis of the current system coupled with the selective analysis of one or more related systems. Thus, by emphasising a broader perspective, extant systems analysis encourages the consideration of a wider range of design alternatives.

Secondly, extant systems analysis should be performed with respect to the target system. Thus, valuable insights may be uncovered regarding the appropriateness of particular design features. In particular, extant designs may be assessed for possible recruitment to the target system, and for possible transfer effects (both positive and negative transfer of learning by current or 'installed' users). These concerns are addressed further at the Generalised Task Model Stage (see later).

Thirdly, the detail to which extant systems are analysed depends on the circumstances of the design project, e.g. the resources available; the designer's familiarity with the domain; etc. Indeed, a related system need not be examined physically if the designer's experience of that particular class of systems is sufficiently rich. Thus, the extent of extant systems analyses should be decided by the designer in each instance. Where limited analysis of related systems is performed, the designer should note the underlying information and rationale of all decisions leading to a design of the target system. In all cases, however, the current system should still be analysed extensively (see above).

A brief account of the design processes and products of this stage follows. (See Figure 4-2 overleaf. The reader is referred to Chapter 3 for an explanation of the representation scheme.) Italics will be used to highlight the design processes shown in the figure.

At the ESA Stage, a statement of requirements is collated from the client's brief, contractual documents, etc., to describe key characteristics of the target system. On the basis of the statement, relevant extant systems (comprising the current system, and appropriate related and partially related systems) may be *identified* for analysis. Using 'off-the-shelf' techniques such as interviews, unobtrusive observations, etc., pertinent information on these systems may be elicited from various sources, e.g. different end-user groups, current job descriptions, user manuals, etc.

Usually, two primary products are derived for each extant system analysed. First, a structured diagram description of the extant system task is derived by decomposing superordinate tasks into sub-tasks. In most cases, a single extant Task Description (TD(ext)) is derived by collating information elicited from diverse sources, e.g. protocols with different task performers, etc. To this end, a basic set of task descriptors or 'building blocks' (e.g. objects and actions that are common across the information sources) needs to be defined by generification (see Chapter 2). Similarly, to support later design analysis and synthesis an appropriate level of task description needs to be derived. Thus, conditions for appropriate termination of task decomposition are specified by the method. In particular, decomposition should be terminated only when the resulting task description conforms to the following criteria:

(a) It is generally understood among designers and end-users. To this end, tasks should be

Figure 4-2:   Block Diagram Summary of the Extant Systems Analysis (ESA) Stage

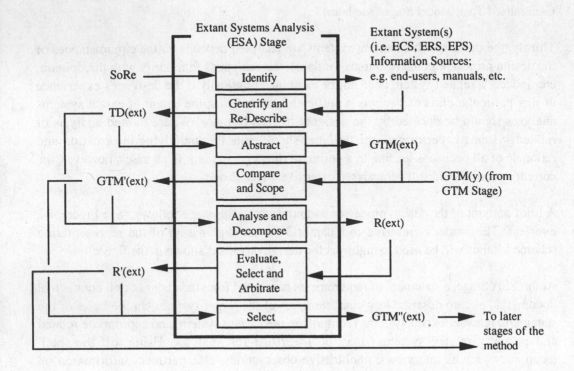

DD = Display Design

DoDD = Domain of Design Discourse

ECS = Extant Current System

EPS = Extant Partial System

ERS = Extant Related System

(ext) = extant system (EXT) descriptions

EXT = Set of Extant Systems = {ECS, ERS, EPS}

GTM = Generalised Task Model

IM = Interface Model

ITM = Interaction Task Model

R = A set of design products of the method

SoRe = Statement of Requirements

STM = System Task Model

SUN = Statement of User Needs

TD = Task Description

UIE = User Interface Environment

UTM = User Task Model

(Note: R(ext) = one or more elements of a set of method descriptions comprising {STM(ext), UTM(ext), ITM (ext), IM(ext), UIE(ext), DD(ext), SUN(ext), DoDD(ext)}. R'(ext) comprises a subset of R(ext) descriptions, identified to be more relevant to the requirements of target system design.)

decomposed to a level that facilitates unambiguous identification with specific system goals.

(b) It is commensurate with the criticality, frequency and centrality of the task (see Johnson and Johnson, 1987).

(c) It supports adequately the identification of performance shaping factors (PSFs).

(d) It supports adequately the identification of training requirements and criteria, e.g. the attainment of satisfactory values of Probability of failure x Cost (or P x C) (Duncan, 1974).

Second, a Generalised Task Model for the Extant System (GTM(ext)) is *abstracted* from the Task Description (TD(ext)). The objective is to remove device-dependent details to facilitate later comparisons between extant and target system designs. Although the level of abstraction should be sufficiently high to reveal the logic underlying the system task, the resulting description need not be homogeneous. For instance, the level of abstraction may be deliberately lower for particular parts of the description to preserve information on design features of interest. Thus, the generalised task model supports human factors analysis of extant system designs vis-à-vis the requirements of the target system.

In addition to the above products, other ESA Stage products may also be derived depending on individual project circumstances. In particular, the full complement (comprising products of all subsequent stages of the method – the set is represented generally as R(ext) in Figure 4-2) may be derived if the design of the extant and target systems are expected to be very similar (as in variant design). Although extant systems are selected on the basis of common domain or task characteristics, it is unlikely that all extant system information would be relevant to target system design. Consequently, a more specific *scope* of extant systems analysis may be identified later by *comparing* the Extant Generalised Task Model (i.e. GTM(ext)) with the Generalised Task Model of the Target System (i.e. GTM(y)[1] – see later). A relevant subset of GTM(ext) (denoted as GTM'(ext) in Figure 4-2) is thus identified. Together, the Extant Task Description and GTM'(ext) support the generation of further ESA Stage products as appropriate.

Lower level *decompositions* of extant designs, referred to generally as R(ext) descriptions, may thus be collated and documented (see Figure 4-2). These descriptions are then *evaluated* to identify potential extant design features for recruitment to target system design at later stages of the method. The set of design features designated for recruitment is represented as R'(ext) descriptions in Figure 4-2. Since R'(ext) descriptions relate to a

---

[1] The suffixes '(ext)' and '(y)' denote method descriptions associated with a particular extant system and the target system respectively. In contrast, human factors descriptions synthesised from parts of extant system descriptions are denoted by the suffix '(x)' (see later).

subset of GTM'(ext), pertinent parts of the latter description are collated to derive a GTM"(ext) description for each of the extant systems analysed. The set of GTM"(ext) descriptions is carried forward to the next stage (the Generalised Task Model Stage) where compatible aspects are synthesised to generate an overall extant system model termed an Extant Composite Task Model or CTM(x).[2] Similarly, other R'(ext) descriptions feed into later stages of the method, where corresponding human factors descriptions are derived for the target system, e.g. Extant Statement of User Needs (or SUN(ext)) descriptions support the derivation of Target Statement of User Needs (or SUN(y)) descriptions, etc.

In other words, to facilitate uptake of the information elicited at the ESA Stage, the information is processed into products corresponding in scope and format to human factors descriptions derived at later stages of the method. (See Figure 4-2 and also later stages of the method for further clarification of the description in this chapter.) The notations applicable at these stages are also used for the description of ESA products; namely structured diagrams, semantic nets, pictorial diagrams and tables.

From the preceding account, it might be concluded (erroneously) that the analyses undertaken at the ESA Stage are intended to address 'variant' design only.[3] Consequently, it cannot be over-emphasised that the method is *not* limited to 'variant' design. On the contrary, 'novel' design is also supported by the combined activities of the ESA, Generalised Task Model and Composite Task Model Stages. At the latter stages, the extent of recruitment of extant features comprises a part of the design decisions (see later).

To support method application, a more detailed account of the ESA Stage follows.

A More Detailed Account of the Extant Systems Analysis Stage
ESA Stage activities may be grouped into three categories, namely:

(a) identification of extant systems for analysis,
(b) elicitation of task information and
(c) derivation of ESA Stage products.

A review of the activities and procedures follows. Case-study examples of the resulting products are also included when appropriate.

---

[2] See Footnote 1.

[3] It may be interesting to note, however, that most system designs currently involve variant design (see Rouse and Boff, 1987).

(a) Identification of Extant Systems for Analysis

The first step in the method is to characterise the purpose (i.e. subject matter) and requirements of the target system.[4] To this end, relevant information may be extracted from the client's brief and other sources such as feasibility reports, informal and contractual documents, transcripts of protocols with stake-holders, existing job descriptions and task manuals, etc. Information concerning target system tasks, hardware requirements, desirable characteristics of the current system and perceived future needs is thus collated to derive a statement of requirements. To define the scope of target system design, the statement should be detailed sufficiently to identify key characteristics of the target system, such as the domain of application (e.g. Network Management), technological and target device constraints (e.g. monochrome computer monitors), end-user characteristics (e.g. novices), etc.

To support the identification of extant systems for analysis, these characteristics of the target system are grouped by the human factors engineer into one or more sets of 'concrete' and 'abstract' concerns of particular interest. 'Concrete' concerns map onto extant systems that operate in the same domain as the target system, i.e. 'variants' of the target system. 'Abstract' concerns, on the other hand, map onto systems operating in different or only partially similar domains. Although the analysis of 'abstract' systems would not generate the same wealth of information (since their relation with the target system is more distant than 'concrete' systems), they may be compared conceptually with the target system to support 'novel' design (as opposed to 'variant' design).

On the basis of these 'concrete' and 'abstract' sets of concerns, three classes of extant systems may be identified for analysis; namely:

(1) The 'extant *current* system' in use in the client organisation, i.e. the system to be replaced by the target system. Aside from domain similarity, device characteristics of the current system may or may not be related to the target system. For instance, a weak relationship would be expected in computerising manual systems. It should be noted that the current system is especially important from a human factors viewpoint since it supports an appropriate address of transfer of learning effects (both positive and negative) during target system design; i.e. to account for the implications of current expectations and experiences of installed end-users.

(2) A class of 'extant *related* systems' whose domain of application is *similar* to the target system. Extant *related* systems include systems in use in other sections of the client organisation, or elsewhere in other organisations.

---

[4] This step is undertaken in collaboration with software engineers.

(3) A class of 'extant *partial* systems' that involve sub-tasks similar to those intended for the target system, but whose domains of application are largely *different* or *unrelated*.

The above relationships between extant and target systems are summarised in Figure 4-3. It should be noted that if project constraints do not permit a wider analysis of extant systems, at least the extant *current* system should be analysed. However, should project resources allow, a number of extant *related* and *partial* systems should be analysed (in that order) to augment the data base for system design. Thus, the derivation of a conceptual design of the target system, may be supported better. It should also be emphasised that the selection and analysis of extant systems is iterative. For instance, the analyst may decide to analyse other extant systems during the course of the ESA Stage and later stages of the method (see Generalised Task Model Stage later).

Figure 4-3:   Extant System Classes Assumed by the Method

System Class	Organisation Status	Domain Status
Extant Current System	Client	Same or very similar to target system
Extant Related System	Client or Other	Similar to target system .
Extant Partial System	Client or Other	Similarities only at sub-task level

The procedures for selecting extant systems for analysis are summarised overleaf.

__Procedures for selecting extant systems for analysis__

1. Consult the statement of requirements and other sources (such as transcripts of interviews with task performers, system manuals, etc.) for information on key target system characteristics such as: the domain of application; technological constraints; task constraints specified by the client; system performance criteria; user characteristics; and environmental factors. These characteristics are then used to identify appropriate extant systems for analysis.

2. Identify and abstract key target system characteristics such as salient features of the domain of application and task. Appropriate characteristics of the extant current system should also be noted.

3. From the generalised set in (2) above, particular sub-sets are then selected to define categories of extant systems of interest, i.e. extant systems that represent potential candidates for analysis. Such generic categories need not include all characteristics of the target system. However, the criteria for selecting a particular set should be made explicit. These criteria are situation-specific, and are determined largely by particular information requirements, e.g. on critical or problematic aspects of the target system task (see (4) below).

4. Select and record a list of extant systems for analysis. The number of extant systems selected is influenced by situational factors such as:

(a) characteristics of the target task, e.g. task criticality, frequency and difficulty;
(b) resources available for analysis, e.g. availability of current system personnel for interview; time constraints; etc.
(c) characteristics of the target system domain, e.g. similarities with the current system; well- or ill-defined system; designer familiarity with the domain; etc.

(b) Elicitation of Information on Extant Tasks

Having selected a number of extant systems for analysis, relevant human factors information is elicited to support later generation of ESA Stage products. To facilitate information elicitation, a number of 'off-the shelf' techniques may be used; such as interviews, observation studies, concurrent and retrospective protocols, critical incident analysis, questionnaires, literature survey, etc. These techniques will not be described since they should be familiar to designers intending to use the method. As an example, procedures for interviewing task performers (which would be conducted in most cases) are described in the next page. The reader is referred to Diaper (1989a, b) for an account of other information elicitation techniques. It suffices to say here that an elicitation technique that meets the requirements of the analysis should be selected.

Procedures for task performer interviews

1. Conduct interviews. To facilitate information elicitation, do the following:
(a) Use graphical representations during the interview. In particular, pertinent design information may be uncovered by asking task performers to describe their task with respect to graphical representations of the device. The descriptions elicited may also be represented graphically to support later confirmation by task performers. The form of graphical representation used would depend on the information to be described, e.g. pictures may be used to describe screens; tree diagrams may be used to represent organisational structure; while structured diagrams, tree diagrams and flowcharts may be used to describe tasks.
(b) Use 'how' and 'why' questions during the interview. Previous research suggests that answers to 'why' and 'how' questions may be related to super-ordinate and subordinate goals respectively. The use of such questions may subsequently facilitate the construction of task 'hierarchies' from interview transcripts.

2. For each task performer, transcribe audio and visual records of the interview (if any).

3. Analyse the interview transcripts. Design information that supports the generation of ESA Stage products may be extracted from the transcripts as follows:
(a) pertinent phrases in the transcripts should be highlighted and summarised;
(b) answers to 'how' and 'why' questions are examined to extract the structure of the task;
(c) relations between domain objects should be noted, e.g. composite objects, task groupings, etc. The information may be used to define the target system domain;
(d) statements describing user needs, problems and possible solutions should be noted. Such information would subsequently support the collation of a set of user requirements.

4. Process the elicited information into ESA products that correspond in scope and format to products derived at later stages of the method. The objective is to facilitate appropriate uptake of ESA information and its later incoporation into the design of the target system.

(c) Derivation of ESA Stage Products

ESA Stage products[5] that may be derived during extant systems analysis comprise some or all of the following:

(1) Extant Task Description (TD(ext)): a device-*dependent* description of the user's task for an extant (ext) system.
(2) Extant Generalised Task Model (GTM(ext)): a largely 'device-*independent*' description of the user's task for an extant (ext) system.
(3) Extant System Task Model (STM(ext)) and User Task Model (UTM(ext)): high-level or conceptual descriptions of the user's on-line (i.e. computer supported) and off-line (i.e. manual) tasks for an extant (ext) system.

---

[5] Henceforth, acronyms for these products of the method will be used.

(4) Extant Interaction Task Model (ITM(ext)): a device-level description of user-computer interactions currently required to perform the on-line task.

(5) Extant Interface Model (IM(ext)): a description of the appearance and behaviours of bespoke objects of the extant user interface, including variant objects of the implemented in-house style or user interface environment (if any).

(6) Extant Display Design (DD(ext)) descriptions: key static and dynamic characteristics of extant displays, e.g. composition, layout and actuation of screens with respect to the user's task (including dialogue and error messages).

(7) Extant Domain of Design Discourse (DoDD(ext)): a semantic net description of the domain of an extant system.

(8) Extant Statement of User Needs (SUN(ext)): a summary of user problems and needs for an extant system.

These products support later assessments of the implications of particular extant system designs (in relation to both their potential recruitment to the target system and possible conflicts with newly proposed designs). To this end, the products of *extant* system analysis are processed into the scope and format of products derived at later stages of the method. In other words, extant and target system descriptions 'mirror' one another, e.g. ITM(ext) and ITM(y); [6] STM(ext) and STM(y); etc. The uptake of extant system descriptions at later design stages is thus facilitated.

It should be noted that in most cases the full complement of ESA Stage products would not be derived. For instance, ESA Stage analysis may be terminated following the derivation of an Extant Generalised Task Model (or GTM(ext)), if more detailed extant systems information is not expected to benefit target system design significantly. Thus, the range of ESA Stage products to be derived should be decided by the human factors designer.[7]

A selective review of ESA Stage products follows.[8] A complete description is unnecessary since some of the extant system products are 'mirrored' by corresponding

---

[6] In general, method products are represented as follows: <Design Stage name><System Designation>. For instance, the product derived at the Generalised Task Model (GTM) Stage for the *target* system (designated generally as (y)) would be denoted as GTM(y). Similarly, the same product derived for an *extant* system (designated generally as (ext)) would be denoted as GTM(ext).

[7] However, the rationale for early termination of ESA Stage analysis should be documented.

[8] Since current understanding of human factors design requirements at the organisational level is limited, its design descriptions have not been addressed extensively by the method. Preliminary case-study attempts at developing a set of potentially useful design descriptions are described in Annex B.

products for the target system (described in Chapters Five and Six). Case-study illustrations of the products are given where appropriate.[9]

(1) Extant Task Description (TD(ext))

TD(ext) is a device-dependent description of the task of the extant system. The purpose of its derivation is to characterise the existing allocation of functions and the tasks currently performed by the user.

When deriving an Extant Task Description, it should be noted that the level of decomposition is determined largely by the purpose of the analysis. In particular, a low-level description (e.g. to the keystroke level) should be derived for an extant *current* system that is significantly similar to the target system in both domain and design characteristics. Alternatively, a high-level description would be more appropriate if the extant systems analysed are less closely related to the target system, e.g. extant *related* systems. In such instances, the Extant Task Description need only be informative enough to support conceptual comparisons between the requirements and designs of the extant and target systems.

The Extant Task Description, or TD(ext), is described using structured diagrams (see Chapter Three and Figure 4-4 later) and an accompanying information table that provides a textual account of important features of the task.

Procedures for deriving an Extant Task Description are summarised overleaf.

---

[9] It should be noted that the primary objective of the case-study is not a complete specification of its design. Instead, the case-study supports a simple illustration of the human factors products derived at each stage of the method. For this purpose, it is only necessary to describe a subset of its design specifications.

Procedures for deriving an Extant Task Description, TD(ext)

1. Take as input information that has been elicited from task performers, manuals, etc. Identify the super-ordinate task (and task goal), and decompose them into sub-tasks (and sub-goals). Note the sequence, frequency and conditions that control the execution of each set of sub-tasks (these will be represented in the Extant Task Description using structured diagrams). The objective is to derive a comprehensive description to support task analysis and design.

2. Continue the decomposition until a satisfactory level of description is derived. The point at which decomposition is terminated will depend on the purpose of the analysis. For example, if target system design involves re-designing the extant current system using similar technology, then it may be informative to continue task decomposition to the keystroke level. In contrast, if target system design involves the use of substitute technology, such a level of decomposition would not be necessary. At a minimum, sub-tasks of an Extant Task Description should detail how superordinate task goals are to be achieved. In particular, it should describe start- and end-points of major tasks and define pre-requisites for the fulfilment of task goals.

3. Analyse task performance from a human factors perspective. Particular attention should be given to:
(a) user problems and needs as well as desirable extant design features that may be recruited later to the design of the target system;
(b) the rationale underlying extant designs. The rationale would help later assessment of the potential for recruiting existing design features.

4. Document the elicited information using structured diagrams and include textual comments in an accompanying table. Note that:
(a) the table structure may vary according to the needs of the structured diagram. In most cases, it should include a column for elaborating boxes of a structured diagram and a column for noting human factors comments on particular features of a task design;
(b) table items should be recorded in the sequence by which structured diagram boxes are read, i.e. from top to bottom and then from left to right;
(c) complete elaboration of all boxes of a structured diagram in the accompanying table is unnecessary. The main objective of the table is to clarify complicated parts of the diagram and not to produce exhaustive documentation. The emphasis on selective elaboration of structured diagram boxes is to balance the requirements for adequate documentation and an economy of effort to accommodate project resource limitations.

Generification and the Derivation of an Extant Task Description

During the derivation of an extant task description, various information sources would be consulted, e.g. different task performers, manuals, etc. The result, on most occasions, is a set of related task descriptions for an extant current system. To derive a consistent and concise extant task description, subjective variations across these descriptions must be identified and removed. To this end, generic descriptors are identified for task elements that share common attributes. Subjective variations across individual task descriptions are then removed by re-describing the tasks in terms of these generic elements. Such a process is termed generification (see Chapter Two). Details of the generification procedure are described below.

Procedures for generification

1. Collate a list of all objects and actions from the task information elicited.

2. Reduce the set by listing each object and action once and once only.

3. Associate all similar terms using one of the following techniques:

Technique 1: The designer associates a particular term with other similar terms iteratively by expressing the original task description in terms of an alternative object or action. If the alternative description is considered 'adequate', then the terms may be considered similar.

Technique 2: Task performers are asked to sort object and action cards into different groups on the basis of task-specific criteria.

4. Subjectively assign a common or generic descriptor to each group of 'like' terms.

5. Validate the generic descriptors by asking task performers to assign them to each item in the original list of objects and actions. If a specific item cannot be located satisfactorily, task performers are free to suggest an alternative descriptor. Thus, a set of suitable generic descriptors (task elements) is identified iteratively.

6. Review the original task description and construct an alternative description using the generic descriptors derived in (5) above (where appropriate). A generic task description is thus derived.

7. Validate the generic task description by asking task performers whether it is equivalent to the description originally elicited from them.

Case-Study Illustration of an Extant Task Description (TD(ext))

Two extant systems were analysed in the network security management case-study, namely an extant *related* system in use at University College London[10] and an extant *partial* system represented by the PC security application, MacPassword.™ The *target* system comprises a hypothetical system to be implemented at a client organisation. For this case-study, the extant *current* system was not analysed since security restrictions imposed by the client organisation prohibited access to documents and staff (see case-study illustration of the Target Generalised Task Model described in Sub-section 4.2).

---

[10] Note that all references to the network management system at University College London and MacPassword™ should be taken as notional rather than actual representations of real systems. The case-study descriptions are intended only for method illustration.

More needs to be said about the extant systems selected for analysis. The network security management system at University College London was selected because it shares the same domain as the target system. Thus, information derived from its analysis would support the generation of a conceptual design for the target system. For instance, it was expected that basic security management tasks for both systems would entail accessing the computer followed by the detection and identification of, and decisions on, appropriate responses to breaches in network security. Similarly, MacPassword™ is selected since its domain (*personal computer* security management) is *partially related* to *network* security management. Its selection for analysis was motivated by the potential recruitment of its low-level design features to the design of the target system.

Examples of the Extant Task Descriptions (TD(ext)) derived are shown in Figures 4-4 and 4-5 for the University College London Computer Centre (TD(UCLCC)) and the MacPassword™ application (TD(MPASS)) respectively. Information tables accompanying each of these descriptions are also shown.

To illustrate how extant system analysis may contribute to target system design, part of the security management task is now examined. The task concerns the identification of, and response to, failed log-on events arising from illegal or incorrect inputs of a user password. These events are important since they may indicate attempted access by a 'hacker' (an illegal network user). In this respect, the TD(UCLCC) description shows that the extant system at University College London does not automatically alert the network manager to the occurrence of such events. Thus, security breaches can only be uncovered by searching manually through volumes of computer logs or network user reports. Such design inadequacies should be rectified by providing better computer support. Thus, following extant system analyses, it was suggested that computer prompts to alert the network manager to failed log-on events should be provided together with both automatic and manager-specified collation of information concerning the events. Similar requirements for computer support were revealed by the Extant Task Description for the MacPassword™ application, i.e. TD(MPASS). In particular, computer owners were prompted to consult a computer generated summary of failed log-on events. The summarised information provides clues on the identity of the hacker, and helps in distinguishing between illegal and incorrect password inputs. Consequently, password mis-keys may be differentiated from actual attempts at hacking. Potentially useful extant design features were thus uncovered by extant systems analysis.

Figure 4-4: Extant Task Description for Network Security Management at University College London Computer Centre (TD(UCLCC)) — Page 1

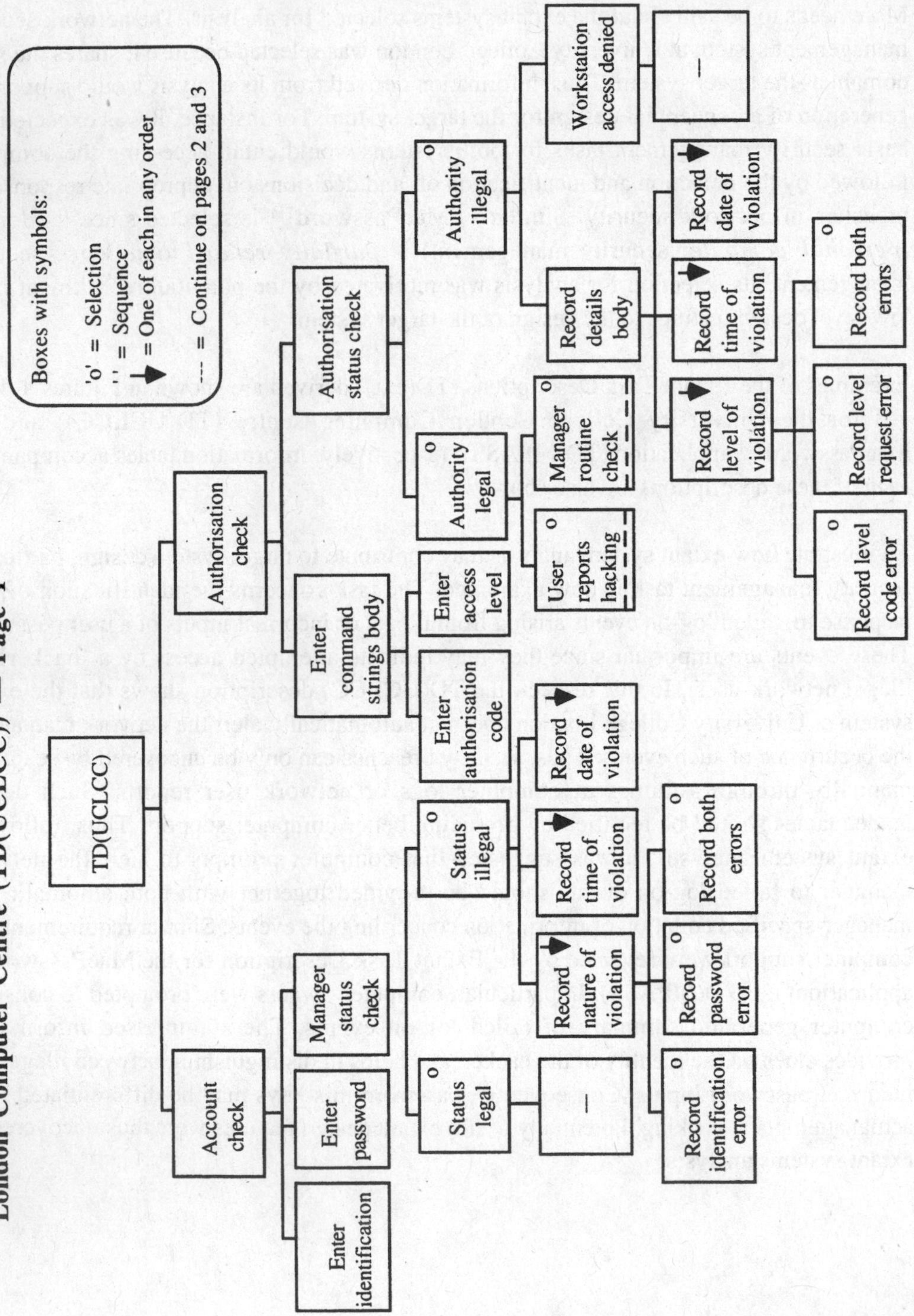

Boxes with symbols:

'o' = Selection
'·' = Sequence
→ = One of each in any order

--- = Continue on pages 2 and 3

Figure 4-4: Extant Task Description for Network Security Management at University College London Computer Centre (TD(UCLCC)) — Page 2

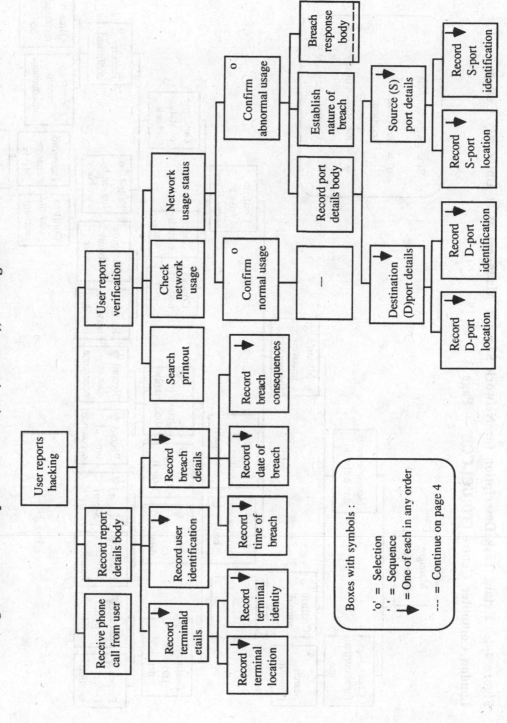

Boxes with symbols :

'o' = Selection

' ' = Sequence

→ = One of each in any order

--- = Continue on page 4

Figure 4-4: Extant Task Description for Network Security Management at University College London Computer Centre (TD(UCLCC)) — Page 3

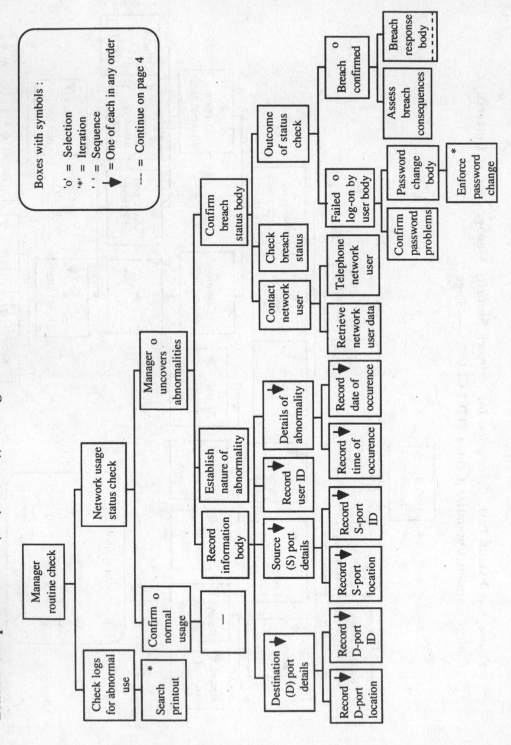

Figure 4-4: Extant Task Description for Network Security Management at University College London Computer Centre (TD(UCLCC)) — Page 4

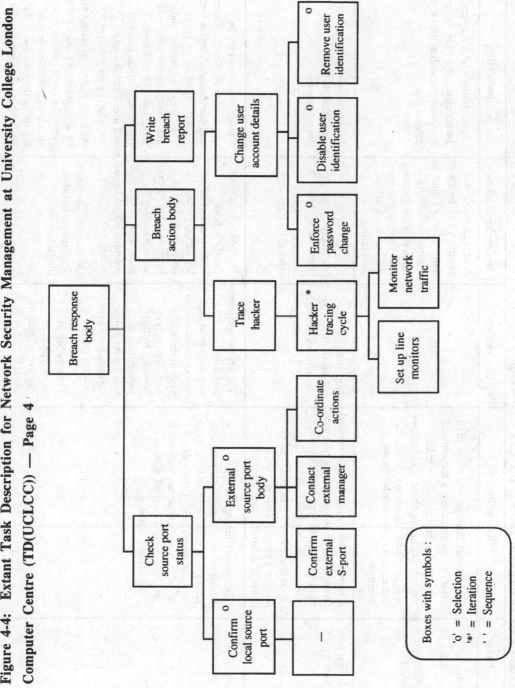

Extant Task Description Table (TD(UCLCC)) — Page 1

Name	Description	Observation	Design Implication	Speculation
Account check / Authorisation check	The network manager was required to clear two checks, namely account and authorisation checks, before access to the network management workstation was permitted. Violation of either of these checks was recorded by the computer.		Access checking was considered necessary as room security cannot be ensured sufficiently. Authorisation checking was required to cover remote access to the workstation.	Authorisation check may not be necessary in a more secure environment such as the target system site.
User reports hacking	A network user may contact the network manager to report a security breach (e.g. an illegal log-on). In most cases, the manager was required to act on the report immediately. The action involves searching through computer print-outs to verify details of the user report.	Report details are recorded off-line by the network manager.	Asynchronous communication between the network manager and user should be supported.	Electronic-mail may support requirements for asynchronous communication.
Manager routine check	The network manager may occasionally scan computer print-outs for signs of possible security breaches (off-line search task). Details of possible security breaches were noted and subsequently verified with the user (both off-line tasks).	The structure, content and layout of computer print-outs were not designed to support the search task. The support provided by line indentations and spacing (to denote separate log entries) is inadequate. Security breaches were typically discovered after the event.	The print-outs should clearly indicate occurrences of failed log-ons. On-line functions should also be provided to support scanning of log-on times to uncover potential illegal log-on events. On-line alert should be provided for failed and illegal log-ons.	On-line functions may be provided to display the source and destination addresses for: (i) each failed log-on event. The time of occurrence and user identification concerned should also be indicated. (ii) particular time intervals and user identifications specified by the manager. Auditory and visual alarms may be used to signal a failed log-on event. An event summary should be displayed on next log-on by the manager, if the workstation was unmanned.

Extant Task Description Table (TD(UCLCC)) — Page 2

Name	Description	Observation	Design Implication	Speculation
Check logs for abnormal use	The log-on address was located by the network manager based on information on the security breach event and user identification. The address may indicate the physical location of the hacker (e.g. a specific room in the college or remote access from other networks).	The structure, content and layout of computer print-outs were not designed to support this task.	On-line support to access details of user identifications and security breach should be provided by the computer.	Network use details should be displayed on input of specific user name and time.
Confirm breach status body	The network manager had to contact the user to ascertain the occurrence of a security breach. If the event is a mistake committed by a legal user (e.g. a mis-key), either no action was taken or a password change was enforced. The user may then choose a password that may be remembered more easily.	It may be difficult to identify specific users if network identifications were shared.	Unique user identification would be required.	
Assess breach consequences	The network manager may search through computer print-outs to determine the consequences of a security breach.	Reported to be a slow and demoralising process.	On-line support to access details of user identifications and security breach should be provided by the computer.	
External source port body	If a hacker has logged onto the network via an external network, the network manager may need to identify the remote source address to determine the hacker's location and identity. The undertaking would involve contacting managers of other networks for information. Contact could be by telephone.	It may be difficult to obtain the required information.	Asynchronous communication facilities should be provided to support remote access.	Electronic-mail may be provided, depending on the facilities of external network concerned.
Trace hacker	The network manager may set up line monitors to trace a persistent hacker in real-time.	Little information was available on this task. However, it was reported to be labour intensive.		

Extant Task Description Table (TD(UCLCC)) — Page 3

Name	Description	Observation	Design Implication	Speculation
Enforce password change	The network manager may enforce a password change on a user in the following circumstances: (a) to rectify a security breach attributed to an illegal log-on. (b) to enable the selection of a more appropriate password following failed log-ons by a user.			
Disable user identification	The network manager may temporarily disable a user identification if: (a) the user cannot be contacted to confirm whether hacking has taken place, or (b) the user cannot be notified that a change of password has to be enforced.			
Remove user identification	The network manager may permanently remove a user identification after contacting the user concerned. A replacement account may be set up if necessary.			
Write breach report	The network manager may require a record of such events in the long term, so that the pattern of hacking attempts by a particular individual may be revealed.			

Figure 4-5: Extant Task Description for PC Security Management for the MacPassword™ Application (TD(MPASS)) – Page 1

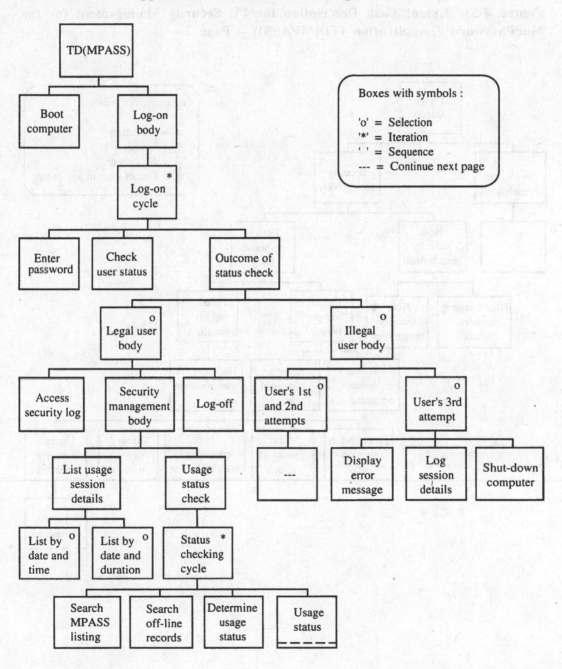

Figure 4-5: **Extant Task Description for PC Security Management for the MacPassword™ Application (TD(MPASS)) – Page 2**

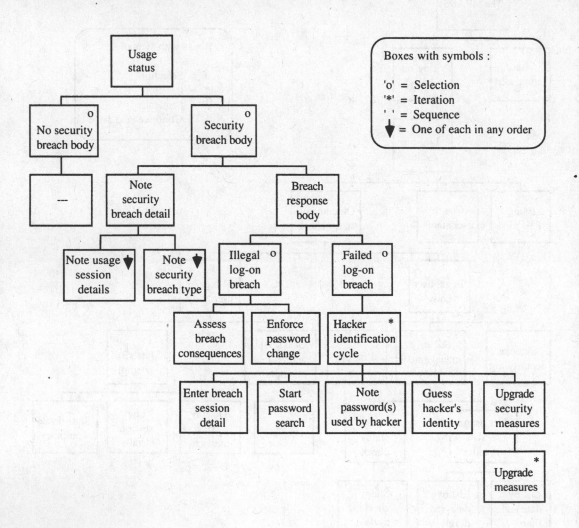

Extant Task Description Table (TD(MPASS)) — Page 1

Name	Description	Observation	Design Implication	Speculation
Boot computer	The user was required to boot the computer to access the system.			
Enter password	A password is entered by the user for verification by the computer.	No user identification was required. Less secure system.		
Legal user status body	A correct password was specified by the user. The user may now access any of the system's services.	Easy access to system logs and other security sensitive information.	Need more stringent controls for sensitive information, e.g. different passwords for different levels of access.	
Access security log	The security log is a file in the system folder.	The log was the only record of hacking activity. It was thus particularly important that logged information is not too easily accessible.	A means of protecting logged information and for facilitating data search may be required.	Define unique password for accessing system logs.
Security management body	As part of a security checking routine, the user must access the database to verify log-on, log-off times and dates against known system usage. If particular usage activities cannot be accounted for, details of the irregular usage were noted as potential hacker activity. Further action may then be taken.	May become cumbersome if many log-ons were involved over a period of time. Usually, a complete off-line record of system usage was not kept by the user. Thus, usage verification against computer logs may be difficult and/or unreliable.	Need support functions to search failed log-on events, user-specified periods of non-use, and its information, e.g. log-on times, dates and passwords used.	A function to search computer usage (i.e. log-on and log-off events) for a specified time interval. Daily print-out of a usage summary.
Enforce password change	The password may be changed following the detection of hacker activity.	For greater security, changes should be enforced regularly, i.e. not only after hacking activity has been detected.	Password changes should be easy to implement. However, accidental password changes should be prevented.	Undo and confirm functions should be provided.

Extant Task Description Table (TD(MPASS)) — Page 2

Name	Description	Observation	Design Implication	Speculation
Failed log-on breach	Failed log-on events were recorded. The user must identify such occurrences from the computer log. Other information of interest includes the date and time of the event and the password used.	A password record and date and time information of the event may provide useful clues to a hacker's identity.	The information recorded should support adequately the task of hacker identification.	
User's 3rd attempt	The session was terminated only after the third invalid input of a user password.	After re-booting the computer, the hacker was free to try again.	This is a security loop-hole. The system should limit multiple attempts by re-booting.	Enforce a period of computer lock out following a failed log-on, e.g. include a time out facility to prevent repeated attempts at computer access.
Log session details	A record of computer access events was kept. The information recorded included: date and time of owner-user and guest-user log-ons; failed log-ons; and password(s) used.			

(b) Extant Generalised Task Model (GTM(ext))

The objective of an Extant Generalised Task Model, or GTM(ext), is to support the assessment of conceptual designs of extant system(s) relative to the requirements of the target system. To this end, Extant Generalised Task Models are usually derived for all extant systems analysed at this stage of the method. Extant design features that may be ported to the target system are thus exposed.

Generally, an Extant Generalised Task Model is derived by eliminating a proportion of the details of an Extant Task Description (TD(ext)) that is specific to a device. In other words, an Extant Task Description may be contrasted with an Extant Generalised Task Model since the latter is abstracted largely towards device-independence. Thus, the logic underlying a particular task is revealed more readily by an Extant Generalised Task Model. Despite this emphasis on device-independence, the level of description of an Extant Generalised Task Model should not be too high, to ensure that sufficient information about relevant extant design features is retained (e.g. their design rationale). Refer to the next page for rules of thumb that should be observed when deriving an Extant Generalised Task Model.

As with an Extant Task Description, an Extant Generalised Task Model is described using structured diagrams. Additional comments on the description are recorded in supporting information tables.

The procedures for deriving an Extant Generalised Task Model are summarised overleaf.

Case-Study Illustration of an Extant Generalised Task Model (GTM(ext))

A case-study example of an Extant Generalised Task Model of the network security management task at University College London (GTM(UCLCC)) is shown in Figure 4-6. The task model is derived by processing the corresponding Extant Task Description (TD(UCLCC)) as follows:

(i) Low-level details of the Extant Task Description were omitted to emphasise a more general description. For instance, the 'Status illegal' sub-node and its leaves (Figure 4-4, Page 1, left-hand side) have been reduced to a single leaf named 'Record violation details' (Figure 4-6, Page 1, right-hand side).
(ii) All task information considered to be device-specific was removed from the Extant Task Description, e.g. the 'Search printout' leaf (Figure 4-4, Page 3, left-hand side) is excluded from the Extant Generalised Task Model (Figure 4-6, Page 2, left-hand side).
(iii) The overall structure of the Extant Task Description was largely carried over to the Extant Generalised Task Model.
(iv) All information beyond the remit of target system design was excluded. In particular,

the 'Check source port status' sub-node (Figure 4-4, Page 4, left-hand side) was omitted since connections with external networks were beyond the scope of the target system.

A new set of design information tables was not generated in this instance since interpretation of the Extant Generalised Task Model was supported adequately by tables accompanying the Extant Task Description.

<u>Procedures for deriving an Extant Generalised Task Model, GTM(ext)</u>

Starting at the top of an Extant Task Description, work through each node as follows:

1. Summarise the semantics of the task (and its sub-tasks) in 'device-independent' terms to reveal its underlying logic. This process is supported by the statement of requirements, which provides guidance on the level of description that is appropriate for the generalised task model of a particular extant system. In general, the more similar the extant and target systems are to one another, the more device-dependent details should be retained in the Extant Generalised Task Model (see rules of thumb below). Note that the information captured by an extant task model should relate directly to salient characteristics of the target system. Later comparisons between extant and target system characteristics are thus facilitated.

2. Continue the above abstraction for each branch of the Extant Task Description. The process may become more difficult lower down the structured diagram, since the branches correspond to more device specific descriptions (e.g. task inputs and outputs).

3. Summarise the Extant Generalised Task Model in a separate structured diagram, and include supporting comments in an information table.

<u>Rules of thumb supporting the derivation of an Extant Generalised Task Model, GTM(ext)</u>

1. The level of description of an Extant Generalised Task Model should be high enough to support conceptual comparison between extant and target systems design.

2. The level of description of an Extant Generalised Task Model should be low enough to retain sufficient information on extant design features of interest for the design of the target system. Thus, complete device-independence in the description of a generalised task model is not always desirable. In this way, information on the relationship(s) between particular task characteristics and specific device design features would not be lost.

3. A one-to-one mapping between device-dependent and device-independent descriptions is unlikely, particularly at lower levels of description. Thus, it may not be possible to abstract directly each structured diagram node of an Extant Task Description (TD(ext)) to a 'device-independent' representation. In such cases, it is necessary to consider the node with one or more adjacent node(s). The group of nodes are then abstracted to generate a single device-independent expression.

Figure 4-6: Extant Generalised Task Model for Network Security Management at University College London Computer Centre (GTM(UCLCC)) – Page 1

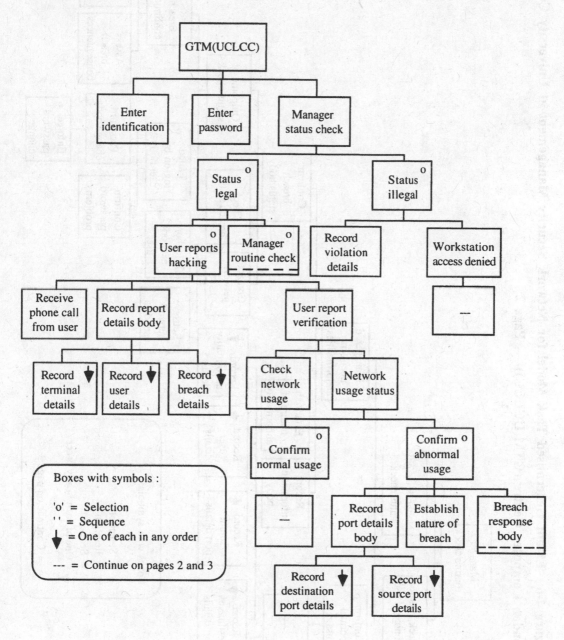

Figure 4-6: Extant Generalised Task Model for Network Security Management at University College London Computer Centre (GTM(UCLCC)) — Page 2

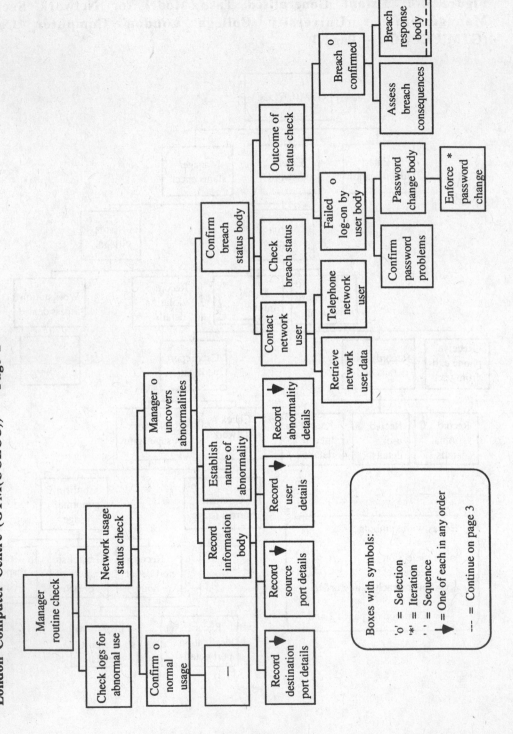

Figure 4-6: **Extant Generalised Task Model for Network Security Management at University College London Computer Centre (GTM(UCLCC)) – Page 3**

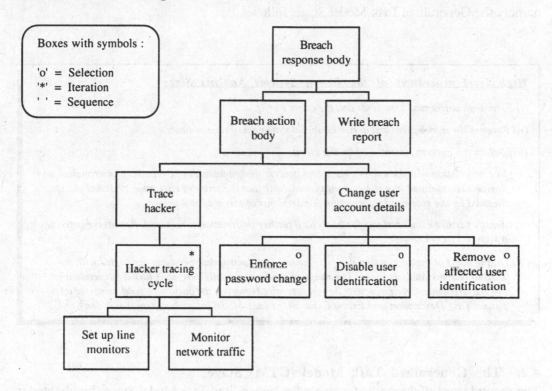

For the MacPassword™ application, an Extant Generalised Task Model was not derived, since the Extant Task Description was simple enough to support an assessment of the potential for porting its design features to the target system. Furthermore, it was anticipated that lower level details of the MacPassword™ application would be of greater interest to target system design. Thus, an abstraction of its Extant Task Description was considered unnecessary.

For this case-study, a wider range of human factors descriptions was also derived at this stage of the method (refer to Sub-section 4.1 and Figure 4-2). However, these products of *extant* system analysis will not be illustrated here, since they are similar in nature to later products that describe the *target* system (see Chapters Five and Six). Nevertheless, for the sake of completeness, an account of the remaining *extant* system descriptions for the case-study is provided in Annex A.

To conclude the account on the Extant Systems Analysis Stage, its main procedures are summarised below. A description of the design activities for the next stage of the method, namely the Generalised Task Model Stage, follows.

High level procedures of the Extant Systems Analysis Stage

(i) Examine contractual documents and the client's brief.

(ii) Process the information and derive an initial statement of requirements.

(iii) Select the current system used by the client.

(iv) In consultation with the user(s), elicit and analyse design features of the task(s), environment and device(s) associated with the current system. Note that the scope of elicitation and analysis is dictated by the scope and information requirements of target system design.

(v) Identify further extant systems for analysis if further information is required. Repeat the activities in step (iv) as necessary.

(vi) On the basis of the information derived, generate the appropriate products associated with the Extant Systems Analysis Stage. The range of products actually derived is largely dependent on the requirements of the particular design scenario. However, the basic set would comprise an Extant Task Description and Extant Generalised Task Model for each system that is analysed.

4.2. The Generalised Task Model (GTM) Stage

The second stage of the method, namely the Generalised Task Model Stage (highlighted in Figure 4-7 by a box outlined in bold), is concerned with the derivation of human factors descriptions to support the conceptual design of the target system. Specifically, device-independent descriptions[11] are derived to facilitate analytic mapping between relevant design features of the extant system and key requirements of the target system. To this end, two products are derived, namely an Extant Composite Task Model (termed CTM(x)) and a Target Generalised Task Model (termed GTM(y)). These models establish the foundation for the recruitment of promising designs of extant system(s), and for the specification of new design features to support task extensions particular to the target system.

---

[11] The extent of abstraction to device-independence is determined by how dissimilar the characteristics of the extant system are to those of the target system. In general, the level of description should be high enough to reveal logical aspects of the task (as opposed to device-specific interaction sequences). Sufficient information on extant design features of interest to target system design should also be preserved.

The task models derived are carried forward to the Composite Task Model Stage, where appropriate elements are synthesised on the basis of a Statement of User Needs. Specifically, by synthesising compatible and complementary subsets of the Extant Composite Task Model with the Target Generalised Task Model (i.e. CTM(x) and GTM(y) respectively), a Target Composite Task Model (or CTM(y)) is derived (see later). Since CTM(x) and GTM(y) describe existing and new task components of the target system respectively, a comparison of their descriptions would provide an early indication of the training required by users of the target system. Such inferences may be drawn by:

(a) assessing the complexity of the Target Generalised Task Model (i.e. GTM(y));
(b) examining the transfer of learning (both positive and negative effects) attributed to the porting of existing design features to the target system (the extent of porting is indicated by the parts of the Extant Composite Task Model that have been recruited to the target system).

Figure 4-7:   A Simple Representation of the Structured Human Factors Method (with the Generalised Task Model Stage Highlighted)

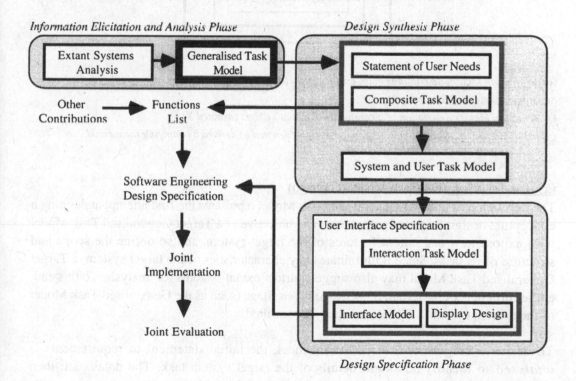

<u>A More Detailed Account of the Generalised Task Model Stage</u>
An account of the derivation of the Extant Composite Task Model and the Target
Generalised Task Model follows. As before, italics will be used to highlight the design
activities shown in Figure 4-8.

Figure 4-8: Block Diagram Summary of the Generalised Task Model (GTM) Stage

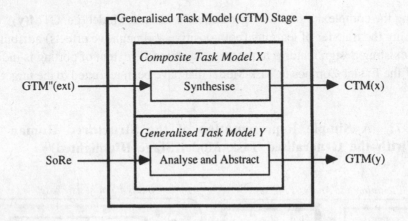

(ext) = human factors descriptions of an extant system (denoted EXT) derived by applying the method
SoRe = Statement of Requirements
(x) = human factors description of a composite of extant systems (denoted X)
(y) = human factors descriptions of the target system (denoted Y) derived by applying the method

<u>(a) Target Generalised Task Model (GTM(y))</u>
The derivation of a Target Generalised Task Model represents the first attempt at defining a
conceptual design for the target system. The objective of a Target Generalised Task Model
is to expose new and salient features of the target system, and so define the scope and
structure of its tasks. Since it illuminates key characteristics of the target system, a Target
Generalised Task Model may also suggest further extant systems for analysis. To this end,
earlier products of the Extant Systems Analysis Stage (such as the Generalised Task Model
of the current system, a GTM(ext)) may be consulted.

To derive a Target Generalised Task Model, the initial statement of requirements is
analysed to identify important details of the target system task. The details are then
abstracted to derive a conceptual level description. Since the statement of requirements

originates from the client, sufficient information to support the derivation of a reasonably complete Target Generalised Task Model cannot be assumed. To address this problem, extensions of the task model are supported by a later stage of the method, namely the Composite Task Model Stage (see Chapter Five). In this way, a reasonably complete conceptual task may be specified for the target system.

Procedures for deriving a Target Generalised Task Model are described below.

Procedures for deriving a Target Generalised Task

1. Take as input task information described in the statement of requirements. Temporal and conditional aspects of task execution should also be noted.

2. Summarise the task (and sub-tasks) in device-independent terms to reveal the logic underlying the design of the task.

3. Re-express the task description using structured diagrams to derive a Target Generalised Task Model, and record additional notes in a supporting table.

Case-Study Illustration of a Target Generalised Task Model (GTM(y))

A simple case-study example of a Target Generalised Task Model is shown in Figure 4-9. The description is derived from the statement of requirements specified by the client. It can be seen from the figure that the statement of requirements provides little information on the task of the network manager. For instance, it fails to distinguish between different types of security breach and the actions that should be taken. Thus, user access is invariably disabled for any occurrence of a security breach (see Figure 4-9).

To support the rectification of inadequacies in the design of the current system, the human factors designer may thus resort to extant systems analysis; e.g. to generate more detailed information on the task of the network manager. Since access to the staff and computer systems at the client organisation was restricted, the extant *current* system could not be analysed. Instead, as indicated earlier, two extant systems were selected for analysis; namely the network management system at University College London (an extant related system) and the PC security application, MacPassword™ (an extant partial system).[12]

---

[12] Refer to Sub-section 4.1 for an explanation of the types of extant systems.

Figure 4-9:   Target Generalised Task Model (GTM(y)) of a Network Security Management System

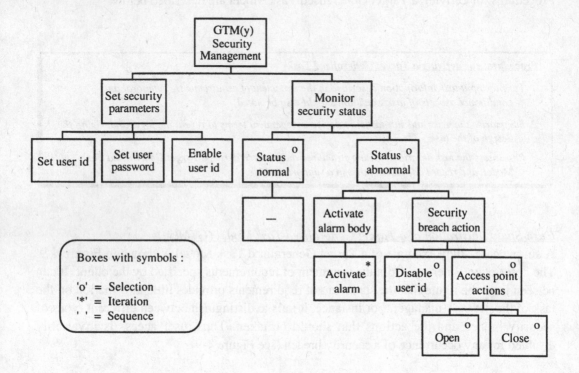

Target Generalised Task Model Table (GTM(y))

Name	Description	Observation	Design Implication	Speculation
Set security parameters	A number of network security parameters may be controlled by the network manager. For instance, the network manager can change a user's password, and either enable or disable a user identification (id) at any time. The original user password is allocated by the computer control centre. On the first log-on, the user may choose a new password.	The client focused only on the security requirements for the network. However, security measures are also required for the network management workstation. A password should comprise an alphabet followed by seven alphanumeric characters.		
Monitor security status	Network activities (e.g. user log-ons) should be monitored by the network management workstation. On detecting abnormal events (e.g. failed log-ons), the workstation should activate an alarm to alert the network manager.	No suggestion from the client on the form of alert required. Also, the requirements for specific responses by the network manager were not defined.		
Access point actions	The network manager should be able to permit or deny access to any network access point (either host or terminal). In particular, the system should be capable of disabling all access to selected host machines if desired, e.g. to secure sensitive information.			

(b) Extant Composite Task Model (CTM(x))

Following the definition of a conceptual task for the target system (described by the Target Generalised Task Model or GTM(y)), a promising subset of the Extant Generalised Task Models (or GTM(ext)s) may be synthesised to derive a composite representation.[13] The

---

[13] Synthesis of GTM(ext)s is only necessary if more than one extant system has been analysed, e.g. when an extant related system and an extant current system have been analysed. In contrast, if only the extant current system is analysed, then the Extant Composite Task Model (or CTM(x)) is equivalent to the Extant Generalised Task Model of the current system (or GTM(ext)).

representation, termed an Extant Composite Task Model (or CTM(x)), encapsulates conceptual designs of extant systems that may be ported to the target system. To this end, low-level design details of the selected subset of Extant Generalised Task Models, are documented.

Procedures for deriving an Extant Composite Task Model are described below.

Procedures for deriving an Extant Composite Task Model, CTM(x)

1. Take as input Extant Generalised Task Models (or GTM(ext)s) of extant systems analysed at the ESA Stage.

2. Compare the Extant Generalised Task Models with key target system requirements represented by the Target Generalised Task Model (or GTM(y)). On the basis of earlier human factors evaluations, identify aspects of extant tasks that are potentially relevant to target system design. In addition, note potential influences from other products of the ESA Stage, i.e. consider other (ext) products that may be relevant.

3. Identify a subset of Extant Generalised Task Models that is mutually compatible, and relevant to target system requirements. The subset represents potentially desirable extant system characteristics that may be ported later to the design of the target system.

4. Synthesise the selected subset of Extant Generalised Task Models into a single representation, termed an Extant Composite Task Model (or CTM(x)).

Case-Study Illustration of an Extant Composite Task Model (CTM(x))

A case-study example of an Extant Composite Task Model (or CTM(x)) for network security management is shown in Figure 4-10. The composite model was derived by synthesising the extant task descriptions derived in the preceding stages of the method, namely TD(MPASS)[14] and GTM(UCLCC) (see Figures 4-5 and 4-6). In particular, computer access characteristics of MacPassword™ (compare the left-hand part of Figure 4-5 and Figure 4-10, Page 1) have been selected and synthesised with the security management tasks at the University College London Computer Centre. (Compare Figures 4-6 and 4-10, Pages 1 to 3. Pages 2 and 3 are carried forward directly from Figure 4-6.)

---

[14] The Extant Task Description of MacPassword (i.e. TD(MPASS)) was used in the synthesis in this instance, because the derivation of its Extant Generalised Task Model was considered unnecessary (see Sub-section 4.1).

Figure 4-10: Extant Composite Task Model (CTM(x)) of a Network Security Management System – Page 1

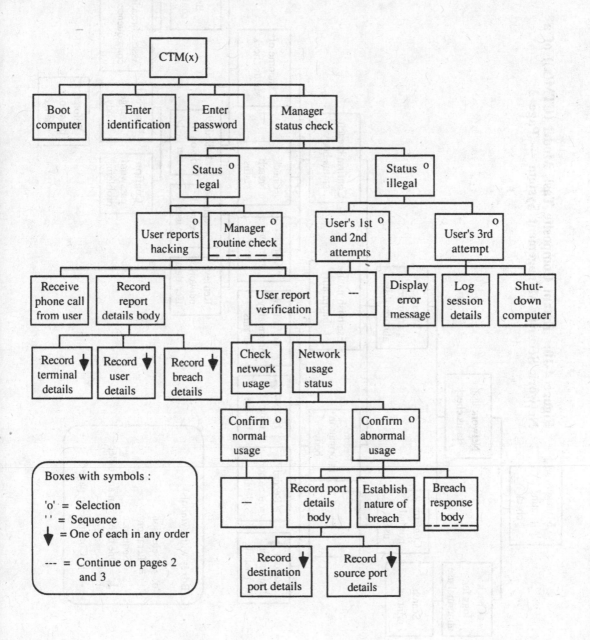

Figure 4-10: Extant Composite Task Model (CTM(x)) of a Network Security Management System — Page 2

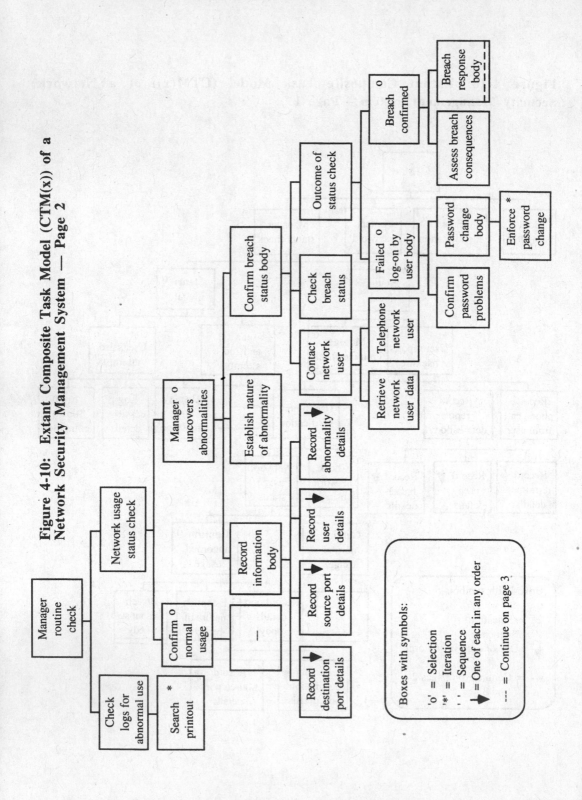

Boxes with symbols:

'o' = Selection
'*' = Iteration
' ' = Sequence
= One of each in any order
--- = Continue on page 3

Figure 4-10: Extant Composite Task Model (CTM(x)) of a Network Security Management System – Page 3

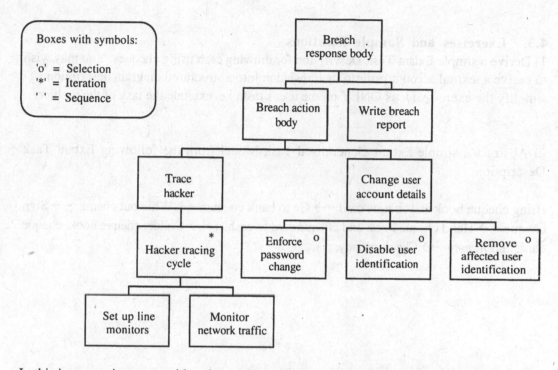

Boxes with symbols:

'o' = Selection
'*' = Iteration
' ' = Sequence

In this instance, it was considered unnecessary to construct a new information table for the Extant Composite Task Model (or CTM(x)). This is because the structured diagram description of the model is sufficiently similar to the original Extant Task Descriptions (see Figures 4-4 and 4-5). Thus, the designer could refer to the tables that accompany the latter descriptions if necessary.

The above account completes a description of the Generalised Task Model (GTM) Stage. Together with the Extant Systems Analysis (ESA) Stage, design activities of the first phase of the method (i.e. the Information Elicitation and Analysis Phase) are now completed. The conceptual design solutions derived are developed further in the next phase, namely the Design Synthesis Phase. To this end, the initial statement of requirements is enhanced so that pertinent design criteria may be defined adequately to support further synthesis and extension of the task models derived at the Generalised Task Model Stage. Such concerns are addressed by the design stages comprising the Design Synthesis Phase; namely the Statement of User Needs Stage, the Composite Task Model Stage, and the System and User Task Model Stage. Design activities and products at these stages are described in the following chapter.

4.3. Exercises and Sample Solutions

1) Derive a simple Extant Task Description for drawing cash using cheques. You may wish to derive a textual account prior to its translation into a structured diagram description. To simplify the exercise, focus ONLY on the user's task, i.e. exclude the task of the cashier.

2) Abstract a simple Extant Generalised Task Model from the following Extant Task Description:

Bring cheque book and cheque card $\longrightarrow$ Go to bank counter $\longrightarrow$ Write out cheque $\longrightarrow$ Sign cheque $\longrightarrow$ Hand cheque book and cheque card to cashier $\longrightarrow$ Collect cheque book, cheque card, and money $\longrightarrow$ Check money.

Sample Solutions to Exercises

Possible solutions to the preceding exercises are given below. It should be noted that more than one 'correct' solution might be applicable for each exercise. In this respect, the appropriateness of particular solutions would depend on the constraints and circumstances of the design project (not specified in the exercise).

Solution to Exercise 1

A textual description may be as follows:

Bring cheque book and cheque card $\longrightarrow$ Go to bank counter $\longrightarrow$ Write out cheque $\longrightarrow$ Sign cheque $\longrightarrow$ Hand cheque book and cheque card to cashier $\longrightarrow$ Collect cheque book, cheque card, and money $\longrightarrow$ Check money.

The textual description may then be translated into a structured diagram description as shown below.

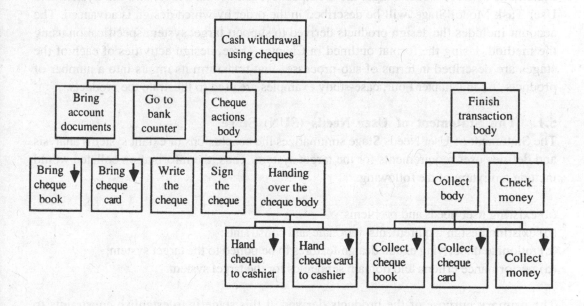

Solution to Exercise 2:

Bring <personal ID> $\longrightarrow$ Go to <money source> $\longrightarrow$ Write out <instructions to withdraw money> $\longrightarrow$ Show <personal ID> $\longrightarrow$ Collect money $\longrightarrow$ Check money.

5
The Design Synthesis Phase of MUSE

To be still searching what we know not by what we know.......

Milton, 1644, ***Areopagitica***

Leaving the old, both worlds at once they view,
That stand upon the threshold of the new.

Edmund Waller, 1606–1687

In this chapter, the stages of the Design Synthesis Phase of the method, namely the Statement of User Needs Stage, the Composite Task Model Stage, and the System and User Task Model Stage, will be described in the order by which design is advanced. The account includes the design products derived to support target system specification using the method. Using the format outlined in Chapter Three, design activities of each of the stages are described in terms of sub-processes that transform its inputs into a number of products. As in Chapter Four, case-study examples are used to illustrate the products.

5.1. The Statement of User Needs (SUN) Stage
The Statement of User Needs Stage summarizes the conclusions of extant systems analysis and defines user requirements for the target system. Thus, the information collated would include a mixture of the following:

(a) existing user needs and problems;
(b) existing design requirements, rationale and constraints;
(c) rationale underlying extant design features to be ported to the target system;
(d) performance criteria and domain semantics for the target system.

The primary purpose of the products derived at this stage is to establish constraints to support later design decisions and extensions, e.g. during the synthesis of task models at the Composite Task Model Stage.

Figure 5-1 shows the location of the Statement of User Needs Stage relative to other stages of the method (the stage is indicated by a box outlined in bold).

Figure 5-1: A Simple Representation of the Structured Human Factors Method (with the Statement of User Needs Stage Highlighted)

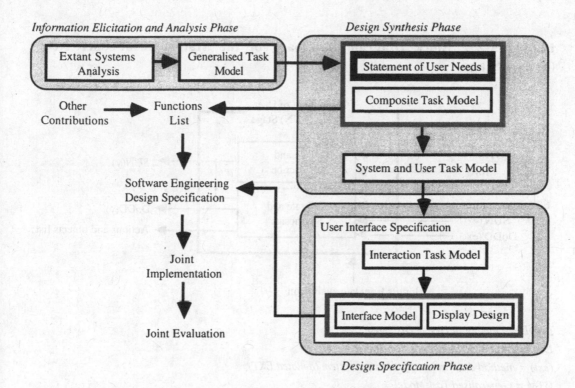

Information Elicitation and Analysis Phase   *Design Synthesis Phase*

- Extant Systems Analysis
- Generalised Task Model
- Statement of User Needs
- Composite Task Model
- Other Contributions
- Functions List
- System and User Task Model
- Software Engineering Design Specification
- User Interface Specification
- Interaction Task Model
- Joint Implementation
- Interface Model
- Display Design
- Joint Evaluation

Design Specification Phase

A More Detailed Account of the Statement of User Needs (SUN) Stage

Design activities and products of the Statement of User Needs Stage are summarised in Figure 5-2. Generally, three design descriptions of the target system are derived at this stage; namely a Statement of User Needs (or SUN(y)), a Domain of Design Discourse (or DoDD(y)), and an actions and objects list (optional product that supports the Domain of Design Discourse description).

A detailed description of the activities involved in the derivation of the above products follows. As before, design processes shown in the block diagram summary of the stage (see Figure 5-2) are indicated in the account in italics.

(a) Statement of User Needs for the Target System (SUN(y))

The purpose of the Statement of User Needs is to establish a human factors basis for conceptual design extension at later stages of the method. For instance, the Statement of

User Needs for the Target System (or SUN(y)) must be defined adequately to support the appropriate synthesis of task models at the Composite Task Model Stage (see later).

Figure 5-2:   Block Diagram Summary of the Statement of User Needs (SUN) Stage

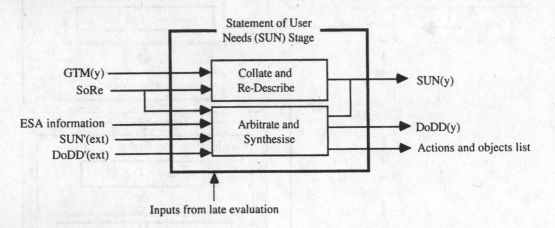

DoDD = Domain of Design Discourse
ESA = Extant Systems Analysis (Stage)
(ext) = method descriptions of an extant system (denoted EXT)
GTM = Generalised Task Model
SoRe = Statement of Requirements
(y) = method descriptions of the target system (denoted Y)

The Target Statement of User Needs is derived by *collating* and *re-describing* design information extracted from the initial statement of requirements and the products derived in preceding stages of the method, e.g. the Extant Systems Analysis Stage. Specifically, suitable parts of the *Extant* Statement of User Needs (SUN(ext), or a more specific subset denoted SUN'(ext) – see Figure 4-2) may be incorporated in the *Target* Statement of User Needs (or SUN(y)). In cases in which the target system requirements are well defined, existing user requirements associated with device interaction (which are more specific and detailed) may also be recruited.

As a rule, the Target Statement of User Needs should address the following:

(i) user requirements, general design constraints and performance criteria associated with the target system;

(ii) user problems with the existing system uncovered by human factors assessments at the Extant System Analysis Stage;

(iii) human factors design recommendations and potential solutions to existing problems described in (ii) above;

(iv) promising features of extant designs and the rationale underlying their potential recruitment to the design of the target system.

The scope of the target system is thus characterised initially by a textual description comprising the Target Statement of User Needs. The description may be shared with software engineers so that user requirements may be included appropriately in early design considerations.

Procedures for deriving the Target Statement of User Needs (or SUN(y)) are summarised below.

Procedures for deriving the Target Statement of User Needs, SUN(y)

1. Take as input the Extant Statement of User Needs (or SUN(ext)) and other information on user problems uncovered at the Extant Systems Analysis Stage.

2. Interpret user problems with extant systems in the context of the target system.

3. Referring to the initial statement of requirements, summarise and extend the statements (e.g. by recruiting descriptions from (1) above) and propose preliminary solutions to the observed problems.

4. Summarise the information textually to derive the Target Statement of User Needs.

Case-Study Illustration of the Target Statement of User Needs (SUN(y))

An extract from the Target Statement of User Needs for the security management task is shown in Figure 5-3. In this case-study, several statements from the initial statement of requirements and the Extant Statement of User Needs (or SUN(ext)) have been incorporated (compare Figure 5-3 with Figures A-1 and A-2 (Annex A)).

<u>(b) Domain of Design Discourse Description for the Target System or DoDD(y)</u>

The Target Domain of Design Discourse description summarises the semantics of the target system by identifying explicit relationships among domain entities (comprising domain concepts, objects, task events and processes). The description establishes a common conceptual scope and vocabulary to support discussions between designers and end-users. For instance, target system solutions may be proposed and interpreted in terms of particular groups of entities of the domain description. In addition, specific relationships among and between entities of *real* and *representation* worlds may be compared using such a description. Thus, promising metaphors may be assessed for their potential incorporation into a user interface design for the target system (see Frohlich and Luff, 1989; Ragoczei and Hirst, 1990).

Figure 5-3: Part of a Target Statement of User Needs for a Network Security Management System

---

Target Statement of User Needs

1. A record of network events should be kept to support the task of following up security breaches. The record should include the following information :

(i) date and time of log-on;

(ii) service requested and outcome of request (either offered or denied);

(iii) user source and destination addresses;

(iv) failed log-on events and the offending password(s).

2. Specific information search and retrieve functions should be provided to facilitate access to logged information. A hard copy log may also be necessary.

3. The network management workstation should notify the manager whenever a security breach is detected, e.g. failed log-ons and service request refusals. Notification criteria should be context sensitive, e.g. frequency, threshold and condition-based triggers; and alarm activation should not unduly interrupt other network management tasks. The alarms should be sufficient to attract the network manager's attention, e.g. both auditory and visual alarms may be used. Security breaches that occur when the network management workstation is unmanned (e.g. outside office hours) should be repeated on next log-on by the network manager.

4. Communication between the network manager and users is often required, e.g. when reporting and confirming a security breach. Although telephones are effective, communication media that support asynchronous communication should be provided to prevent excessive interruptions and work stress, e.g. electronic mail.

The Target Domain of Design Discourse (or DoDD(y)) description is constructed on the basis of information extracted from the initial statement of requirements. The information is summarised as a semantic net, comprising nodes and relations expanded textually in an accompanying table. The description may then be extended further by incorporating relevant parts of the Extant Domain of Design Discourse (or DoDD(ext)) description derived during extant systems analysis.

Procedures for deriving a Target Domain of Design Discourse description are summarised below.

Procedures for deriving a Target Domain of Design Discourse, DoDD(y)

1. *Extract domain and task information from the initial statement of requirements, the Target Generalised Task Model (or GTM(y)) and the products of extant system analysis (such as the Extant Domain of Design Discourse description (or DoDD(ext)), the Extant Statement of User Needs (or SUN(ext)) and the Extant Generalised Task Model (or GTM(ext)). Information relevant to the construction of a Target Domain of Design Discourse description comprises the following:*

   (a) domain objects. Attributes that uniquely define a particular object should be recorded, e.g. 'Network User' attributes = {user id, password};
   (b) task concepts, events and processes, such as 'Hacker Tracing' for network security;
   (c) relations between objects and entities (both composite and taxonomic), e.g. the 'Network User' entity is general to both 'Hacker' and 'Legal User' entities since it is defined by the network status attribute 'network access' = {true/false}.

2. *Collate the information as a semantic net.*

Rules of thumb for deriving a Target Domain of Design Discourse, DoDD(y)

1. *A Target Domain of Design Discourse description should be sufficiently rich in information to support explanations of target system tasks. It should also facilitate scenario construction to support the synthesis of a design solution.*

2. *A Target Domain of Design Discourse description should exclude device-dependent details. The information described is restricted to the semantics of the target system domain.*

3. *To derive a final Target Domain of Design Discourse description, further design iterations may be necessary following consultative meetings between software engineers and human factors designers, and the derivation of a Functions List for the target system (see later stages of the method).*

Case-Study Illustration of a Target Domain of Design Discourse Description (DoDD(y))
A case-study example of a Target Domain of Design Discourse description for a network
security management system is shown in Figure 5-4. In this instance, the description was
synthesised largely from Extant Domain of Design Discourse (or DoDD(ext)s) descriptions
(compare Figure 5-4 with Figures A-3 and A-5 (Annex A)). In other words, a relevant
subset of the domain descriptions of extant systems was incorporated with similar
information extracted from the initial statement of requirements for the target system.

(c) Actions and objects list
To support a Target Domain of Design Discourse description further, an *optional* list of
actions and objects may be derived. The list provides a convenient summary of similar
information derived at earlier stages of the method, e.g. information contained in tables
accompanying structured diagram descriptions, statement of user needs descriptions and
domain of design discourse descriptions. Since it is essentially a listing of actions and
attributes clustered around objects of the target system domain, a case-study example will
not be given. However, the following rules of thumb should be noted:

(i) the focus of the list should be on the domain of the target system, i.e. device-specific
details should be excluded;
(ii) the list should be collated from the initial statement of requirements and products of
extant system analyses. Generally, objects and actions may be identified by noting verbs
and nouns in textual accounts elicited from users or other sources, e.g. contractual
documents, etc.

In conclusion, the objective of the Statement of User Needs Stage is to establish a basis to
support and constrain the specification of an appropriate design solution. Such a basis for
design would include conditions to be satisfied when task models are synthesised to
generate a conceptual model of the target system task (see next stage of the method).

Figure 5-4:   A Target Domain of Design Discourse (or DoDD(y)) Description for a Network Security Management System

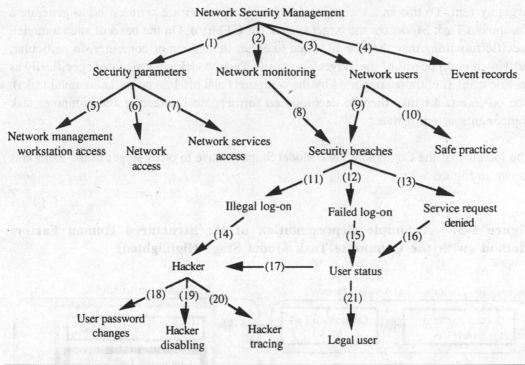

Node	Description	No.	Relation
Network Security Management	The primary concern of network security management is to prevent unauthorised network access.	(1)	To ensure authorised access to the network and its services, the network manager is required to allocate and update security parameters such as user identifications and passwords.
		(2)	Security breaches may be identified by monitoring network access events.
		(3)	Security breaches may be identified by direct liaison with network users. For instance, users may detect and report a security breach on a particular machine to the network manager. Alternatively, the manager may contact the user to ascertain whether suspicious network usage events are attributable to a security breach.
		(4)	The following record of network events should be kept: source and destination addresses; passwords; user identifications; date and time of log-ons and log-offs.
Security parameters	etc.	(5)	etc.

5.2. The Composite Task Model (CTM) Stage

The objective of the Composite Task Model Stage is to generate a conceptual model of the target system. To this end, the task models derived earlier are synthesised to generate a Composite Task Model for the target system (or CTM(y)). On the basis of such a model, specific functions may then be allocated to either the human or computer. In particular, individual components of the Target Composite Task Model are designated specifically as on-line tasks (i.e. those supported by the computer) and off-line tasks (i.e. manual tasks). The on-line tasks may then be decomposed further into interactive and computer task components as appropriate.

The location of the Composite Task Model Stage relative to other stages of the method is shown in Figure 5-5.

Figure 5-5:   A Simple Representation of the Structured Human Factors Method (with the Composite Task Model Stage Highlighted)

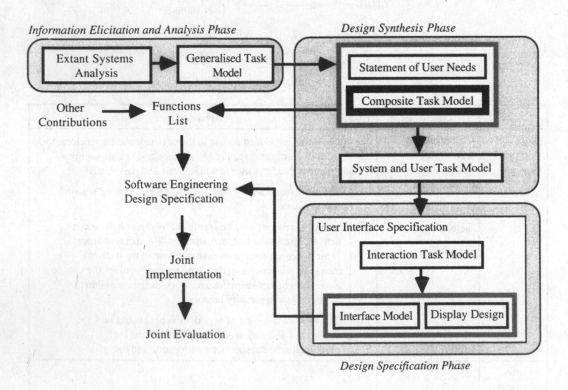

Two other concerns of the Composite Task Model Stage should be noted:

(a) Design iterations may occur between the Statement of User Needs Stage and Composite Task Model Stage. Iterations may be instigated by user feedback resulting in necessary modifications of the products generated in the preceding design stages.
(b) Inter-disciplinary members of the design team should exchange information of mutual interest. The objective is to establish a common design scope, so that subsequent human factors and software engineering design extensions would result in a convergent solution. In other words, the Composite Task Model Stage is a point at which inter-disciplinary design discussions would be required.

Generally, the design products generated thus far should be used to support discussions on the following: user requirements and problems; notable task events; general domain semantics; domain objects and actions; and task support requirements. In addition, a tabular summary of important task events may be derived to facilitate the discussions. A list of functions is thus specified to define the scope of target system design. Subsequent inter-disciplinary design extensions are therefore constrained by adhering to the agreed scope. In this respect, any violation of the constraints should be avoided since additional design iterations would be incurred.[1] For the same reason, necessary changes in the design scope should be discussed immediately with the design team.

A detailed account of the Composite Task Model Stage follows.

A More Detailed Account of the Composite Task Model (CTM) Stage
Details of design activities and case-study illustrations for products derived at the Composite Task Model Stage are addressed in this sub-section. Specifically, human factors descriptions of the target system derived at this stage comprise the following: a Target Composite Task Model (or CTM(y)), an Event Table and a Functions List. The products are described below.

(a) Composite Task Model of the Target System (CTM(y))
The Target Composite Task Model is generated in two steps as shown in Figure 5-6. First, the Target Generalised Task Model or GTM(y) derived earlier, is enhanced as follows:

(i) novel extensions may be proposed to meet new requirements of the target system;
(ii) pertinent extant system tasks may be incorporated on the basis of the statement of

---

[1] In other words, strict adherence to a common design scope obviates unnecessary design iterations. Adherence is vital for ensuring an efficient process of design development.

requirements and user needs. To this end, an appropriate subset of the Extant Composite Task Model (or CTM(x)) is *synthesised* with the Target Generalised Task Model (or GTM(y)).[2] A preliminary version of a Target Composite Task Model is thus derived.

Figure 5-6:   Block Diagram Summary of the Composite Task Model (CTM) Stage

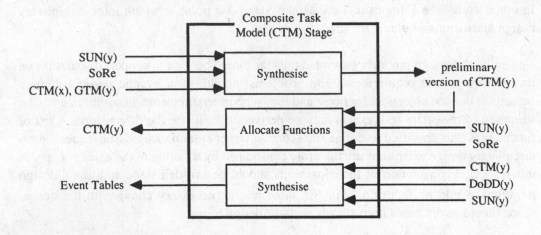

DoDD = Domain of Design Discourse   CTM = Composite Task Model
GTM = Generalised Task Model   SoRe = Statement of Requirements
SUN = Statement of User Needs
(x) = method descriptions of a composite extant system (denoted X)
(y) = method description of the target system (denoted Y)

Second, by applying relevant human factors expertise and declarative design guidelines, *functions* are allocated appropriately to human and computer components of the target system. To this end, on-line and off-line tasks are designated by working systematically through each component of the preliminary Target Composite Task Model. In particular, the on-line components define the scope of the target computer worksystem, while off-line components may be entirely manual tasks. This differentiation of system tasks completes the derivation of a Target Composite Task Model. The task model is then discussed with software engineers and updated as appropriate. The procedures for deriving a Target

---

[2] The rationale for recruiting particular extant design features should be documented to establish explicit links with design criteria defined at the Statement of User Needs Stage.

Composite Task Model are summarised below.

Procedures for deriving a Target Composite Task Model, CTM(y)

1. *On the basis of the statement of requirements and the Statement of User Needs (or SUN(y)), specify appropriate extensions of the Target Generalised Task Model (or GTM(y)). On a similar basis, incorporate appropriate components of the Extant Composite Task Model (or CTM(x)) in the Target Generalised Task Model. To this end, the extant and target task models should be compared to identify and remove (or modify) conflicting designs associated with the Extant Composite Task Model. A preliminary version of a Target Composite Task Model (or CTM(y)) is thus derived.*

2. *Record the design rationale and decisions entailed by the generation of a Target Composite Task Model. Summarise the information in a table accompanying the structured diagram description of a Target Composite Task Model.*

3. *On the basis of earlier human factors evaluation of extant system tasks, the statement of requirements, and the Statement of User Needs (or SUN(y)), allocate functions appropriately between the human and computer. Specifically, components of the Target Composite Task Model are designated as on-line and off-line tasks. Off-line tasks are differentiated in the structured diagram description by boxes outlined in grey. Further decomposition of the Target Composite Task Model may also be undertaken, to derive an appropriate level of description. To this end, products derived at the Extant Systems Analysis Stage may be consulted again as appropriate.*

Case-Study Illustration of a Target Composite Task Model (CTM(y))

Figure 5-7 shows a Target Composite Task Model of the security tasks for a network management system. It may be observed from the figure that off-line tasks are indicated using grey outlined boxes in a structured diagram description of the Target Composite Task Model. On-line tasks comprise the remainder of the boxes. For a more specific case-study illustration, consider the incidence of a failed log-on event during network security management (see Figure 5-7, page 3, left-hand side, box labelled 'Failed log-on by user body'). On detecting the event, the computer disables user access and alerts the network manager of its occurrence. The manager is then expected to access information logged by the computer to determine the user identification (user id) involved and the cause underlying the failed log-on event. In particular, the manager is required to ascertain whether the cause is due to mis-typing a password or 'real' attempts at hacking. These tasks, namely access disabling, and information gathering and interpretation, are designated as on-line tasks. The manager may also contact the user to verify inferences on the event, and thus decide whether the disabled user identification should be restored. In the case-study, such contacts with users are not supported by the computer, i.e. it is an off-line task. Accordingly, the 'Telephone network user' task is represented by a grey outlined box (Figure 5-7, page 2, lower right-hand side).

To illustrate the extent to which products of extant systems analysis have proved useful for supporting system design, the Target Composite Task Model (or CTM(y)) should be compared with human factors descriptions derived previously, namely the Target Generalised Task Model (or GTM(y)) and the Extant Composite Task Model (or CTM(x)). For instance, it may be observed from a comparison of Figures 5-7, 4-9 and 4-10 that responses of the extant system to failed log-on events (Figure 4-10, page 2, lower right-hand side) have been ported to the target system (Figure 5-7, page 3, left-hand side). Specifically, both systems require confirmation (with the user) that the failed log-on event is due to a password problem. Depending on the circumstances surrounding the event, a password change may then be enforced if appropriate. Similarly, specific target system requirements have also been incorporated into the Target Composite Task Model, e.g. automatic functions performed by the network management workstation such as monitoring network security, and enabling and disabling user identifications (see Figure 4-9).

Further information on the Target Composite Task Model is recorded in a table supporting the structured diagram description. Lower level details of the task are thus documented (e.g. the rationale for particular task characteristics) to support stage-wise design evaluation and iteration, and design maintenance following implementation.

Figure 5-7: Target Composite Task Model for a Network Security Management System — Page 1

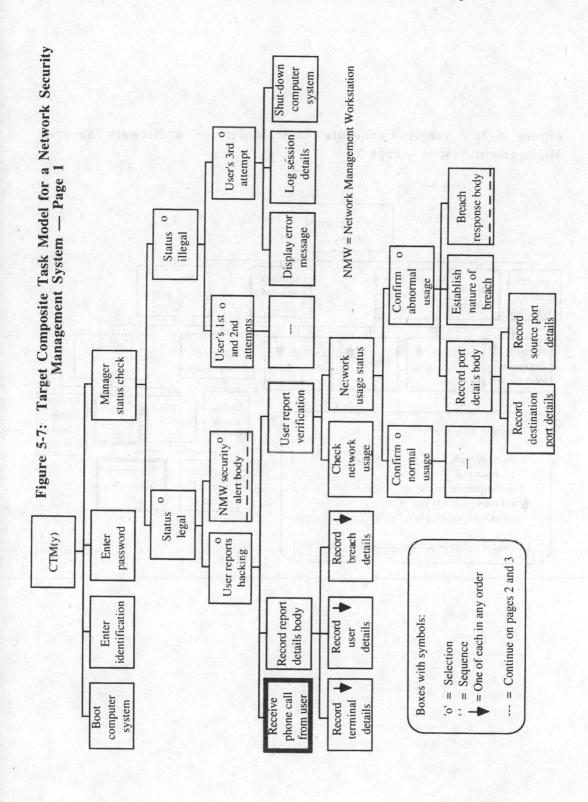

NMW = Network Management Workstation

Boxes with symbols:

'o' = Selection

':' = Sequence

➤ = One of each in any order

--- = Continue on pages 2 and 3

Figure 5-7:   Target Composite Task Model for a Network Security Management System – Page 2

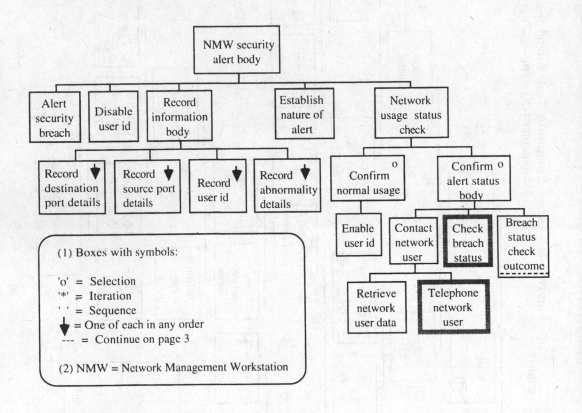

Figure 5-7: Target Composite Task Model for a Network Security Management System – Page 3

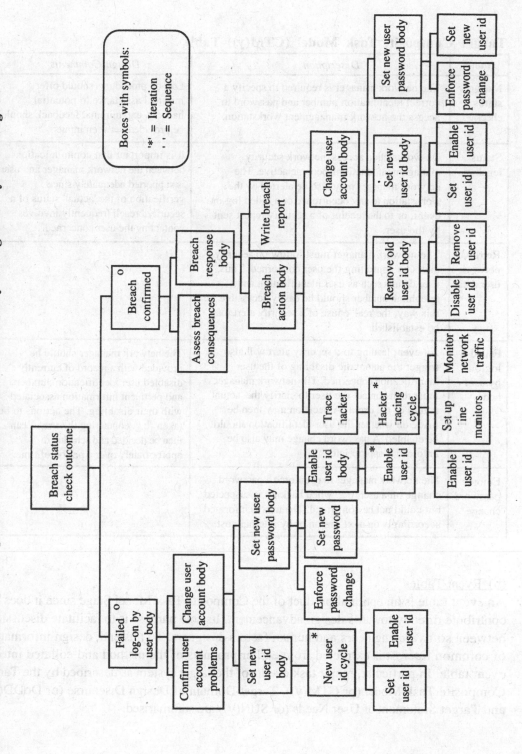

Boxes with symbols:

'*' = Iteration

' ' = Sequence

Target Composite Task Model (CTM(y)) Table

Name	Description	Design Comments
Manager status check	The network manager is required to specify a correct identification number and password to access the network management workstation.	Log-on procedures should offer minimal assistance to potential hackers, e.g. minimal feedback should be provided between inputs.
Status legal	On workstation access, network security management functions become active. The network manager may also be alerted by the workstation to any occurrence of a failed log-on event, or to the receipt of a security report sent by the user.	It is important that communication between the network manager and users is supported adequately since verification of the 'actual' status of a security breach frequently involves contacting the user concerned.
Retrieve network user data	The network manager must follow up security alerts by consulting the user concerned. Thus, user details such as user identification and telephone number should be easily accessible. In this way, the 'real' cause of a security alert may be established.	
Failed log-on by user body	An event leading to a security alert will also trigger the automatic disabling of the user identification concerned. The network manager must then contact the user to clarify the 'actual' nature of the event. A decision may then be made on whether the user identification should be enabled. A password change may also be enforced if appropriate.	The network manager should be provided with a record of currently disabled user identification numbers and pertinent information associated with their disabling. The actions to be taken (e.g. contacting the users) can then be decided and scheduled appropriately over a period of time.
Enforce password change	The network manager may enforce a password change on a user, e.g. when hacking is suspected but could not be confirmed. The user is informed accordingly on next log-on or by internal post.	

(b) Event Tables

An event table is an optional product of the Composite Task Model Stage since it does not contribute directly towards design advancement. Its sole purpose is to facilitate discussions between software engineers and human factors designers. To this end, design information of common interest is extracted from earlier products of the method and collated into an event table. In particular, major task events of the target system as described by the Target Composite Task Model (or CTM(y)), Target Domain of Design Discourse (or DoDD(y)) and Target Statement of User Needs (or SUN(y)) are summarised.

Procedures for deriving an event table are listed below.

Procedures for deriving an event table for the target system

1. Take preceding human factors descriptions as inputs, namely the Target Composite Task Model (CTM(y)), the Target Domain of Design Discourse (DoDD(y)), and the Target Statement of User Needs (SUN(y)). If necessary, refer also to extant system(s) descriptions and the initial statement of requirements.

2. Identify major events such as the completion of key sub-tasks and events resulting in significant changes in status of real world entities. These changes may be associated with the achievement of specific sub-goals of the target system. The objects and actions involved in the event should be noted.

3. Collate the information in a table.

Case-Study Illustration of an Event Table for a Network Security Management System
Figure 5-8 shows part of an event table for the case-study. The table and other human factors products of the method (refer to an earlier account in this sub-section) are used to support discussions with software engineers.

Figure 5-8:   Part of an Event Table for a Network Security Management System

Event	Summary	Attributes	Instances
User notifies security breach	Network user indicates security breach has taken place.	• log-on time and date • user address • user identification number • nature of breach	Network manager receives phone call from user.
Consult network event record	A record of network events is examined for evidence of hacker activity, e.g. unusual log-on times.	• failed log-on • service request denied • log-on time	Network manager consults network logs.
Trace hacker	Attempts made to locate source address of security breach. May involve tracing across a number of machines.	• log-on address • intermediary addresses • source address	Network manager traces hacker via logged data.
Password change	A password change may be enforced on a user following a security breach.	• user identification number	Network manager invalidates user's current password.
Failed log-on	Network user inputs an invalid identification number and/or password. A security breach attempt thus results.	• user identification number • number of attempts • log-on time • destination and source addresses	

(c) Functions List

Following discussions and agreement on the scope of target system design, a Functions List is drawn up collaboratively by human factors designers and software engineers. The list comprises a tabular summary of the initiating trigger, end result and performance characteristics of task support functions. It should be noted that detailed specification of computer support functions is usually excluded at this stage.

On the basis of the Functions List, software engineers and human factors designers may work independently until human factors specification of a software user interface has been derived. However, it should be emphasised that any deviation from the Functions List in the interim should be notified to all designers as soon as it arises.

Case-Study Illustration of a Functions List for a Network Security Management System
An example of part of a Functions List for the case-study is shown in Figure 5-9.

Figure 5-9: Part of a Functions List for a Network Security Management System[3]

Function	Trigger	End result	Performance
Show network user activity	On network manager's request for information on the activity of a named network user over a specified time period.	Display of information for the named network user over the time period t1 to t2. The information should include: log-on time, source address, physical location, destination address, log-off time, failed log-on event at time t.	
Alert security breach: failed log-on	Occurrence of a failed log-on event.	Auditory and visual alert to failed log-on event giving time of occurrence, network user identification, access point and physical location.	Within 10 seconds of the failed log-on event.
Record failed log-on events	Occurrence of a failed log-on event.	Record (for previous two months) of failed log-on events giving time of occurrence, user identification, access point and physical location.	
Enforce a password change	On network manager's request to enforce a password change on a specific network user.	On the next log-on, the named network user will be asked to change his/her password. Failure to effect a password change will automatically disable the user identification.	

---

[3] Figure 5-9 is a modified version of a table constructed by staff at RARDE (see acknowledgements).

5.3. The System and User Task Model (SUTaM) Stage

Having agreed a common design scope with software engineers, human factors designers may then specify independently the high-level functions of the target system. These concerns are addressed at the System and User Task Model Stage, whose location in the method is shown in Figure 5-10.

Figure 5-10: A Simple Representation of the Structured Human Factors Method (with the System and User Task Model Stage Highlighted)

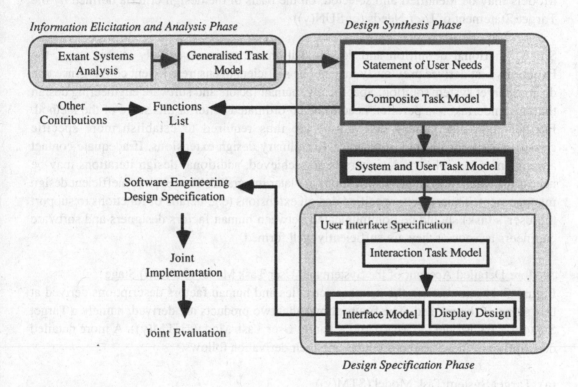

At the present stage, on-line and off-line tasks of the composite task model (designated previously) are decomposed further to generate system and user task models respectively. An account of these models follows.

A Target System Task Model is essentially a high-level description of the cycles of human-computer interaction required to achieve on-line task goals of the target system. In contrast, a Target User Task Model is a summary description of manual or off-line tasks of the target system. Consequently, the functional design of software systems is pursued primarily by decomposing the Target System Task Model. However, in particular instances, decompositions of the Target User Task Model should also be undertaken to support workload assessments and job design. During the derivation of the task models, appropriate subsets of the corresponding extant system descriptions may also be incorporated, namely the Extant System and User Task Models. To this end, appropriate features of extant systems may be identified by examining the parts of the Extant Composite Task Model (or CTM(x)) that have been incorporated into the Target Composite Task Model (or CTM(y)). Thus, corresponding parts of the Extant System and User Task Models may be identified and selected, on the basis of the design criteria defined by the Target Statement of User Needs (or SUN(y))

Since functional definition and decomposition are pursued actively at this stage, the Functions List derived previously may not be sufficient to ensure efficient convergence to a desired target system solution. Specifically, human factors and software engineering design that are undertaken in parallel, need to be co-ordinated better at this stage of the method. Further inter-disciplinary discussions are thus required to establish more specific constraints to ensure consistent inter-disciplinary design extensions. If adequate contact among inter-disciplinary designers is not achieved, additional design iterations may be necessary when individual specifications are later integrated. The result is inefficient design management. Thus, newly specified design extensions (e.g. details of functions to support the user's task) should be communicated between human factors designers and software engineers as soon as they are sufficiently well formed.

A More Detailed Account of the System and User Task Model (SUTaM) Stage
Figure 5-11 summarises the primary activities and human factors descriptions derived at this stage of the method. The figure shows that two products are derived, namely a Target System Task Model (STM(y)) and a Target User Task Model (UTM(y)). A more detailed description of these design products and their derivation follows.

(a) Target System Task Model (STM(y))
A System Task Model of the target system is derived by *decomposing* on-line task components of the Target Composite Task Model (or CTM(y)). In particular, on-line goals of the target system are decomposed to derive a high-level description of the cycles of human-computer interaction required for task performance. During decomposition, due consideration should be given to the design criteria defined earlier at the Statement of User Needs Stage. The interaction cycles are then described using a structured diagram with leaves designated as H (Human) and C (Computer) actions.

Figure 5-11: Block Diagram Summary of the System and User Task Model (SUTaM) Stage

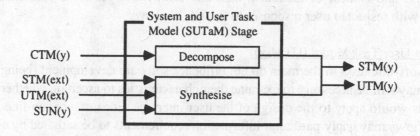

CTM = Composite Task Model   *(ext) = method descriptions of extant systems (denoted EXT)*
SUN = Statement of User Needs   STM = System Task Model
UTM = User Task Model   *(y) = method descriptions of the target system (denoted Y)*

Generally, the objective of deriving a Target System Task Model is to support user interface design at the final phase of the method (see Chapter Six). The design is supported as follows:

(1) H (Human) leaves of a Target System Task Model would be decomposed further to specify lower level human-computer interactions required for performing the on-line task. Such a decomposition is undertaken later at the Interaction Task Model Stage (see Chapter Six). In other words, the purpose of a Target System Task Model is to establish a foundation for the following specifications:

(i) user inputs required to perform the interactive task;
(ii) the context for presenting specific computer functions to support the user's task;
(iii) the context and content of feedback, help and error messages to be presented by the computer, at specific points in the user's execution of the interactive task. Due consideration should be given to the user actions and requirements described in (i) and (ii) above.

(2) C (Computer) leaves of a Target System Task Model may suggest potential user interface objects for the target system. These objects are specified later at the Interface Model Stage (see Chapter Six). In other words, a Target System Task Model establishes a foundation for the following specifications:

(i) behaviour of user interface objects with respect to user inputs and/or state changes of real and representation world entities;

(ii) appearance of user interface objects;

(iii) context and content of feedback, help and error messages to be presented by the computer with respect to user responses to (i) and (ii) above.

(b) Target User Task Model (UTM(y))

Although off-line tasks in the main do not influence software development (being manual tasks), it may still be necessary to examine their characteristics to ascertain whether indirect constraints would apply to the design of the user interface. For instance, on-line and off-line task flows may imply particular information requirements to be satisfied by computer displays; e.g. the content, format and mode of presentation of screen information. Consequently, a Target User Task Model is derived by collating and *decomposing* (if necessary) off-line components of the Target Composite Task Model (or CTM(y)). On the basis of design criteria defined at the Statement of User Needs Stage, appropriate subsets of the Extant User Task Model (or UTM(x)) may also be incorporated into the Target User Task Model (or UTM(y)). A structured diagram description of the Target User Task Model is thus derived. Additional information may be documented in a supporting table as before. Since a Target User Task Model (or UTM(y)) does not contribute directly to user interface design, and is similar in description format to a Target Composite Task Model (or CTM(y)), a case-study illustration is not provided here.

The procedures for deriving Target System and User Task Models are described overleaf.

Case-Study Illustration of the Target System Task Model (STM(y))

An example of a Target System Task Model for the network security management case-study is shown in Figure 5-12. It can be seen from the figure that on-line tasks of the Target Composite Task Model (or CTM(y)) have been decomposed further and assigned to human and computer components of the work system (compare Figures 5-7 and 5-12). For instance, the 'Enter user id and password body' sub-node (Figure 5-12, Page 1, upper-middle part) has been decomposed into Network Manager (NMgr) inputs and Network Management Workstation (NMW) prompts. In some instances, complete decomposition of the on-line task into H (Human) and C (Computer) leaves was considered unnecessary. In particular, the 'Access user data' leaf is described as a sub-task performed collaboratively by the Network Manager and Network Management Workstation (NMgr-NMW) (see Figure 5-12, Page 3, upper left-hand side).

Procedures for deriving Target System and User Task Models, (STM(y) and UTM(y))

1. *Target System and User Task Models are constructed respectively by decomposing on-line and off-line task components of the Target Composite Task Model (or CTM(y)). During decomposition, the structure of the Target Composite Task Model should be maintained as far as possible to facilitate subsequent cross-referencing between Target System and User Task Models.*

2. *The Target System Task Model (or STM(y)) should identify Human (H) and Computer (C) actions required to perform the on-line task. Note that a 'device-independent' description should be maintained as far as possible.*

3. *Describe Target System and User Task Models using structured diagrams. In addition, note further information textually in an accompanying table.*

Rules of thumb for deriving Target System and User Task Models, STM(y) and UTM(y)

1. *Significant off-line tasks may be highlighted in a Target System Task Model if appropriate. In such instances, the tasks should be indicated clearly as off-line tasks, and represented as structured diagram sub-nodes; i.e. without further decomposition to a lower level description. In this way, cross-references between Target System and User Task Models are supported; and a more coherent description of the overall task is afforded by the propagation of a more complete structure of the Target Composite Task Model (or CTM(y)) in the Target System Task Model (or STM(y)).*

2. *In some cases, 'H-C' sub-nodes (rather than decomposition into separate H and C leaves) may be used in a Target System Task Model. For instance, actions associated with a chosen user interface environment need not be described at a lower level since they are usually influenced by decisions external to the method. An 'H-C' sub-node may also be used where intervening interactive transitions may be assumed as understood. For instance, the sequence comprising 'H: activate function XYZ' → 'C: refresh screen to reflect user input' → 'C: carry out function XYZ', may be described equally well by 'H-C: carry out function XYZ'. The H or user input required may then be detailed later in the Interaction Task Model as appropriate. In this way, the Target System Task Model would be less cluttered.*

Figure 5-12: Part of System Task Model for a Network Security Management System – Page 1

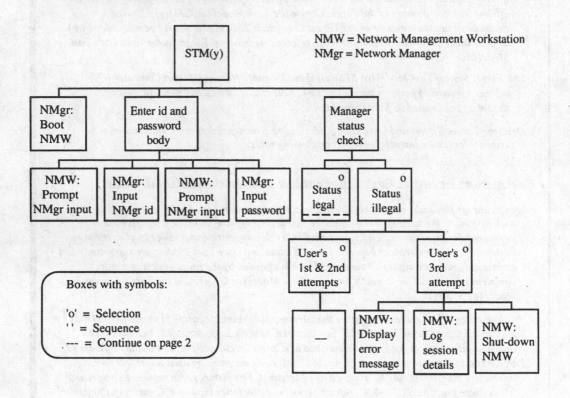

Figure 5-12: Part of System Task Model for a Network Security Management System

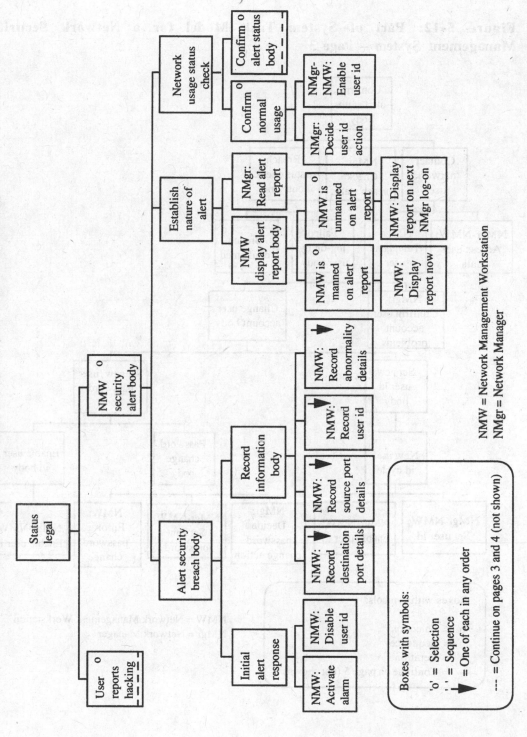

Figure 5-12: Part of System Task Model for a Network Security Management System – Page 3

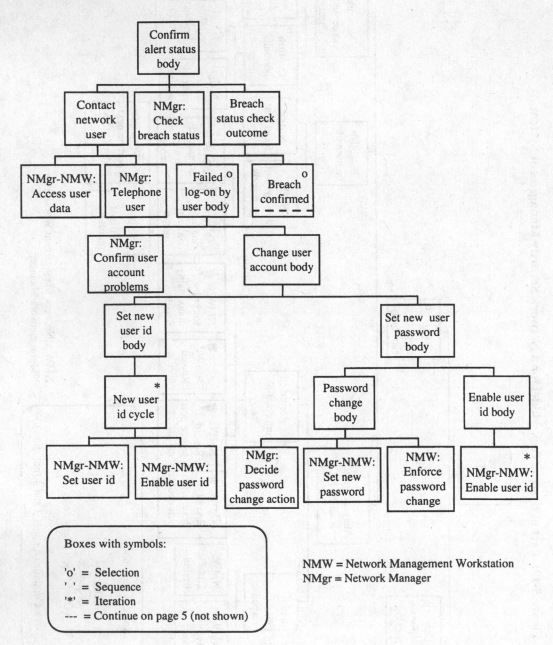

Target System Task Model (STM(y)) Table

Name	Description	Design Comments
NMW : Prompt NMgr input	The network management workstation prompts the network manager to input an identification number and password. These inputs are subsequently verified by the network management workstation before computer access is permitted.	It is important that input prompts by the network management workstation should offer minimal assistance to those unfamiliar with the log-on procedure.
Alert security breach body	The network management workstation may alert the network manager to security breaches including failed log-ons. The workstation may also indicate that a security breach report has been sent by a network user (messaging via the network).	Alerts should be signalled in real time, and should adequately capture the network manager's attention during a log-on session. Alerts to events occurring when the network management workstation is unmanned should be signalled to the network manager on next log-on.
Change user account body	Imposed changes in account details (e.g. passwords) are enforced automatically by the network management workstation.	

The above account completes a stage-wise review of the Design Synthesis Phase of the method. The output of this phase is a conceptual design of the target system that is defined sufficiently to support user interface specification at the next phase of the method; i.e. the Design Specification Phase. In particular, the Target System Task Model is extended to derive two complementary design perspectives of the target system, namely:

(1) 'H' or 'Human' leaves of the Target System Task Model are decomposed to define the device interactions to be performed by the user, i.e. to define the expected *user behaviour*. These design activities comprise the concerns of the Interaction Task Model Stage (see Sub-section 6.1).

(2) 'C' or 'Computer' leaves of the Target System Task Model are decomposed to define the *computer behaviour* that would support appropriately the interactive task to be performed by the user. These design activities comprise the concerns of the Interface Model and Display Design Stages (see Sub-section 6.2).

A detailed account of these design stages is presented in the following chapter.

5.4.   Exercises and Sample Solutions

(Sample solutions to the exercises below are given at the end of the chapter.)

1) It is essential that bank customers remember to collect all items issued by an Automated Teller Machine (ATM). The items issued comprise a withdrawal receipt, an ATM card and cash. Formulate a Statement of User Needs and document the rationale underlying the proposed statement(s).

2) Draw up a Domain of Discourse Description for the following system of cheque encashment:

Bring cheque book and card $\longrightarrow$ Go to bank counter $\longrightarrow$ Write out cheque $\longrightarrow$ Sign cheque $\longrightarrow$ Hand cheque book and card to cashier $\longrightarrow$ Collect cheque book, cheque card, and money $\longrightarrow$ Check money.

3) Given the following Composite Task Model (CTM(y)) for a hypothetical ATM system, derive a corresponding System Task Model. To simplify the exercise, fraudulent attempts at cash withdrawal should be ignored.

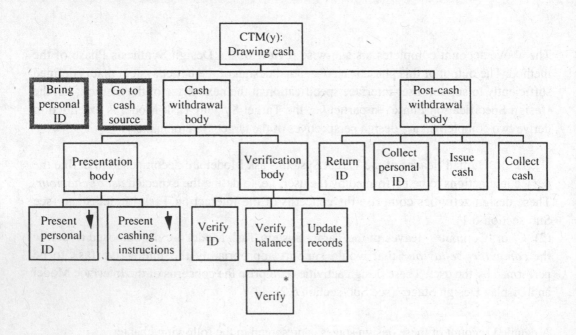

Sample Solutions to Exercises

Possible solutions to the preceding exercises are given below. It should be noted that more than one 'correct' solution might be applicable for each exercise. In this respect, the appropriateness of particular solutions would depend on the constraints and circumstances of the design project (not specified in the exercise).

Solution to Exercise 1

Statement of User Needs: to ensure that bank customers would not forget the items, they should be issued in either one of the following orders:

(a) transaction receipt, ATM card and then cash; or
(b) ATM card, transaction receipt and then cash.

By ensuring that the cash is always issued last, the design of the system is consistent with the requirement to satisfy secondary user goals before primary user goals.

Solution to Exercise 2

A Domain of Discourse Description for cheque encashment is shown overleaf.

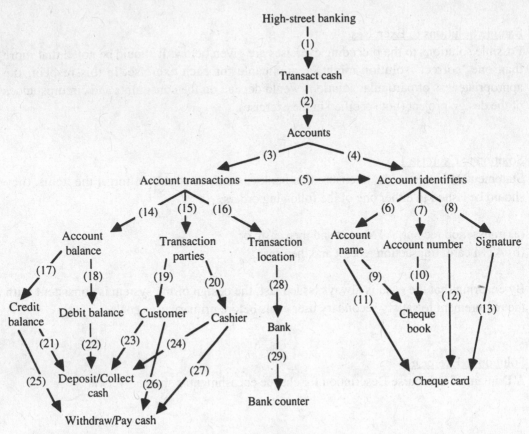

No.	Description
1 to 2	High-street banks transact cash (1) via accounts (2).
3 to 13	Accounts can be transacted (3) and are uniquely identified (4). Account transactions are specific to these identifiers (5). Identifiers comprise an account name (6), number (7) and signature (8). Account name and number may be identified by a cheque book (9, 10) and cheque card (11, 12), while the signature is recorded on the cheque card only (13).
14 to 16	Account transactions are subject to the state of the account balance (14), and take place between parties (15) at a specific location (16).
17 to 18	Account balances can be in credit (17) or debit (18).
19 to 20	Transaction parties comprise a customer (19) and a cashier (20).
21 to 27	Cash can be deposited by the customer (23) whether the account is in credit (21) or debit (22). Deposits are collected by the cashier (24). Money can only be withdrawn by the customer (26) if the account is in credit (25). Withdrawals are paid by the cashier (27).
28 to 29	Account transactions are carried out in a bank (28) at a counter (29).

Solution to Exercise 3

A System Task Model (STM(y), two pages) for a hypothetical ATM system is shown below and on the following page.

Page 1

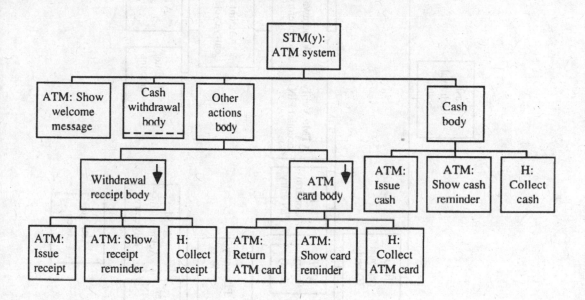

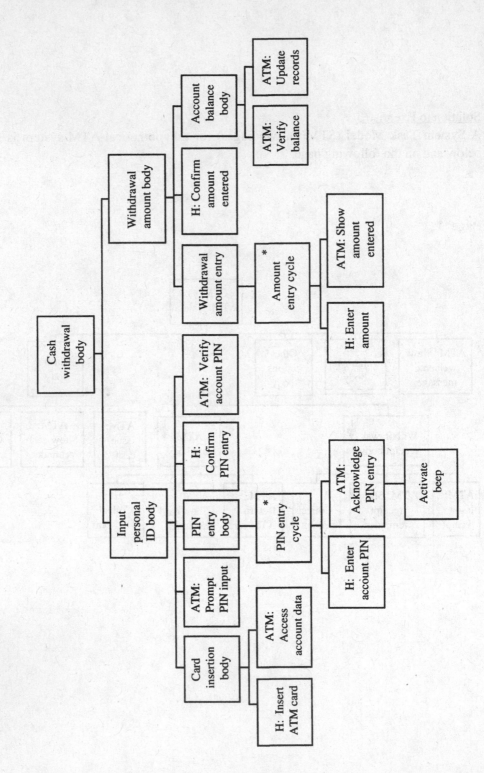

6
The Design Specification Phase of MUSE

The end of our foundation is the knowledge of causes, and the secret motions
of things; and the enlarging of the bounds of human Empire, to the
effecting of all things possible.

Francis Bacon, 1627, **New Atlantis**

Following the derivation of a conceptual design of the target system, user interface specification is undertaken in the Design Specification Phase of the method. Presently, the design stages comprising the phase, namely the Interaction Task Model, Interface Model and Display Design Stages, are described in the sequence performed during design (i.e. in the given order).[1] As before, human factors design activities and products of each of the stages are summarised using a block diagram, and case-study examples are provided where appropriate.

6.1. The Interaction Task Model (ITM) Stage

Having defined the on-line task conceptually in a Target System Task Model, the high-level cycles of human-computer interaction may be decomposed further. The human factors description derived at this stage is termed a Target Interaction Task Model (or ITM(y)). Note that the model is concerned primarily with the description of error-free user-computer interaction. Potential user errors are addressed at later stages of the method (see later). Figure 6-1 shows the location of the Interaction Task Model Stage relative to other stages of the method.

The objective of deriving a Target Interaction Task Model is to specify the device level interactions required to achieve on-line task goals on the computer. The model is described in terms of expected user interactions with the designated hardware, and with bespoke, variant and standard objects and actions of the chosen user interface environment. In this respect, it is essential that an appropriate level of description is derived. As such, iterations may be expected with later design stages of the method.

---

[1] Design iterations are addressed in the account where applicable.

The Target Interaction Task Model establishes a basis for the subsequent design of computer behaviour. In particular, it supports the specification of error recovery, feedback messages and screen displays. To this end, leaves of the structured diagram description of a Target Interaction Task Model (representing user actions) are grouped appropriately into coherent interaction 'units' to define the context and timing for presenting computer support functions.

Figure 6-1:   A Simple Representation of the Structured Human Factors Method (with the Interaction Task Model Stage Highlighted)

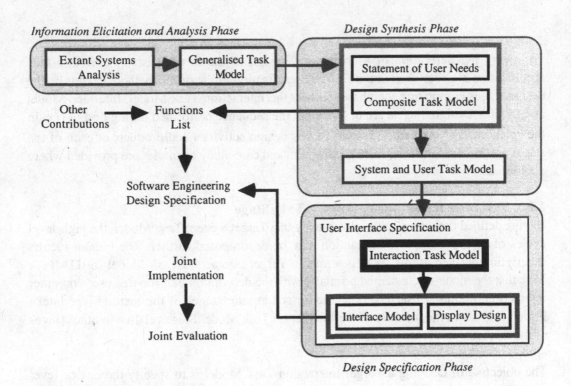

A More Detailed Account of the Interaction Task Model (ITM) Stage
The primary input to this stage is the Target System Task Model (or STM(y)) derived in the preceding stage. Specifically, 'H' or 'Human' leaves of the Target System Task Model (representing on-line actions of the user) are *decomposed* further to derive a device-

dependent description. In particular, the description is expressed in terms of:

(1) basic keystrokes of the designated hardware; and
(2) bespoke, variant and standard object and action primitives of the chosen user-interface environment.

To ensure the derivation of an appropriate and consistent Target Interaction Task Model (or ITM(y)), products of earlier stages of the method should also be considered; namely the Target Statement of User Needs (or SUN(y)) and the Target Domain of Design Discourse (or DoDD(y)). In addition, relevant parts of human factors products derived at the Extant Systems Analysis Stage may be *synthesised* with an initial version of a Target Interaction Task Model (or ITM(y)) (see Figure 6-2). Specifically, the products that may be relevant comprise the existing user interface environment (if any) and an appropriate subset of the Extant Interaction Task Model (or ITM'(ext)). A Target Interaction Task Model that is decomposed to a level understood by all members of the design team may thus be derived iteratively.

Figure 6-2: Block Diagram Summary of the Interaction Task Model (ITM) Stage

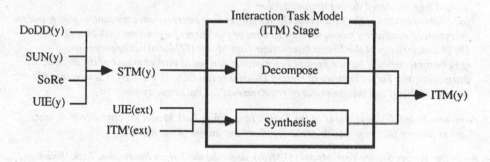

DoDD = Domain of Design Discourse   (ext) =method description of extant systems (denoted EXT)
SoRe = Statement of Requirements   STM = System Task Model
SUN = Statement of User Needs   UIE = User Interface Environment
(y) =method description of the target system (denoted Y)

On deriving a satisfactory description of a Target Interaction Task Model, screen 'boundaries' may be designated at appropriate intervals between coherent groups of structured diagram leaves (see case-study illustration later). The 'boundaries' of the latter leaves correspond to the start- and end-points of appropriate interactive task units to be performed by the user. For all 'boundaries' demarcated on the Target Interaction Task Model, unique numbers are assigned to facilitate cross-references with products derived at later stages of the method; namely the Interface Model and Display Design Stages. Figure 6-3 illustrates the numbering scheme, e.g. Screens 1, 2, 3, etc. denoted by grey 'bubbles' labelled accordingly. Thus, explicit links are established between user inputs (specified by the Target Interaction Task Model) and the static and dynamic presentation of computer supports (specified by products of the Interface Model and Display Design Stages). In other words, the presentation of computerised functions, and error and help messages, is set appropriately against specific task contexts in a stream of user-computer interaction. To this end, the presentation of this computer support is addressed by specifying the context and timing of actuation of major screen displays (whose composition and layout are defined explicitly – see later).

The procedures for deriving a Target Interaction Task Model are described below.

Procedures for deriving a Target Interaction Task Model, ITM(y)

1. Select H and H-C leaves of the Target System Task Model for further decomposition.

2. Decompose each H and H-C leaf to a level that is understood easily by all members of the design team. To ensure the derivation of a consistent Target Interaction Task Model, the following should be considered during decomposition:
   (a) characteristics of the extant and chosen target user interface environment, e.g. to avoid the selection of conflicting names for new actions of the Target Interaction Task Model;
   (b) characteristics of the Extant Interaction Task Model (ITM(ext)) as appropriate;
   (c) characteristics of human factors descriptions derived at earlier stages of the method. In particular, the Target Domain of Design Discourse (DoDD(y)), the Target Statement of User Needs (SUN(y)) and the statement of requirements for the target system.

3. Note important design features of the Target Interaction Task Model for consideration when other human factors products are derived at later stages of the method.

4. As in the Target System Task Model (STM(y)), describe the Target Interaction Task Model (ITM(y)) using structured diagrams. Note additional information in an accompanying table.

5. Iterate with earlier stages of the method as necessary. In particular, re-work earlier versions of the Target Composite Task Model (CTM(y)), the Target System Task Model (STM(y)) and the Target User Task Model (UTM(y)) as necessary. In some cases, wider modifications may involve the task and function allocation adopted originally for target system design. Such changes should be communicated to software engineers as they arise, so as to ensure efficient convergence to the desired design solution. Thus, close contact should be maintained among inter-disciplinary members of the design team.

............continues next page

**Procedures for deriving a Target Interaction Task Model, ITM(y)** _.......continued_

6. _On deriving a satisfactory Target Interaction Task Model (ITM(y)), work through sections of the structured diagram systematically according to the constructs of the notation. Demarcate screen 'boundaries' on the model by identifying the start- and end-points of coherent groups of interactive tasks. During this process, it may also be useful to refer to the Target System Task Model (STM(y)). Assign alpha-numeric identifiers to each screen demarcation so that links may be established between the Target Interaction Task Model and products of later stages of the method, e.g. links with Pictorial Screen Layout descriptions derived at the Design Display Stage. Refer to the design procedures of the latter stage for a more detailed account of the scheme used for assigning alpha-numeric identifiers to screen demarcations. Continue the process for the entire Target Interaction Task Model._

**Rules of thumb for deriving a Target Interaction Task Model, ITM(y)**

1. _It is vital to derive a satisfactory level of description of the Target Interaction Task Model before undertaking later stages of the method. To this end, several versions of the model may be derived before arriving at a satisfactory description. Generally, the derivation of a Target Interaction Task Model (ITM(y)) may involve the decomposition of the Target System Task Model (STM(y)) in two or more steps. Specifically, an initial decomposition may result in a Target Interaction Task Model described in terms of input primitives of the chosen hardware and user interface environment (if any). Following the derivation of human factors descriptions at later stages of the method (namely a set of Target Interface Models (IM(y)) and Target Pictorial Screen Layouts (PSL(y)) at the Interface Model Stage and Display Design Stage respectively), a more detailed description of the Target Interaction Task Model (ITM(y)) may be derived. The latter description of the model should account for user inputs and screen demarcations associated respectively with bespoke user interface objects and potential user errors. Thus, design iterations occur between the Interaction Task Model Stage and later design stages of the method._

2. _Sub-nodes of the Target System Task Model (STM(y)) at two levels (or more) from the bottom of its structured diagram description are likely to remain unchanged. In other words, they would most likely be carried over to the Target Interaction Task Model (ITM(y)) for most cases._

3. _To preserve the uniqueness of sub-node names in a structured diagram description of the Target Interaction Task Model (ITM(y)), it may be necessary to modify the names of sub-nodes that have been carried forward from the Target System Task Model (STM(y)) (see (2) above). Although modified, the original and new names should be semantically similar so that the relationships between the two models remain clearly identifiable._

In conclusion, the objectives of the Interaction Task Model Stage comprise the following:

(a) the specification of device level interactions that a user is expected to perform on the computer;
(b) the establishment of a foundation to support design at later stages of the method; and
(c) the specification of an interaction context to support inter-links with design products derived at later stages of the method. In this way, complementary perspectives of a user interface design may be specified and inter-related.

Case-Study Illustration of a Target Interaction Task Model (ITM(y))

Figure 6-3 shows a Target Interaction Task Model for the network security management case-study. The model was derived after several iterative cycles with later stages of the method. Consequently, the interactive tasks of the user (i.e. inputs required to accomplish on-line task goals) have been specified to a lower level of description, e.g. the clicking of specific buttons. An additional information table was not derived on this occasion since the structured diagram description of the Target Interaction Task Model is reasonably clear.

A case-study illustration of the derivation of a Target Interaction Task Model (ITM(y)) follows. Accordingly, 'H' leaves (human actions) of the Target System Task Model (STM(y)) are decomposed and described in terms of input primitives of the hardware and chosen user interface environment. For the case-study, HyperCard™ was used to simulate the implementation environment.[2] A case-study example of the decomposition of human actions is provided by the 'NMgr-NMW: Access user data' action in the Target System Task Model (Figure 5-12, Page 3, upper left-hand side). Specifically, the action has been decomposed in the Target Interaction Task Model into HyperCard™ primitives, such as 'button objects and clicks' (see Figure 6-3, Page 1, lower left-hand side).

Figure 6-3 illustrates other features of a Target Interaction Task Model; namely:

(a) the demarcation of user actions bounded by particular screens;
(b) a scheme for assigning identifiers to specific screens, e.g. Screen 1 (S1), Screen 2 (S2), etc.

Presently, a case-study example of how the screen demarcations may be linked to pictorial screen layouts (a product of the Display Design Stage) is described for Screens 3A and

---

[2] HyperCard™ is used since it supports the prototyping of WIMP-type user interface designs.

3B.[3] Two scenarios of security alerts may be deduced by referring to the 'NMW security alert body' sub-node for both the Target System Task Model (STM(y)) and Target Interaction Task Model (ITM(y)). As indicated by the screen 'bubbles' in the latter model, the details of computer displays associated with these scenarios may be found in the Pictorial Screen Layout (PSL(y)) descriptions of Screens 3A and 3B. In particular, the scenarios are as follows:

(1) Screen 3A is associated with a scenario in which the network management workstation is unattended. In this case, the workstation is required to monitor automatically security breach events and user reports. It is then required to display the number and classes of security incidents on the next log-on by the network manager (see Figure 6-4).

(2) Screen 3B is associated with an alternative scenario in which security breach events and user reports occur when the workstation is staffed (see Figure 6-5). In this instance, the workstation is required to alert the manager (immediately in certain circumstances) that a security event has occurred in the background of an on-going interactive session.

---

[3] The screens are represented by 'bubbles' labelled S3A and S3B in Figure 6-3, Page 1, lower left-hand side. Note that the location of the screen bubble in the diagram indicates the point at which a particular screen is removed or consumed. The succeeding screen is also presented at the same point.

Figure 6-3: Part of a Target Interaction Task Model for a Network Security Management System — Page 1

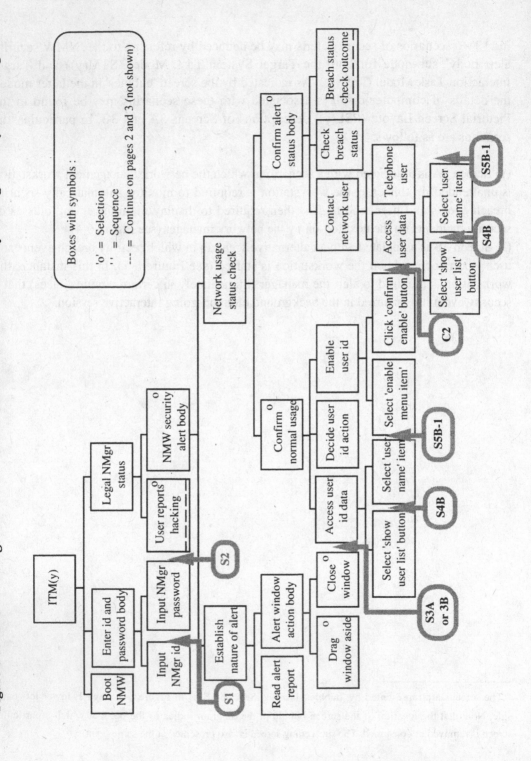

Boxes with symbols :

'o' = Selection

'' = Sequence

--- = Continue on pages 2 and 3 (not shown)

Figure 6-3: Part of a Target Interaction Task Model for a Network Security Management System — Page 2

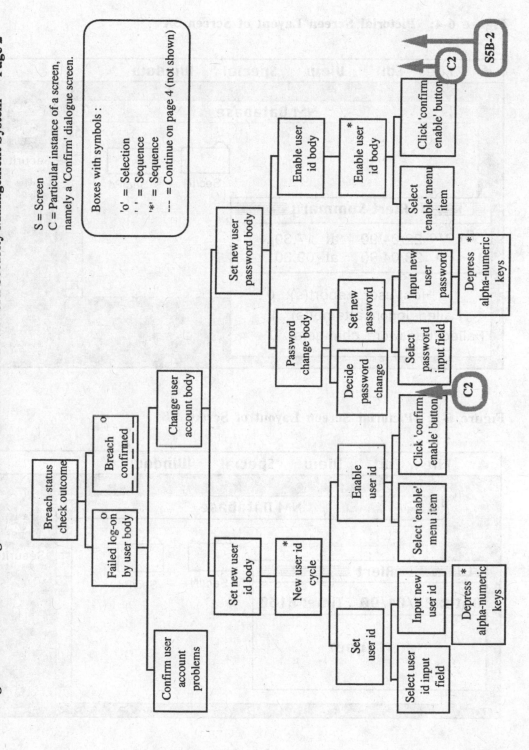

Figure 6-4: Pictorial Screen Layout of Screen 3A

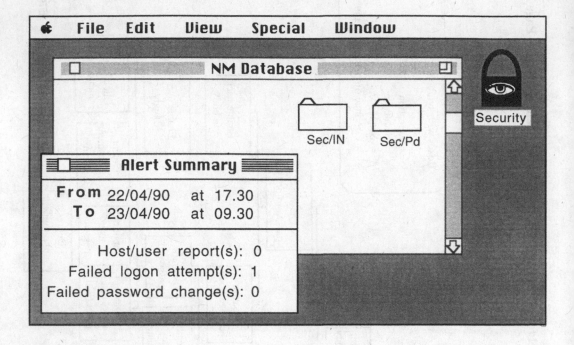

Figure 6-5: Pictorial Screen Layout of Screen 3B

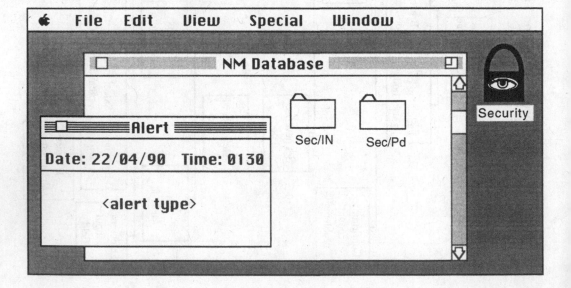

More extensive links between the Target Interaction Task Model and human factors products derived at later stages of the method are addressed in Sub-section 6.2.

Having specified the device-level inputs to be made by the user, a basis for addressing the composition, layout and behaviour of screen displays is established. These user interface design concerns are described in the next sub-section.

6.2. The Interface Model (IM) and Display Design (DD) Stages

To ensure coherent design specification, the two remaining stages of the method (namely the Interface Model and Display Design Stages) are undertaken iteratively. For this reason, the stages are reviewed together.

The objective of the *Interface Model Stage* is to specify the behaviour and changes in appearance of screen objects, following particular user inputs and changes in the state of representation and real world entities. Thus, general design concerns of the stage comprise the following: modelling of user interface objects, specification of command semantics and syntax, and icon design.

The objectives of the *Display Design Stage* are:

(a) to specify the content and layout of screen displays;
(b) to generate a glossary of screen objects; and
(c) to define the contexts for presenting information, help and error messages, and computer functions designed to support the interactive task of the user.

The location of the two stages relative to other stages of the method is shown in Figure 6-6. As shown in the figure, primary inputs to the stages comprise the Target System Task Model (STM(y)) and Target Interaction Task Model (ITM(y)). In addition, further consideration should be given to the following:

(1) Relevant subsets of human factors descriptions derived at the Extant System Analysis Stage; namely extant display design descriptions and Extant Interface Models (IM(ext)). Specifically, subsets of the latter descriptions that are consistent with the contribution of the Extant Composite Task Model (CTM(x)) to the Target Composite Task Model (CTM(y)), are assessed.[4] Appropriate parts of the *extant system* descriptions are then selected and

---

[4] It may be pertinent to add that the design of training programmes and user manuals could also be supported by the human factors products derived between the Generalised Task Model and Interaction Task Model Stages of the method (inclusive).

Figure 6-6: **A Simple Representation of the Structured Human Factors Method (with the Interface Model and Display Design Stages Highlighted)**

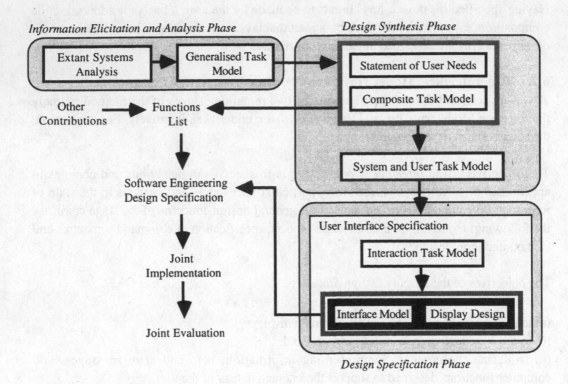

Information Elicitation and Analysis Phase   *Design Synthesis Phase*

Design Specification Phase

incorporated into the *target system* descriptions derived at this stage.

(2) Design requirements and constraints to be satisfied by a user interface design for the target system (including screen compositions and behaviours). In other words, the design basis established by human factors products derived at earlier stages of the method should be observed appropriately during the present stages.

(3) Prototyping and user testing of proposed designs. At the present stage, more comprehensive prototypes and associated user tests should be specified to validate designs that are promising.

The design activities and products of these two stages of the method are summarised in Figure 6-7.

To conclude the present overview, the products derived at the Design Specification Phase of the method constitute human factors specifications of a user interface design. The specifications may then be discussed with software engineers and synthesised subsequently, to generate an overall specification of the target system.[5] Full design implementation, followed by late evaluation, may then be undertaken (see Figure 6-6).[6]

Figure 6-7: Block Diagram Summary of the Interface Model (IM) and Display Design (DD) Stages

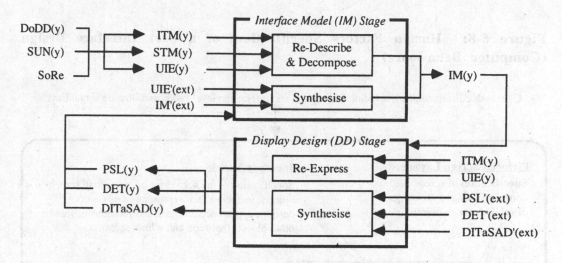

DET = Dialogue and Error message Table
DITaSAD = Dialogue and Inter-Task Screen Actuation Description
DoDD = Domain of Design Discourse
(ext) = method descriptions of extant systems (denoted EXT)   *ITM = Interaction Task Model*
PSL = Pictorial Screen Layout   *SoRe = Statement of Requirements*
STM = System Task Model   *SUN = Statement of User Needs*
UIE = User Interface Environment
(y) = method descriptions of the target system (denoted Y)

---

[5] The integration of target system specifications should be led by software engineers. The assumption is consistent with the current training and role of human factors designers in system development.

[6] Design *implementation* and *late evaluation* will not be reviewed here since the method was developed primarily to address the *'too-little-too-late'* problem of human factors contribution to system development. As such, the main focus of the method is on improving human factors *design*. It should also be noted that design evaluation is already well established in human factors (see Long and Whitefield, 1986). Consequently, the method emphasises the processes, products and descriptions associated with design *analysis* and *specification* rather than design *implementation* and *evaluation*. *Early* and *continuous* human factors contribution to system development is thus facilitated.

<u>A More Detailed Account of the Interface Model (IM) and Display Design (DD) Stages</u>
Figure 6-8 is a schematic summary of the human factors specifications addressed at the
Interface Model (IM) and Display Design (DD) Stages of the method. The design
processes, products and descriptions involved in the derivation of these specifications are
described in greater detail below.

Figure 6-8: Human Factors Specifications of a User Interface Design (Computer Behaviours)

User task considerations (including conceptual and interaction level tasks, and domain semantics)

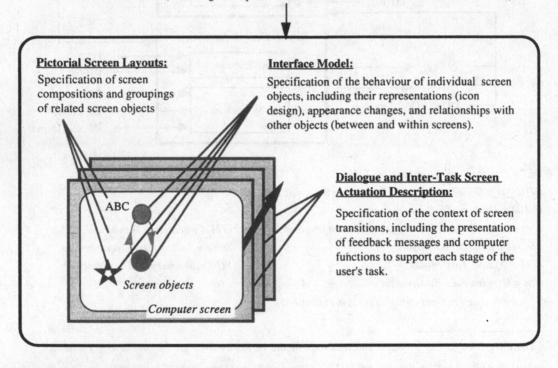

Pictorial Screen Layouts:
Specification of screen
compositions and groupings
of related screen objects

Interface Model:
Specification of the behaviour of individual screen
objects, including their representations (icon
design), appearance changes, and relationships with
other objects (between and within screens).

**Dialogue and Inter-Task Screen
Actuation Description:**
Specification of the context of screen
transitions, including the presentation
of feedback messages and computer
functions to support each stage of the
user's task.

ABC

Screen objects

Computer screen

<u>(a) Interface Model of the Target System (IM(y))</u>
At the Interface Model Stage, a set of human factors descriptions (termed Target Interface
Models or IM(y)) is derived to specify the behaviour and appearance of screen objects.
Two categories of objects are described, namely bespoke objects and variant objects of the
chosen user interface environment (if any). In general, generic or standard objects of the
chosen environment (e.g. scroll bars of a WIMP-interface) need not be described since it

may be assumed that design team members would be conversant with their characteristics.

Target Interface Models are derived by *decomposing* C leaves (representing Computer actions) of the Target System Task Model. The decomposition should be consistent with design constraints defined by human factors products generated at earlier stages of the method; namely the Target Domain of Design Discourse (DoDD(y)), Target Statement of User Needs (SUN(y)) and the statement of requirements for the target system. On the basis of these design constraints, a design of the target system may be developed as follows:

(1) Consider the application of a 'global' conceptual structure to support a user interface design, e.g. the adoption of an appropriate metaphor to structure user-computer interactions for a particular user interface.
(2) Consider the recruitment of Extant Interface Models (IM(ext)) that are consistent with parts of the Extant Composite Task Model (CTM(x)) that have been incorporated into the design of the target system.
(3) Consider the adoption of an appropriate user interface environment or house-style.
(4) Generate new design extensions that would appropriately support the interactive task.

A set of Target Interface Models is thus derived and documented using structured diagrams and pictorially. The rationale underlying important design decisions should also be documented appropriately. The descriptions are then carried forward to the Display Design Stage to support the specification of screen displays. Explicit relationships among the Target Interface Models (IM(y)), Target Interaction Task Model (ITM(y)) and specific screen displays are thus established by assigning common and unique identifiers to overall screen displays and individual screen objects.

Case-study examples of Target Interface Models are provided later.

(b) Display Design Specifications of the Target System
The human factors descriptions derived at this stage of the method address the following aspects of user interface design:

(i) Specification of the 'static' characteristics of screen displays. In particular, the screen composition and layout of functions, and information, error and help messages, are specified. The pictorial descriptions (termed Target Pictorial Screen Layouts or PSL(y)) are supported by two information tables, namely a Target Dictionary of Screen Objects (DSO(y)) and a Target Dialogue and Error Message Table (DET(y)). Generally, the former table provides additional information on the objects of each screen display (e.g. salient characteristics such as inter-screen triggers and permissible user actions); while the latter table is essentially a message index (see later).

(ii) Specification of the 'dynamic' characteristics of screen displays. In particular, the context for actuating screen displays is defined so that the presentation of specific computer support functions and messages is synchronised appropriately to the user's performance of the interactive task. Such a structured diagram description is termed a Target Dialogue and Inter-Task Screen Actuation Description (DITaSAD(y)).

The above human factors products are described in more detail below.

Target Pictorial Screen Layout (PSL(y)) diagrams describe the content, appearance, location and grouping of information, feedback and functional screen objects. Explicit relationships among Target Pictorial Screen Layouts (PSL(y)), the Target Interaction Task Model (ITM(y)), the Target Dialogue and Inter-Task Screen Actuation Description (DITaSAD(y)) and Target Interface Models (IM(y)) are then defined by assigning common and unique identifiers to overall screen displays and individual screen objects. Thus, static and dynamic specifications of a user interface design may be inter-linked as follows:

(i) Target Pictorial Screen Layouts (PSL(y)) may be linked to Target Interface Models (IM(y)) at the *object* level. Thus, static and dynamic descriptions of screen objects are linked. For instance, the behaviour of individual screen objects may be linked to other objects located in the same screen (intra-screen object-object relationships), or across different screens (inter-screen object-object relationships).

(ii) Target Pictorial Screen Layouts (PSL(y)) may be linked at the *screen* level to the Target Dialogue and Inter-Task Screen Actuation Description (DITaSAD(y)) and the Target Dialogue and Error Message Table (DET(y)). Thus, static and dynamic descriptions of screen displays are linked, e.g. by particular contextual relationships and triggers for screen presentation. Target Pictorial Screen Layouts (PSL(y)) may also be linked indirectly to the Target Dialogue and Error Message Table (DET(y)), via references to particular messages in the Target Dialogue and Inter-Task Screen Actuation Description (DITaSAD(y)).

It should be emphasised that the objective of deriving Target Pictorial Screen Layouts is *not* the specification of all possible screen displays. On the contrary, the objective is to specify screen displays associated with important interaction events, such as the computer response to particular user errors and the synchronisation of computer function presentation with particular contexts of interactive task performance. Thus, trivial interaction events such as screen scrolling and refresh, are excluded from the description.

It may be pertinent to note that Target Pictorial Screen Layouts may be composed directly using a computer-supported prototyping tool. In this way, laborious generation and documentation of voluminous paper-based screen diagrams (either drawn to scale or dimensioned – see Figure 6-9) may be obviated.[7] Although Target Pictorial Screen Layouts (PSL(y)) and the Target Dialogue and Error Message Table (DET(y)) may be supplanted by computer-based prototyping, other human factors descriptions should still be documented explicitly as required by the method. In particular, the following human factors descriptions should still be documented: Target Dialogue and Inter-Task Screen Actuation Description (DITaSAD(y)); Target Interface Models (IM(y)); and Target Dictionary of Screen Objects (DSO(y)). Case-study examples of Target Pictorial Screen Layouts are provided later.

Figure 6-9: Dimensioned Drawing of a Pictorial Screen Layout (Screen 3A)

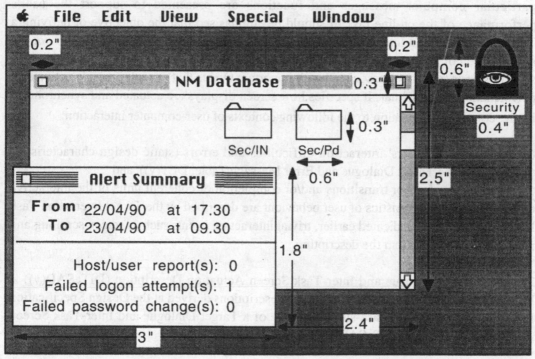

---

[7] Other benefits of using a prototyping tool may include the direct execution of specifications and/or the animation of proposed user interface designs.

The *Target Dialogue and Error Message Table (DET(y))* is essentially an index relating message identifiers and contents. As indicated earlier, the identifiers are part of a scheme that supports the specification of explicit links with other human factors descriptions derived at the Design Specification Phase of the method. In particular, links between the Target Dialogue and Error Message Table (DET(y)) and Target Pictorial Screen Layouts (PSL(y)) of message screens are established by combining message and screen identifiers. Links between the Target Dialogue and Error Message Table (DET(y)) and the Target Dialogue and Inter-Task Screen Actuation Description (DITaSAD(y)) are also specified in this way. A case-study example of a Target Dialogue and Error Message Table (DET(y)) is provided later.

Finally, the *Target Display and Inter-Task Screen Actuation Description (DITaSAD(y))* is derived to specify the context of screen actuation, i.e. appropriate synchronisation of screen actuations with interactive task execution. In other words, it specifies the points at which particular computer messages and functions are presented to support the user's performance of the on-line task. It should be emphasised that the objective of deriving a Target Dialogue and Inter-Task Screen Actuation Description (DITaSAD(y)), is *not* the specification of all the screen actuations that may occur. On the contrary, the objective is to specify screen actuations associated with important events that arise during interactive task performance. In particular, it specifies how screen displays are actuated and synchronised by the computer[8] in relation to the following contexts of user-computer interaction:

(1) occurrence of users' interaction difficulties and errors (static design characteristics described by the Target Dialogue and Error Message Table, DET(y)), and
(2) occurrence of major transitions and/or completion of coherent units of the interactive task (dynamic characteristics of user behaviour are described by the Target Interaction Task Model, ITM(y)). As indicated earlier, trivial interaction events such as screen scrolling and refresh are excluded from the description.

Thus, a Target Dialogue and Inter-Task Screen Actuation Description (DITaSAD(y)) is linked explicitly with other human factors descriptions derived at the Design Specification Phase of the method. A case-study example of a Target Dialogue and Inter-Task Screen Actuation Description (DITaSAD(y)) is provided later.

The procedures for deriving human factors descriptions at the Interface Model and Display Design Stages are described next.

---

[8] The descriptions complement static design specifications, which are documented by Target Pictorial Screen Layouts, PSL(y).

Procedures for deriving Target Interface Models (IM(y)) and human factors products of the Display Design Stage

1. Do not undertake the Interface Model and Display Design Stages until the Target Interaction Task Model (ITM(y)) has been decomposed into input level primitives and screen boundaries demarcated. However, complete decomposition of the task model is unnecessary (see (8) below).

2. A human factors designer may apply either procedure 3(a) or (b), depending on the prevailing design circumstances, such as how familiar the designer is with the chosen user interface environment, and how well defined the environment is. With due references to the Target Interaction Task Model (ITM(y)), Target Pictorial Screen Layouts (PSL(y)) and Target Interface Models (IM(y)) may be derived together and incrementally. It should be noted that design iterations among the three stages of the Design Specification Phase of the method may instigate wider design iterations. In particular, changes to design descriptions derived at the Design Synthesis Phase may be involved. The iterative process is continued until the entire Target Interaction Task Model (ITM(y)) has been considered.

3(a). For each screen boundary demarcated in the Target Interaction Task Model (ITM(y)), specify Target Interface Models (IM(y)) for screen objects involved with the interactive task within that boundary. Note that standard or simple variant objects of the chosen user interface environment need not be described. Referring to the Target Interface Models (IM(y)) and Target Interaction Task Model (ITM(y)), compose a Target Pictorial Screen Layout (PSL(y)) of the screen. The result is a set of structured diagrams and a tabular Dictionary of Screen Objects (DSO(y)) for each Target Pictorial Screen Layout (PSL(y)). Repeat the process as indicated in (2) above until the entire Target Interaction Task Model (ITM(y)) has been considered.

3(b). For each screen boundary demarcated in the Target Interaction Task Model (ITM(y)), compose a Target Pictorial Screen Layout (PSL(y)) of the screen. Specify Target Interface Models (IM(y)) for all screen object constituents of the layout diagram. The result is a set of structured diagrams and a Target Dictionary of Screen Objects (DSO(y)) for each Target Pictorial Screen Layout (PSL(y)). Thus, the latter descriptions are derived iteratively with Target Interface Models (IM(y)). The process is repeated as indicated in (2) above until the entire Target Interaction Task Model (ITM(y)) has been considered.

4. When deriving Target Pictorial Screen Layouts (PSL(y)), note when and how each screen display is to be actuated and the objects involved in triggering the actuation. In other words, note how each screen display is to be triggered and consumed. Such notes would subsequently support the construction of a Target Dialogue and Inter-Task Screen Actuation Description (DITaSAD(y)) (see (9) below).

5. To facilitate reference, each Target Pictorial Screen Layout (PSL(y)) should be collated with its own set of Target Interface Models (IM(y)) and Target Dictionary of Screen Objects (DSO(y)). Note that lower level descriptions of Target Interface Models (IM(y)) may be specified, e.g. to detail object-object relationships within and across screen displays. These descriptions may be related to Target Pictorial Screen Layouts (PSL(y)) if a unique identifier is assigned to each screen object. Thus, the level to which Target Interface Models (IM(y)) is described may be varied, and is largely dependent on the training of the human factors designer.

............continues next page

Procedures for deriving Target Interface Models (IM(y)) and human factors products of
the Display Design Stage............*continued*

6. During the derivation of Target Pictorial Screen Layouts (PSL(y)) and Target Interface Models
(IM(y)), H-C leaves of the Target System Task Model (STM(y)), which represents human and
computer actions that have not been decomposed, may suggest 'generic' computer support
functions, e.g. standard 'house-keeping' functions of text and graphics editors. In such instances,
design features of relevant off-the-shelf packages (which constitute extant partial systems) may
be examined to identify extant screen objects and functions that may be recruited to the user
interface design of the target system. It should be noted that the selected extant screen objects
and functions should be consistent with the Target Interaction Task Model (ITM(y)). In addition,
they should be re-named, and their behaviours and representations modified (as appropriate) in
accordance with the semantics defined by the Target Domain of Design Discourse (DoDD(y)).

7. Since the Target Interaction Task Model (ITM(y)) addresses error-free task performance only,
potential user errors should now be considered. These concerns are addressed by the Target
Dialogue and Inter-Task Screen Actuation Description (DITaSAD(y)) and the Target Dialogue
and Error Message Table (DET(y)). To derive these human factors descriptions, each Target
Pictorial Screen Layout (PSL(y)) is examined to identify potential user errors. In addition,
various error scenarios should be investigated analytically by comparing Target Interface
Models (IM(y)) and the Target Interaction Task Model (ITM(y)). Potential deviations from the
'ideal' interaction prescribed by the latter model are thus uncovered. To rectify the user errors
and difficulties 'discovered' in this way, a re-design should be considered in the first instance. If
a satisfactory design solution cannot be found, appropriate error and help messages should be
composed to support the user. A Target Dialogue and Error Message Table (DET(y)) is thus
derived and linked to the Target Interaction Task Model (ITM(y)). For each item in the message
table, a Target Pictorial Screen Layout (PSL(y)) is composed and labelled in accordance with
the rules of thumb below. To facilitate reference, the set of layout diagrams of the message
screens is collated with the set of Target Pictorial Screen Layouts (PSL(y)) and Target Interface
Models (IM(y)) derived earlier.

8. When Target Pictorial Screen Layouts (PSL(y)), Target Interface Models (IM(y)) and the Target
Dialogue and Error Message Table (DET(y)) have been specified satisfactorily, a further design
iteration may be undertaken (as appropriate) to 'finalise' the decomposition of the Target
Interaction Task Model (ITM(y)). In particular, the latter model may be decomposed to derive a
device-level description expressed in terms of bespoke screen objects and actions that have now
been defined by Target Pictorial Screen Layouts (PSL(y)) and Target Interface Models (IM(y)).

9. Having 'finalised' the human factors descriptions in (8) above, the dynamics of screen
presentation may then be specified. To this end, the Target Interaction Task Model (ITM(y)),
Target Interface Models (IM(y)) and additional notes made in (4) above are consulted.
Specifically, note the context for screen actuations by examining the actions at screen
boundaries demarcated on the Target Interaction Task Model (ITM(y)); i.e. actions between the
boundaries may be ignored. In addition, refer to the Target Interface Models (IM(y)) for each
screen, and note the actions of screen objects that cause the 'consumption' or removal of

............*continues next page*

Procedures for deriving Target Interface Models (IM(y)) and human factors products of the Display Design Stage............*continued*

screens. A structured diagram summary (termed a Target Dialogue and Inter-Task Screen Actuation Description, DITaSAD(y)), is then derived to specify how each screen display is actuated in relation to interactive task execution by the user (as described by the Target Interaction Task Model (ITM(y)).

Rules of thumb for deriving Target Interface Models (IM(y)) and human factors products of the Display Design Stage

1. *Constitutent objects of each Target Pictorial Screen Layout (PSL(y)) should be described further in a supporting table (termed a Target Dictionary of Screen Objects (DSO(y)). In this way, additional information on the behaviours of screen objects may be recorded.*

2. *Whenever possible, each Target Pictorial Screen Layout (PSL(y)) should be uniquely named in a numerical order consistent with the Target Interaction Task Model (ITM(y)), and later with the Target Dialogue and Inter-Task Screen Actuation Description (DITaSAD(y)).*

3. *The names of Target Pictorial Screen Layouts (PSL(y)) should reveal the relationship with other screen displays (if possible). For instance, a parent-child relationship may be highlighted by using screen names such as Screens 3.1 and 3.1A for the 'children' of Screen 3 (with the common root name '3'). In addition, the common root name '3.1' indicates that Screens 3.1 and 3.1A are mutually exclusive screen displays.*

4. *The appearance and name of each screen object should be propagated consistently across screen displays. Instances of an object class may be assigned a composite name comprising a root name (to represent a particular class) and a unique identifier (to represent a particular instance). Such information should be noted in the Target Dictionary of Screen Objects (DSO(y)).*

5. *Target Interface Models (IM(y)) need not be specified for generic or standard screen objects of the chosen user interface environment.*

6. *Error and dialogue message screens are denoted using a composite name comprising a root name to which is appended a '.5', and a unique message identifier (e.g. 'Screen 1.5 — em3'). The latter component of the name indicates its links with the Target Dialogue and Error Message Table (DET(y)) and the Target Dialogue and Inter-Task Screen Actuation Description (DITaSAD(y)). The message name 'Screen 1.5 — em3' should be read as 'Screen 1.5 with error message number 3' (contents of the message are found in the Target Dialogue and Error Message Table (DET(y)). It should be noted that the identifier '1' followed by a '.5' indicates that the screen display is a transition screen that may be triggered when Screen 1 is active. An alternative scheme is to assign distinctive names for error and confirmation screens. For instance, an 'E' or 'C' alphabet respectively may be used followed by a root name and message identifier as before, e.g. 'Screen E(1)1 — em3'. Note that a '.5' label need not be appended in this scheme. The name 'Screen E(1)1 — em3' should be read as 'Error screen format 'E(1)' triggered for screen display '1' with error message number 3'. Note that the name indicates that the contents of the error message, em3, are filled into a text field of a generic error screen display format 'E(1)'; i.e. the only variable in the screen display 'E(1)' is its <message content>.*

............*continues next page*

Rules of thumb for deriving Target Interface Models (IM(y)) and human factors
products of the Display Design Stage............*continued*

7. *The Target Dialogue and Inter-Task Screen Actuation Description (DITaSAD(y)) may be derived in two or more steps. In particular, the designer may exclude error considerations when deriving an initial description. Thus, the screen actuations annotated in a Target Interaction Task Model (ITM(y), a description of error-free performance of the interactive task) are re-described directly using a structured diagram. Potential error scenarios are then considered in a second step, to complete the derivation of a Target Dialogue and Inter-Task Screen Actuation Description (DITaSAD(y)).*

8. *Structured diagram leaves of a Target Dialogue and Inter-Task Screen Actuation Description (DITaSAD(y)) are expected to comprise largely 'consume screen' boxes. Consequently, actions or leaves of the Target Interaction Task Model (ITM(y)) that do not result in a screen actuation are ignored when deriving a Target Dialogue and Inter-Task Screen Actuation Description (DITaSAD(y)). The reason for ignoring intervening actions is because the latter human factors design product is concerned largely with the description of screen actuations that map computer support functions to specific units of interactive tasks, i.e. since screens are actuated to present new functions only when current task units are completed. Although intervening actions may be ignored, the super-ordinate structure of the Target Interaction Task Model (ITM(y)) should be carried forward to Target Dialogue and Inter-Task Screen Actuation Description (DITaSAD(y)).*

Case-Study Illustrations of Target Interface Models (IM(y)) and Human Factors Products of the Display Design Stage

A case-study account of the human factors descriptions derived at the Interface Model and Display Design Stages follows. The descriptions constitute a set of human factors specification of a user interface design. In particular, the set comprises the following: a number of Target Interface Models (IM(y)); a Target Dialogue and Inter-Task Screen Actuation Description (DITaSAD(y)); a Target Dialogue and Error Message Table (DET(y)); a number of Target Pictorial Screen Layouts (PSL(y)); a Target Dictionary of Screen Objects (DSO(y)); and a Target Interaction Task Model (ITM(y), described earlier).

To illustrate the links among the human factors descriptions, the 'failed log-on' scenario for a network security management system (introduced in earlier accounts of preceding products of the method) is used.

(a) Target Dialogue and Inter-Task Screen Actuation Description (DITaSAD(y))

Figure 6-10 shows part of a Target Dialogue and Inter-Task Screen Actuation Description (DITaSAD(y)) that describes computer responses to a failed log-on event.

Figure 6-10:   Part of a Target Dialogue and Inter-Task Screen Actuation Description (DITaSAD(y)) for a Network Security Management System

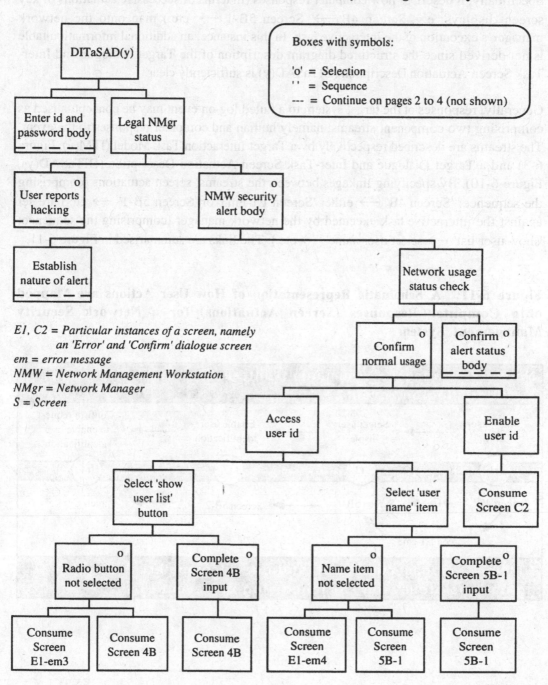

DITaSAD(y)

Boxes with symbols:

'o' = Selection
' ' = Sequence
--- = Continue on pages 2 to 4 (not shown)

Enter id and password body

Legal NMgr status

User reports hacking

NMW security alert body

Establish nature of alert

Network usage status check

E1, C2 = Particular instances of a screen, namely
an 'Error' and 'Confirm' dialogue screen
em = error message
NMW = Network Management Workstation
NMgr = Network Manager
S = Screen

Confirm normal usage

Confirm alert status body

Access user id

Enable user id

Select 'show user list' button

Select 'user name' item

Consume Screen C2

Radio button not selected

Complete Screen 4B input

Name item not selected

Complete Screen 5B-1 input

Consume Screen E1-em3

Consume Screen 4B

Consume Screen 4B

Consume Screen E1-em4

Consume Screen 5B-1

Consume Screen 5B-1

Specifically, it describes how computer responses (in terms of successive actuations of key screen displays, e.g. Screen 4B $\longrightarrow$ Screen 5B-1 $\longrightarrow$ etc.) map onto the network manager's execution of the interactive task. In this instance, an additional information table is not derived since the structured diagram description of the Target Dialogue and Inter-Task Screen Actuation Description (DITaSAD(y) is sufficiently clear.

Generally, responses of the target system to a failed log-on event may be conceptualised as comprising two component streams; namely human and computer responses to the event. The streams are described respectively by a Target Interaction Task Model (ITM(y), Figure 6-3) and a Target Dialogue and Inter-Task Screen Actuation Description (DITaSAD(y), Figure 6-10). By specifying linkages between the streams, screen actuations (comprising the sequence: 'Screen 4B' $\longrightarrow$ either 'Screen E1-em3' or 'Screen 5B-1' $\longrightarrow$ etc.) are set against the interactive task executed by the network manager (comprising the sequence: 'show user list' $\longrightarrow$ select user name' $\longrightarrow$ etc.). The links are summarised in Figure 6-11.

Figure 6-11: A Schematic Representation of How User Actions are Mapped onto Computer Responses (Screen Actuations) for a Network Security Management System

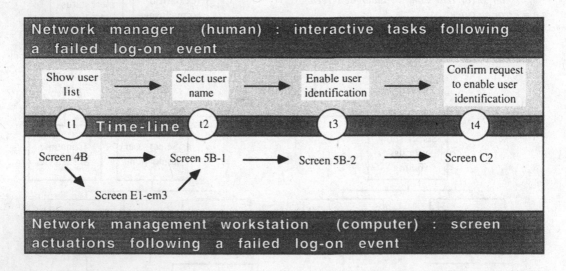

(b) Target Pictorial Screen Layouts (PSL(y)), Target Interface Models (IM(y)), Target Dictionary of Screen Objects (DSO(y)), and Target Dialogue and Error Message Table (DET(y))

On detecting a failed log-on event, the Network Management Workstation alerts the network manager by presenting an appropriate alert screen display (see Figures 6-4 and 6-5). Having been alerted to the event in this way, the network manager is required to access the computer database to gather further information on the user involved. To this end, the manager double-clicks the security icon in Screen 3C[9] to activate the network management application. The input triggers Screen 4B, and a menu offering a selection of three actions, namely 'Search Connection', 'Show User List' and 'Show Access Points', is presented to the network manager (see Figure 6-12).[10] To indicate the desired selection, the manager clicks one of the three radio buttons. The input is then confirmed by clicking the 'Select' button (see Figures 6-12, 6-13 and 6-14 respectively for a Target Pictorial Screen Layout (PSL(y)), a Target Dictionary of Screen Objects (DSO(y)), and a Target Interface Model (IM(y)) for Screen 4B). If a radio button has not been selected before clicking the 'Select' button, an error message screen is activated, namely Screen E1-em3 (see Figure 6-15 for a Target Pictorial Screen Layout (PSL(y)) of the error Screen E1; Figure 6-16 for a Target Dictionary of Screen Objects (DSO(y)) of Screen E1; and Figure 6-17 for the contents of error message 3 (em3)).[11]

---

[9] Screen 3C is not shown here since the screen is very similar to Screens 3A and 3B (see Figures 6-4 and 6-5 respectively). The security icon appears in the diagrams for these screens.

[10] To support a Target Pictorial Screen Layout (PSL(y)), additional information on its constituent screen objects is tabulated in a Dictionary of Screen Objects (DSO(y)). For instance, the Target Pictorial Screen Layout (PSL(y)) of Screen 4B is supported by its Dictionary of Screen Objects (DSO(y)) as shown in Figure 6-12. In addition, the behaviour of individual screen objects is specified by a Target Interface Model (IM(y)). For instance, the interface model in Figure 6-13 describes the radio button objects of Screen 4B.

[11] Error message 3 (em3) shares the same screen format as other error messages, namely screen layout format 'E1'. In other words, the only variable for these screens is their message content.

Figure 6-12: Target Pictorial Screen Layout (PSL(y)) of Screen 4B

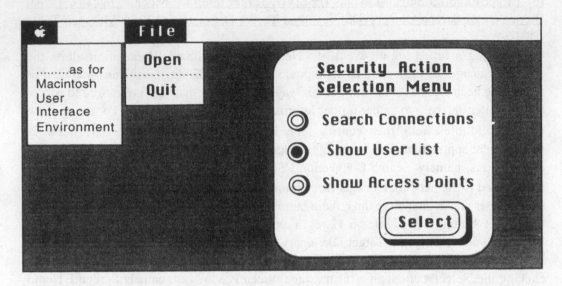

Figure 6-13: Target Dictionary of Screen Objects (DSO(y)) of Screen 4B

Screen Object	Description	Design Attributes
File (menu bar)	Offers 'Open' and 'Quit' menu items. 'Open' allows the network manager to open host and user reports. 'Quit' allows the manager to quit the security application.	Behaviour as per standard Macintosh menu items.
Security Action Selection Menu	Allows the network manager to select an appropriate action, namely 'Search Connections' (for more information on network connections), 'Show User List' (to access a list of network users) and 'Show Access Points' (to access a list of Access points).	
Radio buttons	Allows the network manager to indicate a selection of an action from the menu above.	Behaviour as per standard HyperCard radio buttons.
Select button	Following the selection of a radio button, the network manager has to confirm the input by clicking the 'Select' button. Depending on the radio button selected, one of the screens below is activated following confirmation of input: (1) 'Search Connections' radio button selected: activate Screen 5A-1; (2) 'Show User List': activate Screen 5B-1; (3) 'Show Access Points': activate Screen 5C-1.	Behaviour as per standard HyperCard buttons.

Figure 6-14: **Target Interface Model (IM(y)) of Radio Buttons in the Security Action Selection Menu (Screen 4B)**

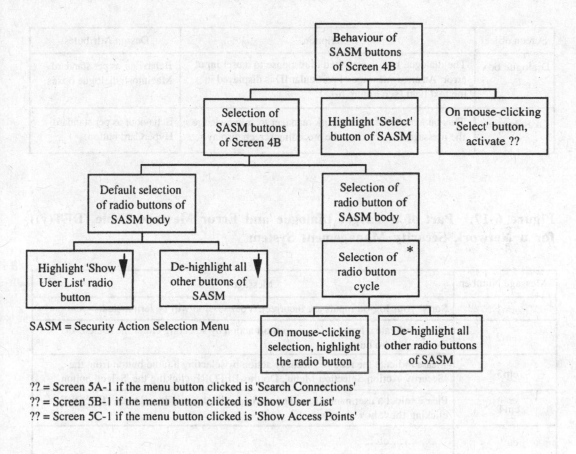

SASM = Security Action Selection Menu

?? = Screen 5A-1 if the menu button clicked is 'Search Connections'
?? = Screen 5B-1 if the menu button clicked is 'Show User List'
?? = Screen 5C-1 if the menu button clicked is 'Show Access Points'

Figure 6-15: **Target Pictorial Screen Layout (PSL(y)) of Screen E1**

Figure 6-16:   Target Dictionary of Screen Objects (DSO(y)) of Screen E1

Screen object	Description	Design Attributes
Dialogue box	The dialogue box is activated in response to a user input error. An error message of particular ID is displayed in the text field (see Figure 6-15).	Behaviour as per standard Macintosh dialogue boxes.
Okay button	This button allows the network manager to acknowledge the message and return to the preceding screen display.	Behaviour as per standard HyperCard button.

Figure 6-17:   Part of a Target Dialogue and Error Message Table (DET(y)) for a Network Security Management System

Message Number	Message
em1	Sorry, your log-on inputs are incorrect. Your session will be terminated.
em2	Please indicate a host and/or user report action by selecting either the 'Delete' or 'Pending' radio button.
em3	Please indicate the required security action by selecting a radio button from the 'Security Action Selection Menu'. Do this BEFORE clicking the 'Select' button.
em4	Please select a user name from the user name display window. Do this BEFORE clicking the 'Show' button.
etc.	................etc.

If all inputs have been made correctly, Screen 4B is 'consumed' and Screen 5B-1 presented (see Figures 6-18, 6-19 and 6-20A and B respectively for a Target Pictorial Screen Layout (PSL(y)), a Target Dictionary of Screen Objects (DSO(y)) and a Target Interface Model (IM(y)) for Screen 5B-1). Using the latter screen display, the network manager may then specify what information on the network user should be extracted from the database and displayed. For instance, the manager may request a list of user identifications that have been disabled temporarily. Following an examination of the list, the manager may access further information on a particular user by clicking the desired user name item in the 'User Name Display' window (inside the 'User List' window – see Figure 6-18). Screen 5B-2 is thus activated to display personal details and usage information of a particular user (see Figures 6-21 and 6-22 respectively for a Target Pictorial Screen Layout (PSL(y)) and a Target Dictionary of Screen Objects (DSO(y)) for Screen 5B-2). Having assessed the information in the 'User Details' window, the manager would then decide whether the user should be contacted to establish possible causes of the failed log-on event. Appropriate actions may thus be taken. For instance, the manager may decide to restore the network account of the affected user via the 'Enable' command in the menu bar, if the event is ascertained to be due to a password mis-key (see Figure 6-21). On detecting such a request, the network management workstation will seek confirmation from the network manager. Thus, Screen C2 is activated (see Figures 6-23 and 6-24 respectively for a Target Pictorial Screen Layout (PSL(y)) and a Target Dictionary of Screen Objects (DSO(y)) for Screen C2). Although Screen C2 may be considered a redundant step, it was included to make the interaction cycle more consistent with other regulatory actions, e.g. 'Disable User' and 'Mark User' actions. Specifically, consistency is maintained by requiring additional confirmation for all regulatory actions to be imposed by the network manager.

The above account completes a review of the entire method. To conclude, the method contributes to system development as follows:

(a) As a human factors design method, it specifies explicitly the scope, process and notation of human factors contributions to system design *specification.* Together with the already well-established human factors contributions to system design *evaluation,* the method facilitates greater and more efficient support of the complete system development cycle.

(b) As a *structured* human factors method, its explicit methodological characteristics support the integration of human factors and software engineering methods. Consequently, the method provides the following:

(i) It supports timely and contextually relevant human factors input to system development.
(ii) It facilitates explicit accommodation of human factors design needs by the overall agenda for system development. Appropriate design resources to support effective human factors input may then be planned and budgets allocated. With better planning, the tendency to encroach on resources set aside for human factors design is minimised.
(iii) It defines explicit roles and design relationships between human factors designers and software engineers. Thus, the method supports better design communication and co-ordination among members of a design team.

In summary, by engendering a better understanding of inter-disciplinary design concerns and needs, a more effective uptake of human factors contributions may be expected from the application of the method.

Figure 6-18: Target Pictorial Screen Layout (PSL(y)) of Screen 5B-1

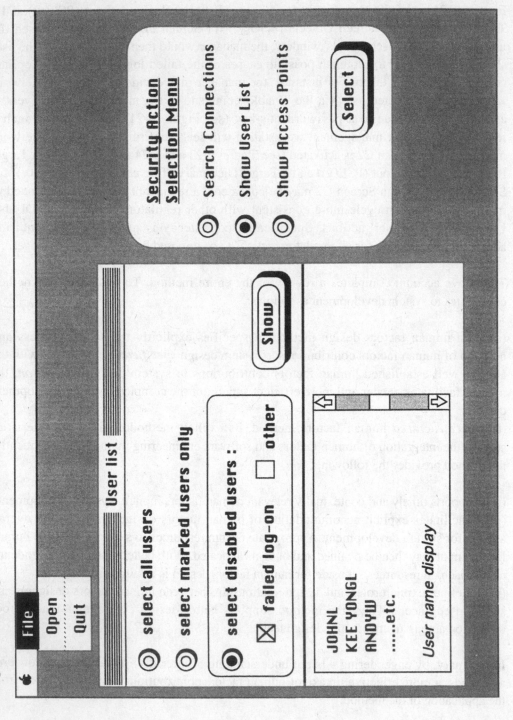

Figure 6-19: Target Dictionary of Screen Objects (DSO(y)) of Screen 5B-1

Screen object	Description	Design Attributes
User list window	The window is used to indicate specific name lists to be displayed (e.g. display a list of disabled user names only).	Activated by selecting 'Show User List' from the 'Security Action Selection Menu' (see Screen 4B for further information).
Radio buttons	Radio buttons are used to specify which user names should be listed in the 'User Name Display' window. Possible lists are 'All Users', 'Marked Users Only' and 'Disabled Users Only' (this selection includes two sub-lists, which may be chosen by checkboxes in Screen 5B-1).	Behaviour as per standard HyperCard buttons. Default display is to list all user names in the user name display. Selecting a radio button would blank out the name display, and when the 'Show' button is clicked, the specified user name list is displayed.
User name display	The display is used to show user names, and is activated by clicking the 'User List' radio buttons (see above) followed by the 'Show' button.	Default display is to list all user names in alphabetical order. A user name item may then be selected (causing it to be highlighted) to indicate that further user information should be displayed in the 'User Details' window (see Screen 5B-2).
Show button	The 'Show' button is used to activate the display of user names following the selection of a particular 'User List' radio button (see above).	Behaviour as per standard HyperCard buttons.
Security Action Selection Menu	Information described previously for Screen 4B.	

Figure 6-20A: Target Interface Model (IM(y)) of Names Item(s) in the 'User Name Display' Window (Screen 5B-1)

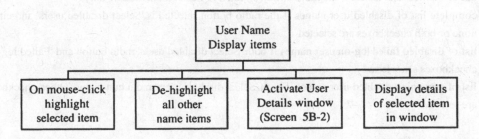

Figure 6-20B: Target Interface Model (IM(y)) of Radio Buttons for the 'User List' Window (Screen 5B-1)

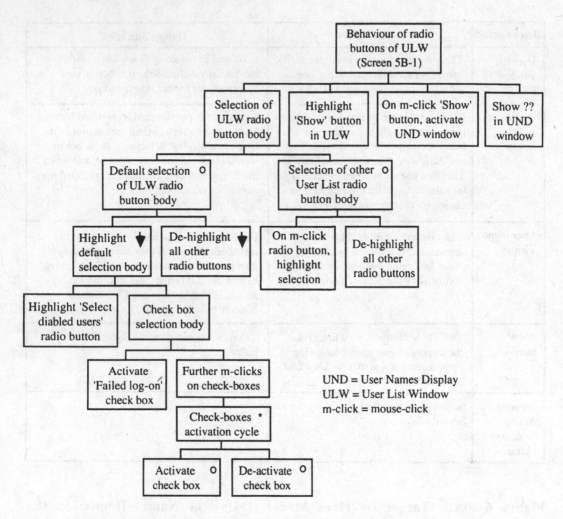

UND = User Names Display
ULW = User List Window
m-click = mouse-click

?? = complete list of user names if the radio button selected is 'Select all users'

?? = list of marked user names if the radio button selected is 'Select marked users only'

?? = complete list of disabled user names if the radio button selected is 'Select disabled users' and either none or both checkboxes are selected

?? = list of disabled failed log-on user names if both 'Select disabled users' radio button and 'Failed log-on' checkboxes are selected

?? = list of remaining disabled user names if both 'Select disabled users' radio button and 'Other' checkboxes are selected

Figure 6-21: Target Pictorial Screen Layout (PSL(y)) of

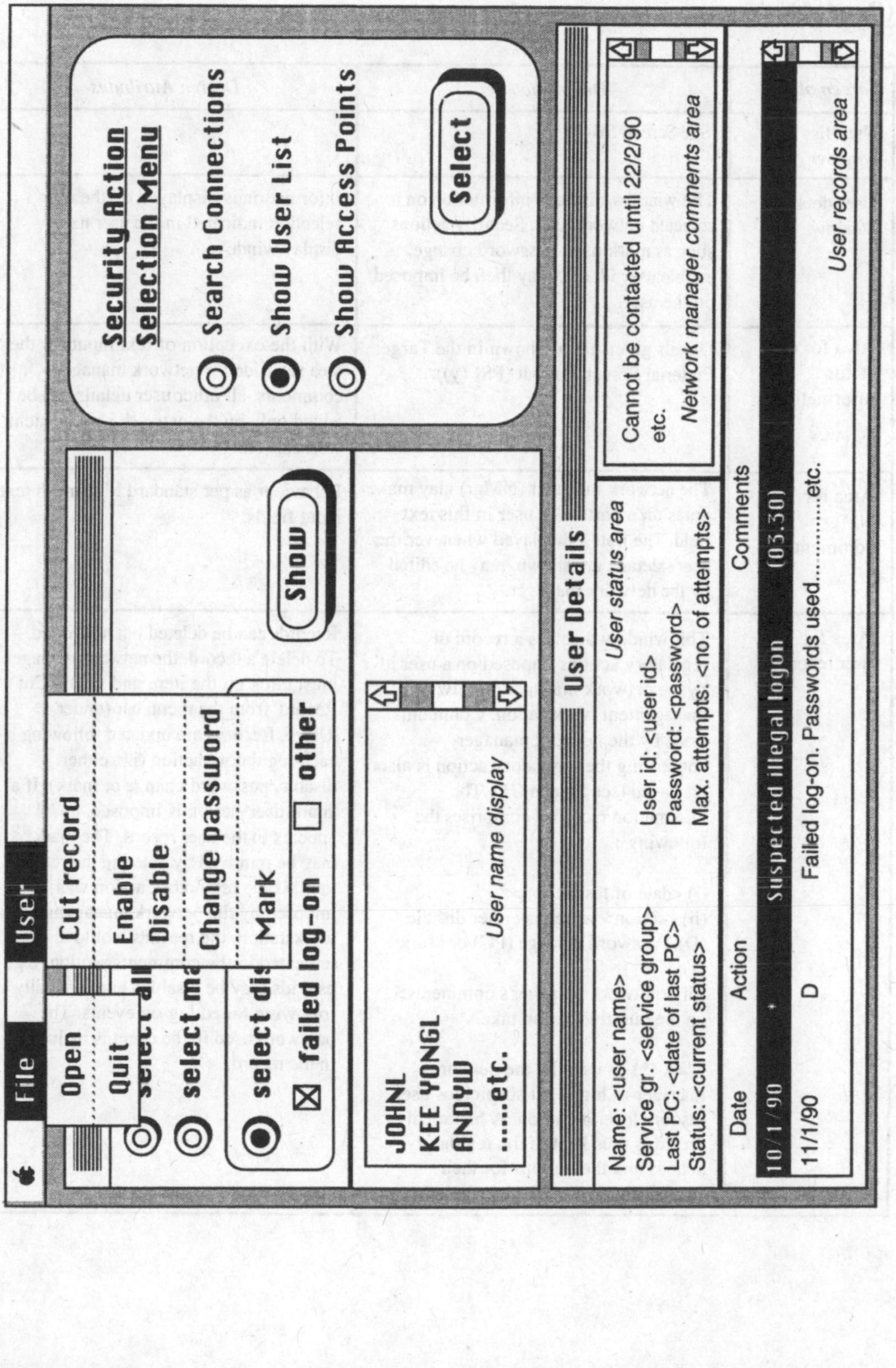

Figure 6-22: Target Dictionary of Screen Objects (DSO(y)) – Screen 5B-2 (Page 1)

Screen object	Description	Design Attributes
User list window	See Screen 5B-1.	
User details window	The window displays information on a selected network user. Security actions such as mark user, password change, enable user id, etc. may then be imposed on the user.	Information is displayed on the user selection indicated in the user name display window.
Area for user status information	Details given are as shown in the Target Pictorial Screen Layout (PSL(y)).	With the exception of text inputs in the area set aside for network manager's comments, all other user details can be edited only by the network management workstation.
Area for NMgr comments	The network manager (NMgr) may make notes on a particular user in this text field. The notes, displayed whenever the user's details are shown, may be edited by the network manager.	Behaviour as per standard Macintosh text input fields.
Area for user records	This window displays a record of regulatory actions imposed on a user id by the network manager or network management workstation. Comments made by the network manager concerning the regulatory action is also displayed (see Screen C1). The information recorded comprises the following : (i) <date of last action>; (ii) <action> which is either disable (D), Password Change (PC) or Mark (*); (iii) <network manager's comments> on the punitive action taken. Mark (*) is used by the network manager to highlight suspicious user ids for closer attention. A historical record is thus kept of the regulatory actions and the reasons for their imposition on a particular user id .	Records can be deleted but not edited. To delete a record, the network manager must click on the item and select 'Cut Record' from the menu bar (under 'User'). Records are updated following each regulatory action (i.e. either disable, password change or mark). If a 'mark user' action is imposed, an '*' appears in the user record. The mark may be removed by deleting the record item. If the regulatory action was imposed by the network management workstation, the reasons would also be indicated in the comments section, e.g. user ids may be disabled automatically following failed log-on events. The password used in the event is included in the record.

Figure 6-22: Target Dictionary of Screen Objects (DSO(y)) – Screen 5B-2 (Page 2)

Screen object	Description	Design Attributes
Security Action Selection Menu	See Screen 4B.	
Cut record	This command is used by the network manager to remove a 'record' from the 'User Details' window.	Available only after the record item in the 'User Details' window is selected for deletion. Behaviour as per standard Macintosh menu bar items.
Enable	This command is used to enable a (previously disabled) user id.	Available only when the 'User Details' window is displayed (i.e. after a user name item has been selected). Activates Screen C2. Behaviour as per standard Macintosh menu bar items.
Disable	This command is used to disable a user id. Comments on the action should be recorded (see Screen C1 for more information).	Available only when the 'User Details' window is displayed (i.e. after a user name item has been selected). Activates Screen C1. Behaviour as per standard Macintosh menu bar items.
Change password	This command is used to enforce a password change on a user id. Comments on the action should be recorded (see Screen C1 for more information).	Available only when the 'User Details' window is displayed (i.e. after a user name item has been selected). Activates Screen C1. Behaviour as per standard Macintosh menu bar items.
Mark	This command is used to 'mark' a user id so that suspicious activities are highlighted. Comments on the action should be recorded (see Screen C1 for more information).	Available only when the 'User Details' window is displayed (i.e. after a user name item has been selected). Activates Screen C1. Behaviour as per standard Macintosh menu bar items.

Figure 6-23:   Target Pictorial Screen Layout (PSL(y)) of Screen C2

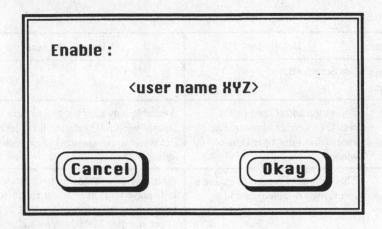

Figure 6-24:   Target Dictionary of Screen Objects (DSO(y)) – Screen C2

Screen object	Description	Design Attributes
Dialogue box	The dialogue box displays the user id, and confirm and cancel options after an 'Enable' action has been selected. In contrast with Screen C1, comments are not recorded for this action.	The dialogue box displays the enable action and the user name concerned. Behaviour as per standard Macintosh dialogue boxes.
Okay and Cancel buttons	Used to confirm or cancel an 'Enable' action.	Behaviour as per standard HyperCard buttons.

6.3.   Exercises and Sample Solutions
(Sample solutions to the exercises below are given at the end of the chapter.)

1) Using the System Task Model (STM(y) – two pages shown below) for the Automated Teller Machine (ATM), derive a corresponding Interaction Task Model (ITM(y)). Taking the latter model further, specify appropriate screen boundaries and assign identifiers to these boundaries. Describe the contents of the screens briefly. For simplicity, the following should be assumed:

(a) the withdrawal receipt is issued before the ATM card;
(b) the amount of cash requested would not exceed the account balance.

Page 1

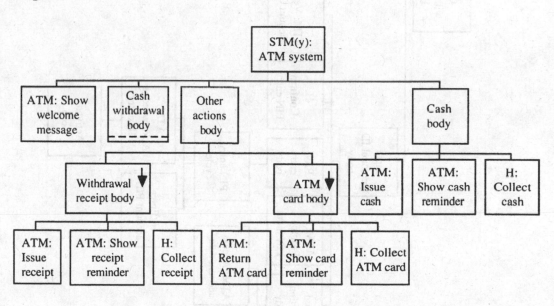

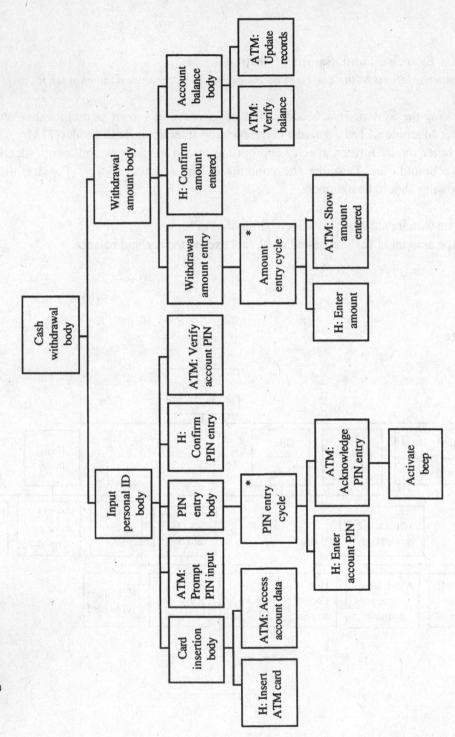

2) The diagram below shows a 'toolbox' associated the MacDraw™ package (version 1.9.8 – you may use any other software package for this exercise if the latter is not available). Explore the behaviour of the 'toolbox' components and generate the following descriptions:

(a) A small part of a set of Interface Models (IM(y)) describing the deactivation behaviours of 'toolbox' components Q, R and S.

(b) A larger part of an Interface Model (IM(y)) for 'toolbox' component Q describing, in one structured diagram, its behaviour for the following (a complete model need not be derived for this exercise):

(i) what happens on mouse-clicking its icon?

(ii) what types of inputs (e.g. keyboard, mouse-menu, etc.) may be made after its selection?

(iii) how the mouse-pointer display would change for the inputs in (ii) above?

(iv) what happens when alphanumeric keys are pressed?

(v) where its deactivation behaviour described in (a) above should be incorporated?

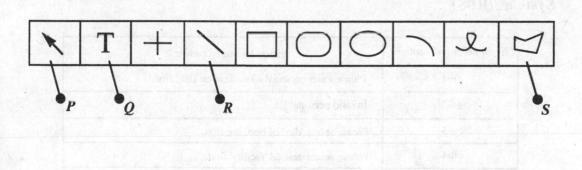

3) This exercise is intended to reinforce the reader's understanding of how human factors specifications of a user interface design should be interpreted. It emphasises the nature of the specifications (namely the Interaction Task Model (ITM(y)), Dialogue and Inter-Task Screen Actuation Description (DITaSAD(y)) and Dialogue and Error Message Table (DET(y))) and highlights important links among them. Read these specifications as described in the three figures below, and answer the following questions:

(a) What actions are required to input booking day, facility and time-band values?
(b) What error message numbers and contents may be triggered between Screen 4(2) and Screen 5(2)?
(c) Which message is displayed if the user were to click the 'Okay' button in Screen 2, *without* making any input?
(d) Which button(s) should be clicked to consume Screen 4(2)?
(e) What inputs are required to trigger Screen 6(2)a? (Note that Screen 6(2)a is the screen activated on selecting the 'Search within time-band' option.)

Dialogue and Error Message Table (DET(y)) for the Recreation Booking System (RBS)

Error Message Number	Error Message Content
em1	Please enter personal identification (ID) first.
em2	Invalid personal ID.
em3	Please select 'day' of booking first.
em4	Please select desired 'facility' first.
em5	Please select 'time from' before activating 'search'.
etc.	etc.

Interaction Task Model (ITM(y)) for the Recreation Booking System (RBS)

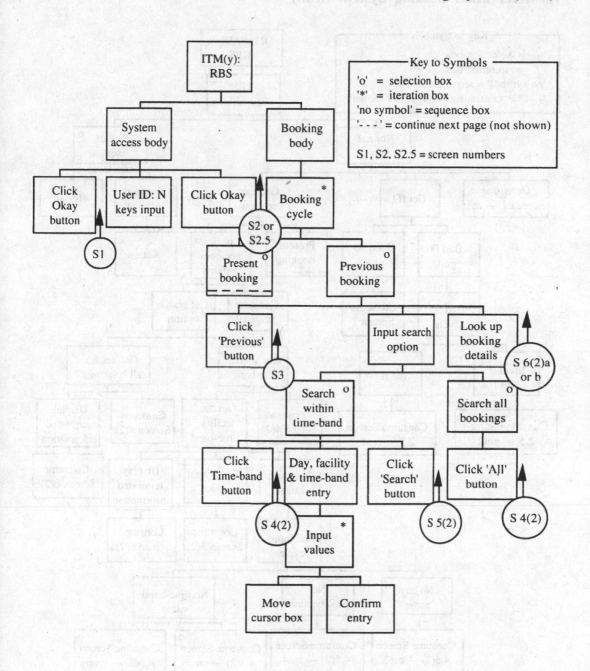

Dialogue and Inter-Task Screen Actuation Description (DITaSAD(y)) for the Recreation Booking System (RBS)

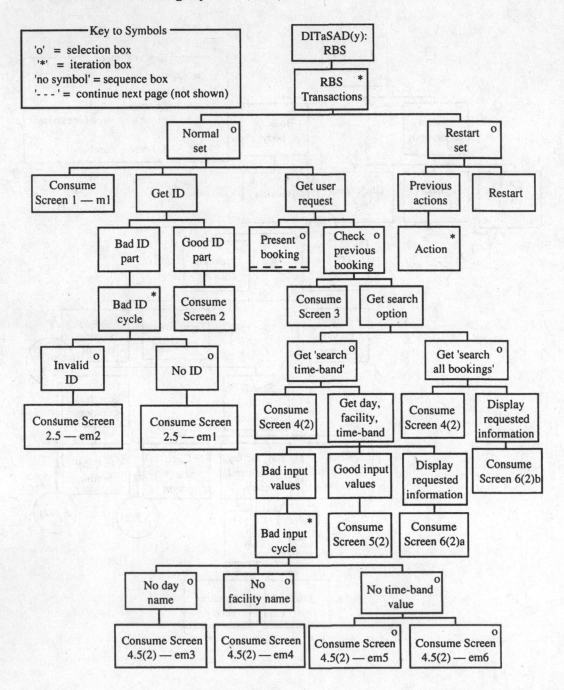

4) The Pictorial Screen Layouts (PSL(y) – (1) to (12) below) describe how specific screen displays and messages are to be actuated in response to user inputs. On the basis of these descriptions, construct a Dialogue and Inter-Task Screen Actuation Description (DITaSAD(y)) and a Dialogue and Error Message Table (DET(y)) for the recreation booking application.

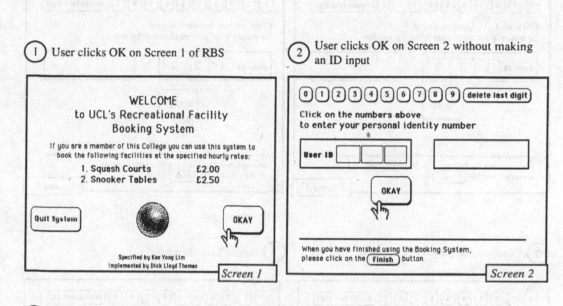

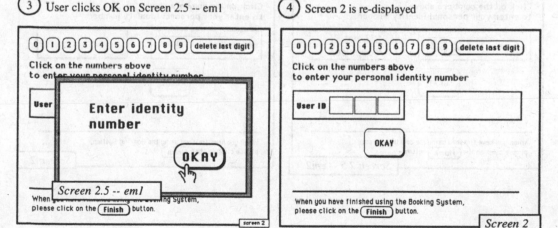

⑤ User inputs an invalid ID number 123

⑥ User confirms the input

⑦ Computer displays error message

⑧ Screen 2 is re-displayed

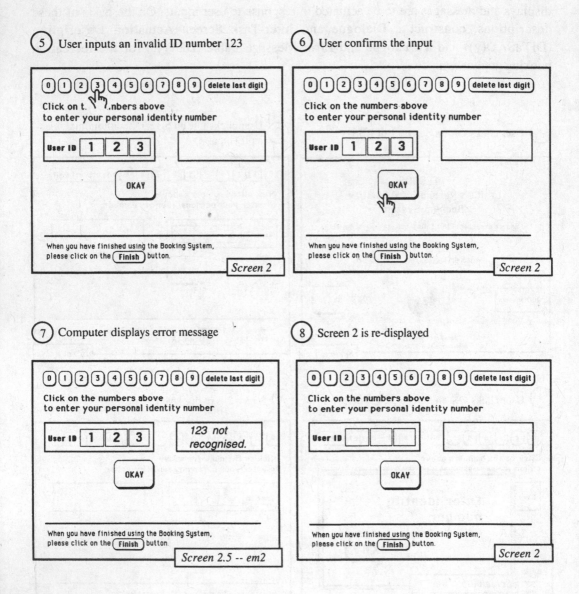

(9) User inputs a valid ID number 111

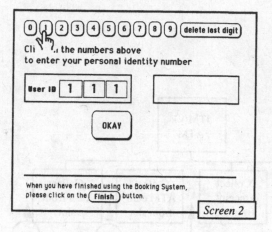

(10) User confirms the input

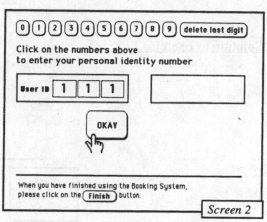

(11) Computer acknowledges valid input

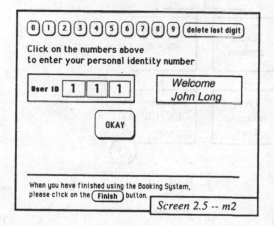

(12) Computer displays Screen 3

Please indicate whether you wish to make a
new booking or to check a previous booking

New Booking   Check Previous Booking   OKAY

You may return to this screen at any time by clicking
on the (Restart) button.

Screen 3

Sample Solutions to Exercises

Possible solutions to the preceding exercises are given below. With the exception of Exercise 3, note that there may be slightly different versions of a 'correct' solution for each of the exercises, e.g. different labels for the boxes of a structured diagram description.

Solution to Exercise 1

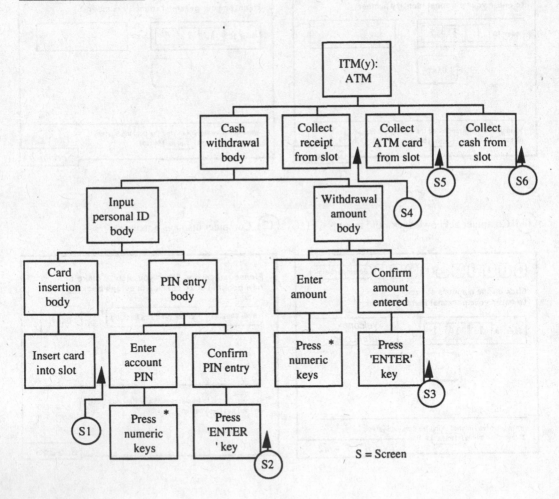

Contents of Screens 1 to 6 are:

Screen 1 (S1):   general welcome message; information about Automated Teller Machine
(ATM) facilities available; prompt for insertion of ATM card
Screen 2 (S2):   prompt for PIN input; numeric, CANCEL and ENTER keys
Screen 3 (S3):   prompt for withdrawal amount input; numeric, CANCEL and ENTER keys
Screen 4 (S4):   collect receipt reminder
Screen 5 (S5):   collect ATM card reminder
Screen 6 (S6):   collect cash reminder

Solution to Exercise 2(a)

Part of a set of Interface Models (IM(y)) describing the deactivation behaviours of
'toolbox' components Q, R and S.

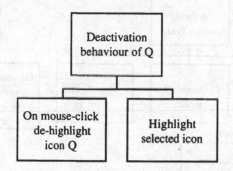

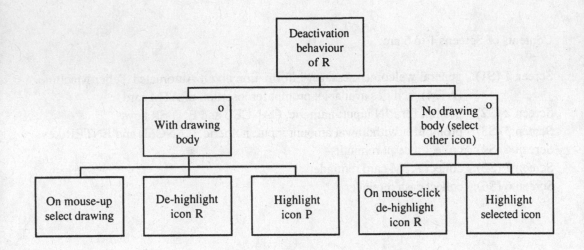

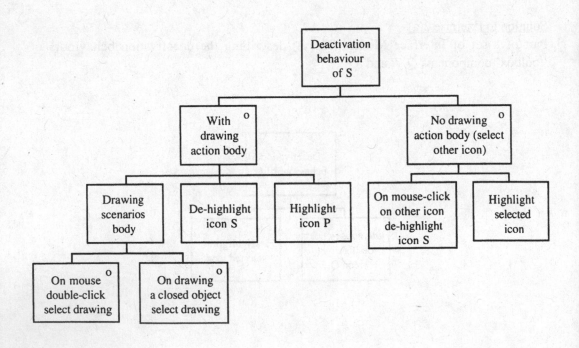

Solution to Exercise 2(b)

Part of an Interface Model (IM(y)) describing particular behaviours of 'toolbox' component Q.

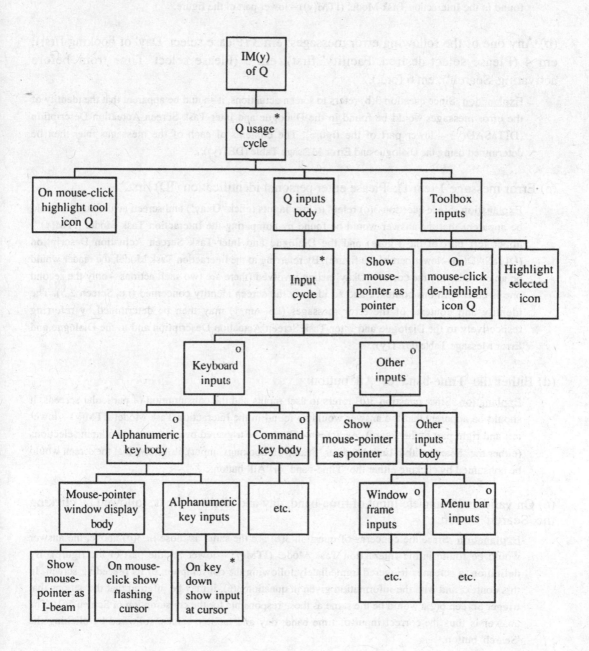

Solution to Exercise 3

(a) An iteration of the action sequence: 'Move Cursor Box' $\longrightarrow$ 'Confirm Entry'.

> Explanation Since question 3(a) refers to user inputs, it should be apparent that the answer would be found in the Interaction Task Model (ITM(y)) – lower part of the figure.

(b) Any one of the following error messages: em 3 (Please select 'Day' of booking first); em 4 (Please select desired 'Facility' first); em 5 (Please select 'Time from' before activating 'Search'); em 6 (etc.).

> Explanation Since question 3(b) refers to screen actuations, it should be apparent that the identity of the error messages would be found in the Dialogue and Inter-Task Screen Actuation Description (DITaSAD(y) – lower part of the figure). The contents of each of the messages may then be determined using the Dialogue and Error Message Table (DET(y)).

(c) Error message 1 (em 1): 'Please enter personal identification (ID) first.'

> Explanation Since question 3(c) refers to user inputs (click 'Okay') and screen actuations, it should be apparent that the answer would be found by comparing the Interaction Task Model (ITM(y) – upper left part of the figure) and the Dialogue and Inter-Task Screen Actuation Description (DITaSAD(y) – lower part of the figure). By referring to the Interaction Task Model, the reader would be able to identify the correct 'Okay' action involved (there are two such actions – only the second one is correct in this context), and so identify the screen identity concerned (i.e. Screen 2.5). The identity and contents of the error messages (i.e. em 1) may then be determined by referring respectively to the Dialogue and Inter-Task Screen Actuation Description and to the Dialogue and Error Message Table (DET(y)).

(d) Either the 'Time-band' or 'All' button.

> Explanation Since question 3(d) refers to user inputs and the consumption of particular screens, it should be apparent that the answer would be found in the Interaction Task Model (ITM(y) – lower left and right part of the figure). As Screen 4(2) may be triggered by any one of two input selections (either the 'Search within time-band' or 'Search all bookings' input), it follows that the screen would be consumed by clicking either the 'Time-band' or 'All' button.

(e) On valid and complete input of time-band, day and facility values, followed by clicking the 'Search' button.

> Explanation Since the concerns of question 3(e) are the same as those in 3(d) above, the answer would be found in the Interaction Task Model (ITM(y) – lower middle part of the figure). By definition, a screen is triggered immediately following the consumption of its preceding screen. In this context and with the information given in question 3(e), it may be inferred that the actions that trigger Screen 6(2)a would be the same as those responsible for the consumption of Screen 5(2). The answer is thus the correct input of time-band, day and facility values, followed by clicking the 'Search' button.

Solution to Exercise 4

The Dialogue and Inter-Task Screen Actuation Description (DITaSAD(y)) for the Recreation Booking System is given below.

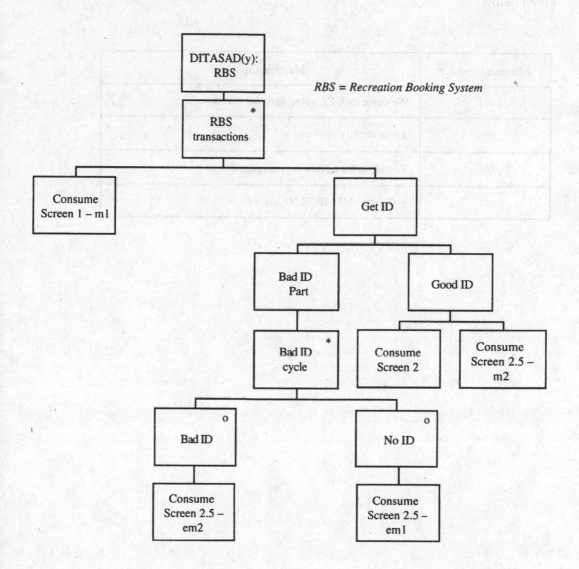

The Dialogue and Error Message Table (DET(y)) for the Recreation Booking System is given below.

Message Identifier	Message Content
m1	Welcome to UCL's Recreational Facility..............
em1	Enter identity number.
em2	Number <ID# NNN> not recognised.
m2	Welcome <MEMBER NAME> !

PART FOUR:

THE INTEGRATION OF HUMAN FACTORS WITH STRUCTURED SOFTWARE ENGINEERING METHODS

7

Pre-requisites and Examples of the Integration of Human Factors with Structured Software Engineering Methods

The last thing one knows in constructing a work is what to put first.

Blaise Pascal, 1909, ***Pensées***

The meaning of things lies not in the things themselves but in our attitude towards them.

Antoine de Saint-Exupéry

Having developed a structured method that supports human factors specification at each stage of system development (namely MUSE), its explicit integration with similarly structured software engineering methods may be considered. In this way, the problems associated with the 'too-little-too-late' contribution of human factors to system development may be addressed more completely (see Chapter One). To this end, the following concerns of methodological integration are discussed in this chapter:

(a) A conception of what constitutes an integration of structured human factors *and* software engineering methods. The requirements to be satisfied by the integrated method are thus defined.
(b) The pre-requisites and issues to be addressed during the integration of structured human factors *and* software engineering methods.

The above concerns are reviewed generally, followed by an illustration of how they have been addressed in the integration of MUSE (the structured *human factors* method) with the Jackson Systems Development (JSD) method (a structured *software engineering* method). For completeness and to provide a contrast with the latter work, other integrations of human factors with structured software engineering methods (work undertaken elsewhere) are also reviewed. Three structured software engineering methods are covered in the latter review, namely the Jackson System Development (JSD) method; the Structured Systems Analysis and Design Method (SSADM); and the Structured Analysis and Structured Design (SASD) Method.

7.1. General Requirements for Integrating Structured Human Factors and Software Engineering Methods[1]

The most basic requirement of integration relates to the definition of a structured method. Generally, such a method is expected to possess the following characteristics (see also Carver (1988); Maddison (1983); Hartson and Hix (1988)):

(a) The method should provide a reasonably *complete coverage* of the system development cycle. Its design activities should be grouped coherently into *stages*, which should then be operationalised appropriately to support a systematic address of the design concerns involved at each stage of system development.

(b) The *scope* of individual design stages should be well defined. In particular, the *design inputs* and *products* to be derived at each stage should be specified explicitly.

(c) The *process* of individual design stages should be adequate to support satisfactory application of the method. In particular, the design *procedures* at each stage should be sufficiently explicit.

(d) The *notation* and *documentation scheme* of individual design stages should be sufficiently powerful to describe the design products that are derived.

Thus, these characteristics should remain unaltered by an integration of structured methods. To this end, the requirements to be satisfied by an integration of structured human factors and software engineering methods are as follows:

(1) *Design stages* originating from structured methods of the human factors and software engineering disciplines should be intersected and timed appropriately. The stage-wise design scope and process of the methods are thus interwoven coherently to define an integrated agenda or schedule of system development.

(2) Appropriate *design notations* originating from structured software engineering methods (with extensions as necessary) should be used for the description of human factors design products. By maximising the use of a common notation, discussion and communication among inter-disciplinary design team members would be facilitated. Thus, the assimilation and uptake of human factors design contributions may improve.

---

[1] The integration of structured human factors *and* software engineering methods (i.e. the methods of both disciplines are structured – see Sub-section 7.3), may be contrasted with the integration of *disparate* human factors *techniques* with structured software engineering methods (see Sub-section 7.4). Generally, the latter integration would not satisfy the stringent methodological requirements described in Sub-sections 7.1 and 7.2.

(3) Appropriate *co-ordination of design contributions* from the two disciplines.[2] In particular, design inter-dependencies should be identified at appropriate stages *across* the component design streams of the integrated method (i.e. design streams originating from the individual disciplines). To ensure efficient project management, the design streams of an integrated method may be co-ordinated as follows:

(a) Design stages across component streams of the integrated method may be inter-linked serially. Obligatory contact points are thus established at the beginning and end of such design stages, to accommodate inter-disciplinary discussion and agreement on inter-dependent design constraints and information.

(b) Design stages across component streams of the integrated method may be undertaken in parallel. For such design stages, periodic checks to ensure adherence to the agreements indicated in (a) above are needed. By checking potential 'designer drift' at appropriate stages, design specifications generated by component streams of the integrated method would converge more efficiently. To this end, check points should be specified at stages where extensive design extrapolations are expected.[3] Thus, unnecessary design iterations are avoided by obviating mismatches between software engineering and human factors specifications.

To satisfy the above requirements, three options for integrating structured human factors and software engineering methods may be considered, namely:

(i) direct integration of existing human factors methods with existing structured software engineering methods;
(ii) the development of a structured software engineering method for subsequent integration with a structured human factors method;
(iii) the development of a structured human factors method for subsequent integration with a structured software engineering method.

Although there is a wealth of human factors methods (Gould, 1988), the methods on their own are either insufficiently complete or explicit in their coverage of the system development cycle (see Chapters One and Two). Consequently, direct integration using

---

[2] Large system development projects are generally undertaken by multi-disciplinary design teams, each responsible for their own stream of work. Thus, an integrated method should specify how design contributions from the individual disciplines should be co-ordinated.

[3] To maintain general applicability and flexibility, situation-specific check points (e.g. those peculiar to a particular organisation or design team) should be excluded from the method.

existing human factors methods (as described in option (i) above) would not satisfy adequately the above-mentioned requirements, unless extensive modifications and extensions of a complementary set of methods are involved. The route for methodological integration thus approximates to that described in option (iii) above. As for option (ii) above, none of the few newly developed structured human factors methods are accepted widely enough to justify a leading role in methodological integration. On the contrary, the choice of such an option for methodological integration would conflict directly with the existing design support role played by human factors in system development. Thus, to support effective uptake of human factors contributions, software engineering design practices that are well established should be accommodated appropriately. In particular, to improve assimilation of human factors design, its stages should be located against design reference points that are already familiar to software engineers, i.e. the design stages of existing structured software engineering methods. Furthermore, the stage-wise design scope, process and notation of the latter methods are better formed than any existing human factors method. Consequently, option (iii) represents a more sensible option for integration. Another argument for selecting option (iii) is that computer-based tools have already been developed for many structured software engineering methods. Such tools may also support human factors design. For instance, graphics editors may facilitate the documentation of human factors design products in cases in which software engineering notations have been recruited for the description.

Although (iii) is the most amenable option for methodological integration, its selection incurs an overhead. Specifically, a constraint is imposed, which requires existing structured software engineering methods to be left largely unchanged by integration. However, the consequences of such a constraint would not be severe since the latter class of methods is generally well developed. Thus, it is anticipated that the benefits arising from a more explicit representation of human factors design in the integrated method would more than compensate for the consequences of the constraint (see later).

Now, the research entailed in the development of a structured human factors method for integration with a structured software engineering method (option (iii)) is described. Generally, the requirements of such an undertaking are as follows:

(a) An extension of the design scope of the structured software engineering method to include a similarly structured human factors method. The extension is not necessarily a simple addition of methods, since some aspects of human factors design may already be included in the scope of a particular structured software engineering method, e.g. requirements analysis.
(b) An integration of design stages attributed to both the structured human factors and

software engineering methods. Thus, human factors design processes and products are located and timed appropriately in relation to those of the structured software engineering method. Design inter-dependencies may then be identified across the component streams of the integrated method.

(c) An extension of the notations of the structured software engineering method, to include the description of human factors design products. As in (a) above, the extension is not necessarily a simple addition, since existing notations of the structured software engineering method may already be suitable for the latter class of descriptions.

These requirements of methodological integration may be compared with the pre-requisites for effective human factors input reviewed in Chapter Two. In particular, human factors contributions should be contextualised to design support requirements associated with each stage of system development. The scope, timing, granularity and format of human factors contributions may then be configured more appropriately. Greater uptake of the latter contributions is thus supported by improvements in the applicability, relevance and communicability of its design products.

A more detailed account of the above requirements follows.

7.2.   Pre-Requisites and Concerns to be Addressed during the Integration of Structured Human Factors and Software Engineering Methods

It was indicated in the preceding sub-section that a pre-requisite of the integration of multi-disciplinary structured methods is the development of a structured human factors method to complement the design scope of the chosen structured software engineering method. The pre-requisite may be decomposed into the following requirements:

(1) Derivation of an explicitly structured conception of human factors design. The latter may be constructed by extending existing design conceptions. The satisfaction of this requirement (addressed in Chapter Two), led subsequently to the development of MUSE.

(2) Identification of the required human factors support for the chosen structured software engineering method. The design support required may be identified by comparing the design scope of the structured software engineering method with MUSE. Alternatively, a comparison could be made with the conception of human factors design referred to in (1) above, if a structured human factors method similar to MUSE has not been developed. More specific design support requirements may then be identified for each stage of the chosen structured software engineering method.

(3) Specification of a structured human factors method to support the chosen structured

software engineering method.[4] To this end, existing human factors methods may be reviewed and recruited to meet the requirements for design support as identified in (2) above. For instance, existing methods for requirements analysis would be reviewed if such design considerations are excluded from the scope of the chosen structured software engineering method. Relevant parts or whole methods are then modified and recruited to the development of a structured human factors method. This emphasis on recruiting existing methods is motivated by two reasons, namely:

(a) to facilitate faster convergence to an acceptable structured human factors method by building upon existing human factors knowledge;
(b) to maximise positive transfer of training with respect to the subsequent application of the structured human factors method for the same reason as in (a) above.

Prior to their recruitment, existing human factors methods may be developed further to satisfy the requirements of a structured method. For instance, the design scope of the methods may be extended, and their stage-wise design products, process, procedures and notation may be defined more explicitly (see Chapter Two).
(4) Integration of the structured human factors method with the chosen structured software engineering method. Following the development of a satisfactory structured human factors method as described in (3) above, explicit integration with a chosen software engineering method[5] may then be undertaken. The integration should satisfy the requirements specified in the preceding sub-section, namely:

(a) the design stages of the methods should be inter-woven;
(b) design notations of the chosen structured software engineering method should be exploited for human factors description;
(c) design inter-dependencies should be specified between the methods.

(5) Evaluation and iterative development of the integrated method. More needs to be said about the method evaluation tests to be applied. Specifically, appropriate tests may be configured to address the concerns listed below:

(a) *Demonstrating* the utility of the integrated method using design case-studies. In particular, case-studies may be used to show how design at each stage of system

---

[4] Since MUSE is already developed broadly according this step, its design scope need only be extended to meet additional support requirements (if any) of the chosen structured software engineering method.

[5] Note that the chosen structured software engineering method remains essentially unchanged.

development could be supported by the method;

(b) *Validating* the utility of the integrated method in the context of 'real world' design. Specifically, field studies may be conducted to establish how project pressures and social interactions among members of a design team may affect the utility of the integrated method.

(c) *Validating* the efficacy of the integrated method. Specifically, field studies may be conducted to ascertain whether the integrated method supports the development of superior system designs.

For economy of effort, concern (a) is usually addressed before concerns (b) and (c), since field studies generally require significant resources. Thus, appropriate measures should be observed during method development to ensure that a positive outcome for concern (a) would be more likely to lead to the same outcome for concerns (b) and (c). In particular, the following measures should be observed:

(1) Only established human factors methods and knowledge should be recruited. By building upon established research and design practice, it would be reasonable to expect field validity for the structured human factors method being developed.

(2) The explicit, systematic and comprehensive characteristics of existing structured software engineering methods, should be emulated by both the structured human factors method and the integrated method. Since such an orderly design process encourages more complete problem analysis, it would be reasonable to expect that superior system designs would result from the application of these methods. [6]

(3) The intended user of the method should be identified at an early stage.[7] Explicit user requirements may then be defined and satisfied during method development, e.g. the scope and level of proceduralisation required by the user of the method.

(4) Proposed versions of the method should be developed iteratively, and tested on more than one case-study.

(5) Human factors and software engineering design contributions should, at a minimum, be simulated during case-study tests of the method. In this way, design inter-dependencies proposed between the disciplines may then be assessed for their pertinence in ensuring

---

[6] Note that such premises have also been assumed by established structured software engineering methods.

[7] MUSE is intended for a designer trained appropriately in human factors. The training is necessary since MUSE does not presently include reference manuals on the substantive human factors knowledge required to support system development. Similarly, MUSE*/JSD is targeted at a human factors designer with a working knowledge of the JSD method.

efficient design collaboration and management.

Following the development of an acceptable structured method, field studies may then be considered. In particular, longitudinal and lateral studies may be conducted to control for the following variation across system development case-studies:

(a) level of experience and competence of individual system designers;
(b) contractual requirements of the project, e.g. design pressures;
(c) organisational and social influences on the conduct of the design project;
(d) composition of the design team;
(e) characteristics of the particular system design problem (and domain).[8]

Two further concerns of method evaluation need to be addressed, namely the type of evaluation and test beds to be selected. Firstly, the characteristics of the method could be evaluated in terms of their functionality and usability. In this respect, functionality evaluation should take precedence over usability evaluation during method development, since concerns associated with the provision of pertinent system design support commands a greater priority at this stage. Following the development of a satisfactory method, the evaluation focus may then shift onto usability assessments of the appropriateness of methodological formulation. In addition, subjective assessment of the method takes precedence over objective assessment in the shorter term. Methodological characteristics that may be assessed subjectively include the following: completeness of design scope; flexibility; utility; acceptability; learnability; and compatibility with the chosen structured software engineering method and other established design methods and practices; etc. In the longer term, sufficient data may be accumulated from the application of the method to support more objective assessment. For instance, the method could be assessed in terms of its efficacy for facilitating improvements in design performance, e.g. quality of design management, documentation and solution; amount and seriousness of errors committed and detected at each stage of design development (e.g. early or late discovery of errors); project turn-around time; overall project resource requirements; etc.

---

[8] Such scientifically controlled field studies have not been reported for existing structured software engineering methods. The methods were taken up without the requirement for such studies, since such system design support methods were much needed at the time of their introduction. In addition, many of the structured methods were developed, applied and tested iteratively by in-house design teams, prior to their introduction to the wider design community. MUSE is presently at this stage of methodological development.

Secondly, to manage more effectively the complexities of method development and integration, appropriate case-study test beds should be identified and used at initial stages of the undertaking. To this end, the following case-study selection criteria may be applied at the initial stages of method development and integration:

(a) The case-study system domain should not be unnecessarily complex or unfamiliar to the method developer. In particular, the domain of the initial case-study system should not be ill defined. The criterion is intended to ensure that resources (time and effort) are expended appropriately on developing the method rather than on supporting familiarisation with the case-study domain. To broaden the scope of evaluation tests, a wider range of domains may be considered later when an acceptable method has been derived. The notation of the method may thus be tested on its capability for supporting the description of various system domains.

(b) The scale of the case-study system should be incremented progressively as the method is developed. Alternatively, successively larger size modules of a case-study system may be used as test beds when the method becomes better formed.

(c) A simpler design scenario should be selected. For instance, at early stages of method development, a *variant* design scenario would be more suitable than a *novel* design scenario. When the method becomes better developed, evaluation tests under a novel design scenario may be introduced. Thus, by increasing the complexity of the case-study design scenario, the procedures of the method may be tested more fully.

During method tests, answers to the following questions may be sought:

(i) Is the system design scope supported by the method reasonably complete? Does its design support cover system development from requirements definition to user interface specification?

(ii) Are design processes and products of the method defined sufficiently to support human factors design? Are its design steps manageable, and are they decomposed into activities that are sensibly organised to support design reasoning? Are the activities grouped into coherent design stages and operationalised appropriately?

(iii) Are notations of the method powerful and comprehensive enough to support descriptions of both intermediate and final human factors design products? Are they adequately usable to facilitate discussions between designers, and between designers and users? In addition, are they specific enough to ensure unambiguous implementation of human factors specifications? Would the documentation schemes generate a sufficiently detailed record of the design decisions and rationale of design products derived at each stage of the method?

(iv) Are design inter-dependencies of the integrated method specific enough to support effective design co-ordination and management; i.e. to ensure efficient convergence in the design undertaken in component streams of the integrated method ? Would the inter-dependencies impose unnecessary design constraints and hamper creativity ?

Thus, by seeking appropriate answers to the above questions, necessary upgrades of a particular version of the method may be inferred. In this way, progressively refined versions are developed in successive iterations. The process is continued until an acceptable version of the method is derived.

7.3. MUSE*/JSD – Structured Integration of MUSE with the Jackson System Development (JSD) Method
The objectives of this sub-section are as follows:

(1) to describe the methodological constraints imposed on an in-house integration of MUSE (a structured human factors method) with the Jackson System Development (JSD) method (a structured software engineering method);
(2) to identify the requirements for human factors support in respect of the Jackson System Development method;
(3) to review and assess a conception of an integrated method (termed MUSE*/JSD) derived on the basis of (1) and (2) above.

An expanded account of the objectives follows.

7.3.1. A Brief Review of the Jackson System Development (JSD) Method
The Jackson System Development method is concerned with the technical specification of software systems based on an event model.[9] The method is thus most suitable for the development of real-time systems (Renold, 1989).

Generally, the Jackson System Development method comprises three design stages; namely Modelling, Network and Implementation Stages. Each of the stages is decomposed into explicit design activities and products to guide the user of the method. The scope of the stages is as follows:

(1) *Modelling Stage:* the purpose of this stage is to capture the subject matter of the target system. Thus, an abstract model of the users' world is defined using a set of entities and their actions. A JSD entity must exist in the real world and is a person, organisation or

---

[9] Although the Jackson System Development method does not include specialised techniques such as physical database design, it highlights where they should be accommodated within its framework.

object that performs and/or suffers a series of actions described using one or more structured diagrams. A JSD action is an atomic event in the real world (with specific start- and end-points), about which the system must produce or use information. Each *model process* communicates with its *real world* process via inputs associated with its actions. The model is realised in the computer as a set of sequential processes. Since model processes define the functions a system can support, they are differentiated from function processes which are concerned only with the production of system outputs (see (2) below).
(2) *Network Stage:* this stage is concerned with the functional definition of the target system. Specifically, function processes (comprising input sub-systems, information processes and interactive functions) are specified and connected by information flows, to model processes defined in the preceding stage. Thus, a network of function and model processes is derived. The timing of information flows and outputs, and linkages with external world processes are also defined.
(3) *Implementation Stage:* the purpose of this stage is to transform JSD specifications into sequential programs that may be executed more efficiently by the target hardware. Thus, its concerns include the scheduling of processes and data storage and access. Specifically, a set of one or more processes are grouped together and delegated to a physical or virtual processor. It should be noted that the external behaviour of the system would not be affected by these transformation processes; i.e. JSD specifications are conserved during implementation (Zave (1984); Renold (1989)). In addition, the following characteristics of JSD implementation may be pertinent:

(a) Since it is a very well regulated (Zave, 1984) and mechanistic process, most of its transformations could be automated (Renold, 1989). Thus, human factors input during JSD implementation may be limited. [10]
(b) It is different from other implementations since it involves transformations of design specifications rather than only the physical construction of a system.

Since software realisation is beyond the scope of legitimate human factors concerns, JSD implementation is not addressed here.

In summary, the Jackson System Development method involves a separation of what the system is about from what the system has to do. Thus, it advocates the derivation of a real

---

[10] Possible human factors contributions at this stage may include the specification of additional feedback cues to be provided by the device (e.g. in cases in which a particular JSD implementation results in longer than expected transient response time); and an assessment of implementations involving batch and on-line processing (e.g. the frequency of computer data updates and the resulting impact on the user's task).

world model of the problem domain, before the functional specification of a design solution. Similarly, it emphasises the separation of design specification from design implementation. This account completes a brief review of the Jackson System Development method. For a more complete description, the reader is referred to Jackson (1983) and Cameron (1989).

7.3.2. Rationale for Selecting the Jackson System Development Method for Integration with MUSE

Generally, the Jackson System Development method was selected for integration with MUSE for two reasons; namely the good reputation of the method and the preferences of the project sponsor. Since the latter preferences were influenced by the former, subsequent discussions are focused on the strengths of the method.

In addition to the general arguments in favour of structured methods (see Chapter One), strengths specific to the Jackson System Development method include the following:

(1) It is a well-established structured software engineering method, and is among the more popular methods used in the development of real-time systems (Morrison (1988); Wilson et al. (1989)).

(2) Its specifications are in principle directly executable (Carver and Cameron, 1987). Thus, its descriptions of a system may be considered to comprise a simulation of particular aspects of the real world, with functions to present outputs from the simulation (Carver et al. 1987). Such an emphasis on simulating the real world may be more amenable for the accommodation of an appropriate user's model of the system. In particular, the method starts by modelling the proposed system in terms of real world objects and events (this approach may be contrasted with structured methods that focus immediately on data flow description). Since its specifications are developed from an understanding of the user's world, explicit links with user requirements capture, and task description and analysis may be identified. Thus, the integration of human factors with the Jackson System Development method may be facilitated.

(3) Since its design focus may be considered object-oriented, it is compatible with other object-oriented methods (Birchenough and Cameron (1989); Cameron (1987)). For instance, its more complete methodological framework could potentially support the design of object-oriented user interfaces. Since such graphical user interfaces are becoming increasingly popular, it would be pertinent to consider the integration of human factors with the method.

(4) Its well-developed methodological characteristics facilitate the explicit location of human factors contributions. For instance, its specifications of the input sub-system has been intersected with human factors contributions to user interface design (Sutcliffe (1988b);

Carver et al. (1987)). General design concepts of the Jackson System Development method may also be recruited, namely:

(a) its input sub-system specification includes a taxonomy of input errors, e.g. context error, simple input error, etc.;

(b) its information functions may be linked to domain semantics, e.g. the context for system outputs is defined by the JSD model;

(c) its specification of information flow includes different categories (e.g. state vector inspection and data-streams) and time grain markers. Information flows may thus be specified in detail, e.g. information content; direction of flow; timing; and duration of display; etc.

(5) Its structured diagram notation can support precise description of users' tasks (see Carver (1988); Carver and Cameron (1987); Sutcliffe (1988a)). Specifically, its well-developed constructs support the description of sequential, selection, iteration, concurrent, inter-locking, backtracking and uncertain events (see Chapter Three; and Carver and Cameron (1987)). The notation has also been shown to be:

(a) a graphical equivalent of grammar-based notations such as BNF (Reisner, 1977). For further information, the reader should refer to Boldyreff (1986);

(b) at least equal in descriptive power with TAG (Payne and Green, 1986), Generalised Transition Networks (Kieras and Polson, 1985), flowcharts (e.g. Drury, 1983) and tree hierarchies (e.g. Annett and Duncan, 1967). For further information, the reader should refer to Walsh (1987a and b);

(c) understood easily by users (Carver, 1988; Finkelstein and Potts, 1985). Specifically, the graphical nature of the notation may facilitate the elicitation of user feedback.

Other benefits of recruiting the notation for human factors description[11] may include the following:

(a) The specificity of current human factors contributions would improve, since the notation supports more precise design descriptions.

(b) Communication problems between software engineers and human factors designers would be reduced through the use of a common notation. Since the primary motivation for

---

[11] For these reasons, the structured diagram notation of the Jackson System Development method was recruited, extended and incorporated into MUSE.

integrating human factors with structured software engineering methods is to support early and continuous human factors involvement (i.e. collaborative design), effective and unambiguous communication is essential between designers representing the two disciplines. The potential of a common notation should therefore be exploited.

(c) *Formal* human factors specification may accrue in the future, since the structured diagram notation has been mapped onto formal notations such as Communicating Sequential Processes (CSP) – see Sridhar and Hoare (1985).

These desirable characteristics indicate that the Jackson System Development method would be a good candidate for the first integration of MUSE with a structured software engineering method.

7.3.3. Constraints Imposed on the Integration of MUSE with the Jackson System Development Method

Generally, the constraints on the present integration of MUSE with the Jackson System Development method comprise the following:

(1) The integration should not unduly disrupt design practices of the Jackson System Development method. Specifically, the integrity of the latter method should be preserved and its notations should be exploited for human factors description. These constraints should not be considered adversely. On the contrary, the configuration of a structured human factors method around an essentially unchanged structured software engineering method implies that human factors concerns would be located against design reference points and practices that are familiar to software engineers. The assimilation of human factors contributions is thus facilitated.

(2) The present scope of the project is limited to the derivation and case-study demonstration of an integrated method. Specifically, the project is focused on establishing the viability and capability of the integrated method, as opposed to a field validation of its efficacy for supporting the development of superior system designs. By applying the measures described in Sub-section 7.2, the constraints would not necessarily affect the project adversely. The reasons are as follows:

(a) A superior design may be expected by improving the uptake of human factors contributions. Such improvements may be expected since the integrated method supports orderly and timely incorporation of human factors design processes and products.

(b) Only design methods and practices that are well established are incorporated into the integrated method. Thus, it would be reasonable to expect that the method would support the specification of better system designs.

(3) The scope of the integrated method addresses only the main concerns of human factors design. In other words, secondary design concerns, e.g. organisational and job design; training and personnel selection; and late evaluation (already well established), will be referenced but not addressed in detail.

(4) The human factors designer intending to use the integrated method is expected to have a working knowledge of the Jackson System Development method. Similarly, the software engineer is expected to be generally knowledgeable about MUSE, the human factors component of the integrated method.

In the remaining sub-sections, the Jackson System Development method is reviewed briefly, followed by an account of the development and a conception of the integrated method (termed MUSE*/JSD).

7.3.4. Identifying the Human Factors Design Support Required by the Jackson System Development Method

Figure 7-1 shows a list of human factors design concerns that have not generally been addressed by existing structured software engineering methods. The list, compiled by Anderson (1988), is examined presently in the context of the Jackson System Development method.

Generally, Anderson's observations are mostly true for the Jackson System Development method, but the following qualifications should be noted:

(a) Point 4 (Figure 7-1) is not strictly correct, since the Jackson System Development method may be used to support other object-oriented approaches for user interface design (Birchenough and Cameron (1989); Cameron (1987)).

(b) Point 5 (Figure 7-1) is debatable for the Jackson System Development method, since there are conflicting reports on the ease of assimilation and use of its structured diagram notation. In any case, prototyping is encouraged by the method.

(c) Point 6 (Figure 7-1) is also debatable for structured software engineering methods in general. For instance, it may be argued that the emphasis of such methods on in-depth analysis and specification before implementation may reduce the project time available for design iterations. In addition, the emphasis of the methods on comprehensive design documentation may foster a greater reluctance towards the acceptance of necessary design modifications. The opposite argument would be that a thorough design analysis phase would support faster convergence to a design solution (see Chapter One). These conflicting arguments were put forward during the initial introduction of structured software engineering methods. With the emergence of computer-based support for such methods (e.g. PDF™ and SpeedBuilder™ for the Jackson System Development method), the negative arguments have become weaker.

Figure 7-1:   Human Factors Deficiencies of Existing Structured Software Engineering Methods (Anderson, 1988)

---

1. Existing structured software engineering methods may not specify the procedures to be applied for eliciting the operational requirements of the system, e.g. information concerning user roles, tasks, etc.

2. Existing structured software engineering methods may not address appropriately the allocation of function between user and computer. The tendency is to computerise functions that can be automated and leave the remainder to the user.

3. Existing structured software engineering methods generally do not indicate how system design specifications and implementation (e.g. computer functions) should be assessed against the user's task.

4. Existing structured software engineering methods may not support the design of object-oriented user interfaces.

5. The notation of existing structured software engineering methods may be too difficult for users to understand. Thus, without prototyping, the elicitation of user feedback may be supported poorly.

6. Existing structured software engineering methods may discourage iterative design.

7. The scope of existing structured software engineering methods generally does not address the design of the human-computer dialogue.

8. Physical dialogue design is addressed poorly by existing structured software engineering methods. Usually, there is no reference to style kits and screen design is left to common sense.

Having considered these qualifications duly, human factors deficiencies of the Jackson System Development method may be inferred from Anderson's list. It was thus concluded that the method is essentially deficient in two areas of human factors design; namely requirements and task analysis, and user interface design. Similar observations were reported by Finkelstein and Potts (1985); McNeile (1986); Carver et al. (1987); Carver and Cameron (1987); Sutcliffe (1988a); Renold (1989); and Sutcliffe and Wang (1991).

The scope of human factors design support required by the Jackson System Development method, is thus defined by analysing the above deficiencies of the method. MUSE may then be suitably extended (or a new structured human factors method may be developed) for integration with the Jackson System Development method. These concerns of methodological integration are addressed next.

7.3.5. The Integration of MUSE with the Jackson System Development Method

It was stated earlier that methodological integration would involve extending the design scope of the Jackson System Development method to include human factors design. The undertaking should be contrasted against making the Jackson System Development method more usable, e.g. by enhancing its procedures for deriving JSD model and function processes (both software engineering design concerns).

To facilitate methodological integration, MUSE would be required to support human factors design deficiencies in the Jackson System Development method.[12] Specifically, the scope of MUSE should include requirements analysis, task analysis and user interface design. To this end, MUSE should satisfy the following requirements:

(1) It should facilitate the development of a superior system design. In the case of structured methods in general, a superior design artefact is ensured by encouraging an orderly design process and a well-defined set of design deliverables. The requirement entails the specification of an explicit scope, process and notation for each design stage of MUSE.

(2) It should address human factors design from user requirements definition to user interface specification. In this respect, the design descriptions of MUSE should be defined sufficiently to inform software engineers and users. The requirement may be satisfied by specifying the methodological characteristics of MUSE explicitly as described in (1) above, and by ensuring that its design scope provides a reasonably complete coverage of the system development cycle.

A more detailed account of the above methodological requirements follows. Firstly, the *design scope* of MUSE should satisfy the following:

(a) It should indicate how human factors design parameters, namely the environment, device, task and user, should be addressed during system development. To this end, intermediate design products should be defined adequately to support reasoning. In addition, the stage-wise process by which such products are derived should be specified explicitly, so that appropriate design inter-dependencies may be identified with software engineering concerns addressed by the Jackson System Development method. Obligatory

---

[12] Although the requirements of methodological integration are described here with respect to MUSE, they are generally applicable to any similar attempt at integration involving any other structured human factors method.

meeting points and information exchanges may then be specified to co-ordinate system design undertaken in individual streams of the integrated method.

(b) It should compensate for the currently incomplete state of human factors knowledge. In particular, it should emphasise and support prototyping and user testing activities required to ascertain the validity of design assumptions. Since MUSE involves the derivation of explicit design products at each stage of system development, such activities would be supported.

Secondly, the *design process* of MUSE should satisfy the following:

(a) It should uphold design principles advocated by the Jackson System Development method; such as model before functional specification and separate addressing of distinct concerns of system development (e.g. separation of specification from implementation). In the case of MUSE, such principles are exemplified by setting requirements analysis and task modelling before function allocation, conceptual task design before interaction task design, and the separate addressing of human factors and software engineering design.

(b) It should facilitate early and continued human factors involvement throughout system development.

(c) It should support various scenarios of system design, e.g. variant design, novel design and the computerisation of manual systems.

(d) Its procedures should be comprehensive enough for application by human factors designers. However, they should not be too rigid that design creativity is stifled. In addition, appropriate existing human factors design techniques should be incorporated into MUSE to maximise positive transfer of training (see Chapter Two).

Thirdly, the *design notation* of MUSE should satisfy the following:

(a) It should be powerful enough to support a comprehensive record of design decisions and rationale, and the subject matter of human factors products derived at each stage of the method.

(b) Its documentation schemes should support adequate records of human factors design products derived at each stage of the method. The records should be explicit enough to support assessments of alternative designs of a system.

(c) It should recruit existing design notations of the Jackson System Development method, with as little modification as possible. The benefits of a common notation may thus be maximised.

In summary, the development and integration of MUSE with the Jackson System

Development method would involve the following concerns: [13]

(I) identification of the human factors design stages and products required to support the Jackson System Development method. Required extensions of MUSE (if any) are thus defined;

(IIa) definition of explicit processes and procedures to support each stage of human factors design as prescribed by MUSE;

(IIb) extension of the notations of the Jackson System Development method, to support the description of human factors design;

(III) specification of design inter-dependencies between MUSE and the Jackson System Development method.[14] The two component methods are thus integrated to derive an inter-disciplinary structured method termed MUSE*/JSD.

A work plan comprising a number of research strategies[15] was devised to address systematically the above requirements of human factors integration with the Jackson System Development method. In particular, the following activities, conducted *before* the development of MUSE, should be noted:

(1) A set of well-established structured software engineering methods was reviewed, to identify a broader set of requirements to be satisfied by MUSE.[16] Thus, methods such as Structured Systems Analysis and Design Method (SSADM), Structured Analysis and Structured Design (SASD) Method, etc., were reviewed in addition to the Jackson System Development method (see Walsh and Lim, 1987). The human factors design support required by these methods, was then collated as a set of requirements to be accommodated by MUSE (concern (I) was thus addressed). In this way, MUSE was developed into a reasonably complete and general structured human factors method (concern (IIa) was thus addressed – see Chapter Two; Lim, 1992);

(2) Suitable notations from the set of structured software engineering methods reviewed were extended and incorporated during the development of MUSE. In particular, the structured diagram notation (and to a lesser extent, the network notation) of the Jackson

---

[13] The method development activities are undertaken in the given order. Iterations are also performed as necessary.

[14] Design inter-dependencies exclude situation-specific and informal exchanges of design information, since the basic requirement of a method is that it should be sufficiently general for application across various design domains and project circumstances.

[15] The reader is referred to Lim et al. (1990a and b) and Lim (1992) for a detailed account of the research plan and strategies applied in the development of MUSE.

[16] Thus, it would be reasonable to expect that MUSE could potentially support human factors integration with a number of structured software engineering methods.

System Development method was found to be useful. Consequently, the notation was extended and incorporated into MUSE (see Chapter Three and Sub-section 7.3.2). To this end, specific extensions of the notation entailed by concern (IIb) comprise the following:

(a) Addition of a hierarchy construct to the structured diagram notation. The construct provides a more convenient representation of non-sequential events of a task (see Chapter Three).

(b) Relaxation of a number of rules associated with the structured diagram notation (to accommodate the 'inexact' nature of some human factors descriptions – see Lim (1988e)), namely the following:

(i) 'Actions should be atomic.' This rule is relaxed to permit the specification of task actions at different levels of description. Thus, 'chunking' of sub-tasks may be accommodated.

(ii) 'Actions should have detectable start- and end-points.' Although the rule is applicable to the description of overt actions, it cannot be used when cognitive processes are involved.

(c) Adaptation to support wider application of the structured diagram notation. In particular, the notation was adapted for the description of human factors specifications as follows:

(i) Behaviour and changes in appearance of screen objects. Since the structured diagram notation is already suited for such descriptions, the extensions were generally minor. Figure 7-2 shows a simple extension to link the behaviour of screen objects to changes in their appearance.

Figure 7-2: Structured Diagram Description of Screen Object Behaviour and Changes in Appearance

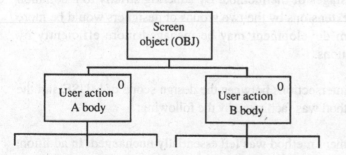
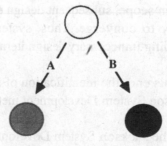

A and B are permissible selections of user actions on a screen object named OBJ (lower level operations of A and B not shown).

Changes in appearance of screen object OBJ in response to actions A and B.

(ii) Screen actuation of important computer functions and messages to support the user's task. This structured diagram description is linked to screen layout diagrams and message index tables (see Chapter Three).

(d) Adaptation to support wider application of the network diagram notation. In particular, the notation was adapted for the description of control, timing and direction of information flows among system entities. It should be noted that, unlike the structured diagram notation, the utility of the network diagram notation for such human factors description remains to be established (see Chapter Three and Annex B). In this regard, further research is necessary to develop the potential of the notation for the following description:

(i) Information exchanges among human, computer and other real world entities. The notation may be used to specify continuous, periodic and on-request type information flows.
(ii) Information exchanges between users in an organisation. Such descriptions may be useful when socio-technical concerns are addressed during system development.
(iii) Display duration of screen objects, e.g. whether a particular computer function should be displayed continuously or periodically.

The above review completes an account of how intrinsic characteristics of MUSE have been developed to support its integration with the Jackson System Development method. Now, the specification of explicit design inter-dependencies between MUSE and the latter method (i.e. concern (III)) is addressed.

Generally, a common design scope (including system design criteria, assumptions and constraints) should be established by human factors designers and software engineers at each inter-dependency point of the integrated method. The agreed design scope should then be carried forward through later stages of the method. By adhering strictly to a common design scope, subsequent design extensions by the two groups of designers would be more likely to converge. Thus, system development may be managed more efficiently by avoiding unnecessary design iterations.

To this end, the identification of intersections between the design scope of MUSE and the Jackson System Development method was facilitated by the following:

(a) The Jackson System Development method was left essentially unchanged. In addition, its methodological characteristics were accommodated appropriately during the development of MUSE, e.g. its structured diagram notation.

(b) Both MUSE and the Jackson System Development method are structured methods. Since the design stages and concerns of such methods are well defined, their design processes could be intersected unambiguously on the basis of expected design inter-dependencies; i.e. overlaps in design information used and generated at each stage of system development.

A 'basic' number of design inter-dependency points was thus identified by comparing the stage-wise design scope of MUSE with that of the Jackson System Development method. To assess the pertinence of these design inter-dependencies, case-study applications of the integrated method (i.e. MUSE*/JSD) were conducted, during which human factors and software engineering design roles and relationships were simulated. In particular, the design inter-dependencies were assessed on the support they provide towards ensuring convergent contributions from the two design streams. Modifications and/or new design inter-dependencies may then be specified as appropriate,[17] and the integrated method re-assessed using further case-studies. An acceptable integrated method may thus be derived incrementally. Such a method is reviewed in the next sub-section.

7.3.6.   MUSE*/JSD – An Integration of Structured Human Factors and Software Engineering Methods

Figure 7-3 shows a schematic representation of the integrated structured method. Since MUSE and the Jackson System Development method are both largely unchanged (the design stages should be undertaken following the original methods), it suffices to say that design stages of the integrated method (termed MUSE*/JSD) have been operationalised as follows (specific design iterations are not indicated):

(1) Design stages of MUSE prior to the Composite Task Model Stage are performed to completion.
(2) The System and User Task Model Stage of MUSE is performed in parallel with the Model and Function Stages of the JSD method. Close consultation between the design streams should be maintained.
(3) Human factors design is suspended at the Composite Task Model Stage, while the JSD Model and Function Stages are performed to completion. JSD analysts may continue to consult human factors designers as appropriate.
(4) Design stages of MUSE following the System and User Task Model Stage are

---

[17] To maintain general applicability of the method, only high-level design inter-dependencies would be specified. Appropriate lower level design inter-dependencies (e.g. informal design contacts and discussions) may be established later by the design team (with particular working habits and relationships) following repeated application of the integrated method.

performed to completion. Human factors designers may continue to consult JSD analysts as appropriate.

(5) The Implementation Stage of the JSD method is performed to completion.

(6) The design is evaluated jointly.

A more specific account of the design inter-dependencies between the component methods of MUSE*/JSD follows.

Figure 7-3:   Schematic Representation of MUSE*/JSD, the Integrated Human Factors and Software Engineering Method

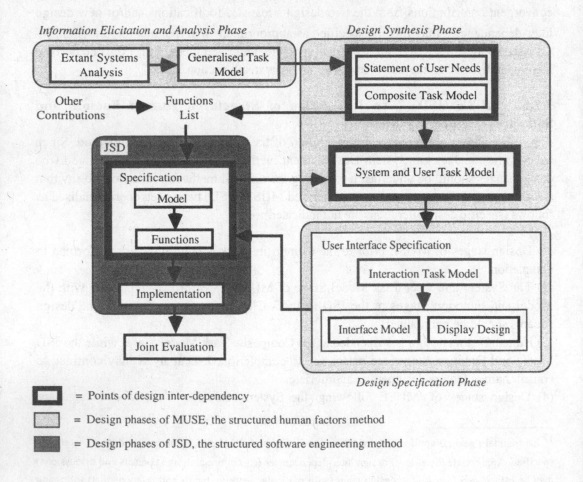

Generally, there are two primary points of design inter-dependencies between MUSE and the Jackson System Development (JSD) method; namely:

(a) between the Model Stage of the JSD method and the Composite Task Model Stage of MUSE;

(b) between the Functions Stage of the JSD method and the System and User Task Model Stage of MUSE.

At the first design inter-dependency, both component methods of MUSE*/JSD are concerned primarily with defining an appropriate scope and design basis for the target system. In particular, the JSD Model is concerned with describing the purpose and subject matter of the target system. The focus of the JSD Model is on what is to be performed by the system, rather than on how work goals may be achieved by the user; i.e. user tasks are excluded from the scope of a JSD Model. Although the design perspectives entailed by JSD modelling and task analysis are different, the derived viewpoints are largely complementary. For instance, although the JSD Model of a library system describes permissible actions on a book rather than librarian tasks, the actions suffered by a book correspond largely to those initiated by a librarian. Consequently, indirect overlaps in information captured by the component methods would occur; e.g. common domain entities and actions such as to 'shelve' a 'book'.

To determine the pool of design information of common interest to be shared, the main concerns of human factors designers and JSD analysts at this design stage should be considered. Specifically, in addressing task and user interface design requirements, human factors designers would be interested in capturing information about the users and the 'real-and-representation' world relationships assumed by the current system. In contrast, JSD analysts would be concerned only with modelling real world entities. Since the human factors information captured at this stage may not be entirely relevant to JSD modelling, the pool of inter-dependent information should, *at a minimum,*[18] be dictated by the needs of JSD analysts.[19] Thus, information associated with the generation of a JSD Model should be shared and agreed at this design inter-dependency point. In other words, human factors designers should take account of the information assumed by JSD analysts at this point of inter-dependency, while converse considerations need not apply. Instead, the information captured by human factors designers at this stage may be deferred by JSD analysts for

---

[18] Wider sharing of human factors design information may be encouraged at this inter-dependency point, e.g. pre-emptive support of design information required at the JSD Functions Stage.

[19] In particular, the JSD Model is not concerned with the user task requirements addressed by human factors products derived at this stage.

accommodation later at the Functions Stage of the method.[20]

To support the derivation of a JSD Model, the following design products of MUSE (originating from the Composite Task Model and Statement of User Needs Stages) should be discussed and agreed with JSD analysts at this inter-dependency point:

(a) Target Statement of User Needs, SUN(y): user problems and task support requirements are addressed by this human factors product (see Figure 5-3). By identifying the key functions to be supported by the target system, the statements provide a means of assessing the scope of a particular JSD Model. In this way, alternative target system boundaries may be investigated.

(b) Target Domain of Design Discourse, DoDD(y): the semantics of the target system are described by this human factors product (see Figure 5-4).

(c) Target Composite Task Model, CTM(y): a conceptual design of the target system is established by this human factors product (see Figure 5-7). In addition, on-line and off-line tasks are demarcated explicitly. Since the model identifies the functions to be supported by the target system, it provides a means of assessing the scope of a particular JSD Model. In this way, alternative target system boundaries may be investigated.

(d) Event table: notable events of the target system are listed in the table to characterise the target system scope (see Figure 5-8).

(e) List of objects and actions (and their attributes): the list characterises the domain of the target system and identifies its ancillary devices (if any).

The result of the discussions is a Functions List, specified collaboratively by human factors designers and JSD analysts. Thus, it represents the 'agreed' scope of target system design. The design information summarised in the List should include the initiating trigger, end result and performance characteristics of task support functions (see Figure 5-9). However, detailed computer functions are usually excluded at this stage.

On the basis of the Functions List, the Target Composite Task Model (CTM(y)) is then updated by human factors designers (as appropriate). Similarly, a JSD Model is derived by JSD analysts. These products are discussed again in another design meeting to confirm

---

[20] This deferral is possible because additional functional support requirements that may be identified later should not affect the JSD model if an appropriate system design scope was defined. In such instances, the additional functions may be accommodated at the Functions Stage of the JSD method. To this end, the Functions List (see later) is incremented, and a design iteration performed to update all human factors products that may be affected.

appropriate adherence to the agreed design scope. Any deviation from the Functions List should be highlighted immediately, so that efficient convergence in design contributions may be ensured from the human factors and software engineering streams of MUSE*/JSD. In this way, the two groups of designers may work independently (until the next inter-dependency point) on design products to be derived at succeeding stages of the method. To conclude, the design information shared at this inter-dependency, is summarised in Figure 7-4.

Figure 7-4: Products of MUSE and the JSD Method Shared at the First Design Inter-Dependency

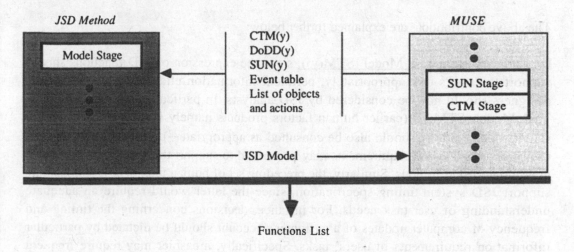

CTM = Composite Task Model   DoDD = Domain of Design Discourse description
JSD = Jackson System Development   SUN = Statement of User Needs
(y) = human factors descriptions of the target system (Y)

A second design inter-dependency occurs between the Functions Stage of the JSD method, and the System and User Task Model Stage of MUSE. This inter-dependency point is important since it is concerned with the following specifications:

(a) human-computer interactions required to perform the on-line task;
(b) appropriate computer functions and messages to support the user's task;
(c) appearance and behaviour of screen displays and their constituent objects.

Since these specifications involve extensive design synthesis and decomposition, the Functions List (defined at the previous inter-dependency) alone would not be specific enough to ensure convergent design extensions, undertaken independently by human factors designers and JSD analysts. Consequently, more specific design constraints have to be established at this stage. In particular, the design information to be shared and agreed comprises the following:

(i) Human factors design information – a Target System Task Model (STM(y)) that describes the cycles of human-computer interaction required by on-line tasks of the target system. The sequence for presenting functional supports may thus be defined.
(ii) JSD design information – specifications of input and output streams, JSD function processes and the input sub-system.[21]

The above contributions are explained further below:

(a) Target System Task Model (STM(y)): since the expression of JSD functions should support the user's task appropriately, pertinent information elicited by human factors designers should now be considered by JSD analysts. In particular, the Target System Task Model (STM(y)) (earlier human factors products namely DoDD(y), SUN(y) and CTM(y) descriptions, should also be consulted as appropriate[22]). Thus, a better view of user problems and task requirements may be derived to support the specification of more appropriate JSD functions. Similarly, the preceding set of human factors descriptions may support JSD system timing specification, since the latter would require an adequate understanding of user task needs. For instance, decisions concerning the timing and frequency of computer updates of a customer's account should be dictated by particular information requirements of users' tasks. Specifically, a cashier may require frequent account updates to support enforcement of withdrawal limits, while a bank clerk may only require daily updates to verify interest computations.
(b) JSD function specifications: the converse contributions in (a) above may apply. In such instances, JSD function specifications may provide confirmation of the completeness of a functional design proposed by human factors designers.

---

[21] Input sub-system specifications contribute later to the design of error and feedback messages (undertaken by human factors designers).

[22] Although the design considerations entailed by the last three human factors products may be deferred by JSD analysts at the first design inter-dependency, their requirements should now be accommodated appropriately.

(c) JSD input and output streams: since JSD input and output streams[23] may indicate information flows across the user interface, they should be discussed with human factors designers. The specification of screen displays and associated constituent objects is thus supported. In return, human factors designers could contribute by specifying the sequence of the information flows, according to the requirements of the interactive task.

(d) JSD input sub-system specifications: since these JSD specifications include the identification of errors and their recovery mechanisms, they should be discussed with human factors designers to support later specifications of error and feedback messages. In this respect, JSD specifications concerning error types (e.g. simple errors and false inputs) and context filters would be particularly relevant.

The products of MUSE and the JSD method to be shared at this design inter-dependency are summarised in Figure 7-5.

Figure 7-5:   Products of MUSE and the JSD Method Shared at the Second Design Inter-Dependency

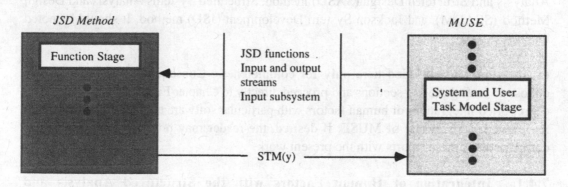

JSD = Jackson System Development   STM = System Task Model
(y) = Human factors descriptions of the target system (Y)

Following discussion and agreement on the above, a common pool of design information is established to support the derivation of a convergent design. Human factors designers may then proceed to work independently at the Design Specification Phase of MUSE. However, close contact with JSD analysts should be maintained as far as possible, to avoid incurring

---

[23] Information flows *between* JSD model and function processes are excluded.

unnecessary design iterations when integrating human factors and software engineering specifications. Thus, human factors design specifications should be communicated to JSD analysts as soon as they are well formed. These specifications may then be integrated appropriately and later implemented according to the original JSD method.

In conclusion, human factors and software engineering design activities of MUSE*/JSD are managed by specifying obligatory contact between designers at two points of design inter-dependency. Although further inter-disciplinary contact points may be specified to meet the requirements of particular organisations and design teams, they are not addressed here to maintain the general applicability of the method. In this context, the present conception of MUSE*/JSD was assessed and potential developments identified. An account of these concerns is presented in Chapter Eight.

7.4. Examples of Other Integration of Human Factors with Structured Software Engineering Methods

In the following sub-sections, attempts by other researchers at integrating human factors with established structured software engineering methods are reviewed; namely Structured Analysis and Structured Design (SASD) method, Structured Systems Analysis and Design Method (SSADM), and Jackson System Development (JSD) method. It should be noted that:

(a) the review is included here only for completeness. Consequently, the reader may choose to omit these sub-sections and proceed directly to Chapter Eight;
(b) reported integrations of human factors with particular software engineering methods are reviewed independently of MUSE. If desired, the reader may refer to Lim (1992) for a comparison of these reports with the present work.

7.4.1. Integration of Human Factors with the Structured Analysis and Structured Design (SASD) Method

Blyth and Hakiel (1988, 1989) undertook this integration in response to commercial in-house requirements to include human factors design (in particular user interface design) in their software engineering method, namely the Structured Analysis and Structured Design (SASD) method. A review of their concerns follows.

As in most structured software engineering methods, a key activity of the SASD method is the derivation of a context diagram termed the Essential System Model. The model defines events to which the system must respond, and specifies data that should flow from the system to the external world (via terminators). Thus, the model determines implicitly the scope of subsequent system analysis and design activities. In this respect, the SASD method (as is the case for most software engineering methods), excludes users from the boundary of the system. Specifically, user requirements are unaddressed by the context diagram since they are considered 'external event generators'. Consequently, the scope of system development is already confined inappropriately, at a very early stage, to the specification of a *computer* system rather than a *human-computer* system (Hakiel and Blyth, 1990a and b). The result of such a limited design scope would be an ineffective system, since user tasks would not be addressed sufficiently. Thus, the functionality and usability provided by the computer system may not be appropriate. To be more specific, the exclusion of users from the Essential System Model leads to an allocation of function[24] that is unsupported by an analysis of the overall performance of the *human-computer* system. Consequently, design considerations pertaining to human-computer interaction tend to be expressed only in terms of event lists and data elements of a context diagram. Thus, interaction specification tends to be machine-centered, since it is subsumed in the design of communicating sub-systems. Furthermore, since system operations are specified in the absence of a task context, appropriate considerations on how human-computer interaction may be supported more effectively are precluded. In particular, design considerations tend towards a premature definition of low-level input and output actions. As a result, the design of the software user interface is confined to the optimisation of individual screen displays.

To avoid these problems, Blyth and Hakiel (1989) emphasised that system design should begin with task analysis. On the basis of such an analysis, design decisions may then be made appropriately concerning the deployment of system resources (organisational and individual level) and the exploitation of new technologies. In other words, early activities of system design should comprise the following:

(a) decomposition of system goals into system tasks;
(b) conceptual definition of a system model;
(c) further decomposition of system tasks to support function allocation;
(d) function allocation and description of user tasks, computer tasks and collaborative tasks;
(e) specification of context diagram terminators and event list.

It was suggested that the above design activities would support the definition of a more appropriate Essential System Model to constrain the scope of system development. In this way, the expected level of user-computer performance is more likely to be realised.

---

[24] Including function allocation between users and/or between users and computers.

To augment these design activities, Blyth and Hakiel (1989) conducted a review of existing literature to derive a conception of how human factors design may be integrated with the SASD method (see Figure 7-6). The conception was then developed into a human factors method comprising eight sequential levels of system design. The design scope and levels of description are detailed below:

(a) Goal and Task levels: detailed analysis of goals, tasks, and function allocation of the system. A set of task models is derived from abstractions of the domain (see Steps 1 to 4 later).
(b) Conceptual level: definition of conceptual objects to be represented at the user interface (see Step 5 later).
(c) Semantic, Syntactic, Lexical, Alphabetic and Physical levels: top-down specification of human-computer interaction.

These levels of design are addressed in a number of steps in Blyth and Hakiel's (1989) method. A step-wise description of their human factors method follows.

Step 1: Analysis of extant systems
(i) Identify functional goals of the target system by consulting the initial statement of requirements.
(ii) Identify existing human-machine systems that share some or all of the target system goals. Real world tasks may then be established for each goal of the target system, by analysing a range of existing systems. Technological equivalence between existing and target systems is not required as the subsequent creation of an abstract task model would remove all device-specific details at the implementation level. Where computer-based support is already in use, both computer and human sub-tasks should be described.

Blyth and Hakiel's (1989) emphasis on analysing a range of existing systems (see (ii) above), may be contrasted with the common practice of focusing only on the current system, i.e. the system used by the client organisation. An account of the rationale for such an emphasis may be found in Lim (1986, 1988d). Generally, a broader analysis of extant systems could support the following:

(a) A wider consideration of design alternatives. Thus, it helps to avoid premature commitment to a design solution (i.e. 'blinkered' design); in particular, the tendency towards excessive replication of the current system.
(b) An earlier assessment of transfer of learning effects (both positive and negative).

Figure 7-6: Schematic Representation of Blyth and Hakiel's (1988) Integration of Human Factors with the SASD Method

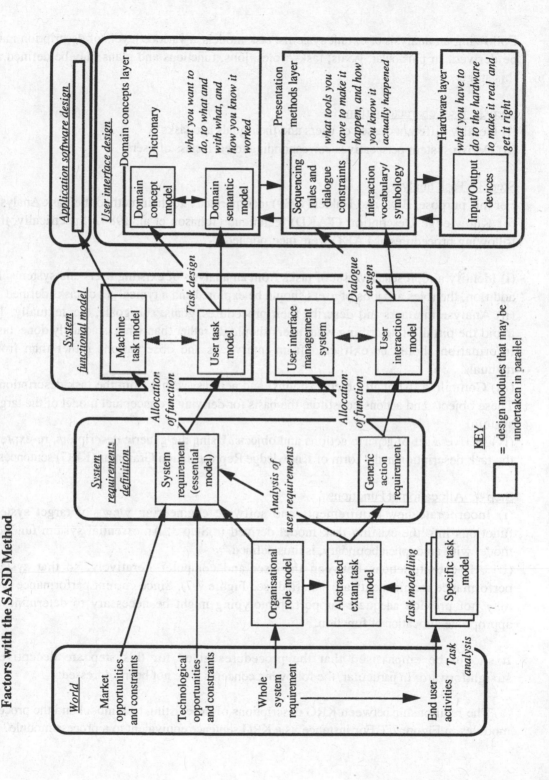

Following an analysis of extant systems, task models at various levels of description may be derived. In particular, goals, tasks, roles, jobs, functions and plans may be defined at this stage.

Step 2: User characterisation
(i) Identify different classes of users and their goals and tasks.
(ii) Derive system perspectives corresponding to each class of users.

Step 3: Task analysis
For this purpose, Blyth and Hakiel (1989) incorporated into their method the Task Analysis for Knowledge Description (TAKD) technique (Johnson et al. 1984). Specifically, the following procedures of TAKD were incorporated:

(i) Identify a representative set of tasks from an analysis of existing users and systems. In addition, the roles and jobs of users should be explored and a typical set of tasks defined.
(ii) Analyse the tasks and describe their procedures, goals, sub-goals, etc. textually. To avoid the pitfall of describing what users should do rather than what is actually done, task information should be extracted from interviews and observations rather than from manuals.
(iii) Compile a list of all objects (nouns) and actions (verbs) from the task descriptions. These objects and actions constitute the basis for deriving a conceptual model of the target system.
(iv) Derive a set of generic actions and objects. Using the generic descriptors, re-express the task description in the form of Knowledge Representation Grammar (KRG) sentences.

Step 4: Allocation of Functions
(i) Incorporate new requirements and software engineering views of target system functions into the existing task model derived in Step 3. An essential system function model with an explicit boundary, is thus defined.
(ii) Allocate functions between the user and computer iteratively, so that system performance requirements are satisfied (see Figure 7-7). Since current performance data may not provide adequate support, prototyping might be necessary to determine an appropriate allocation of function.

It should be emphasised that the procedures given for this step are deceptively straightforward. In particular, the following concerns have not been addressed:

(a) The relationship between KRG descriptions of the existing task model and the process modules in Figure 7-7. For instance, is a KRG sentence equivalent to a process module?

Figure 7-7: Allocation of Function using a System Function Model (Hakiel and Blyth, 1990a)

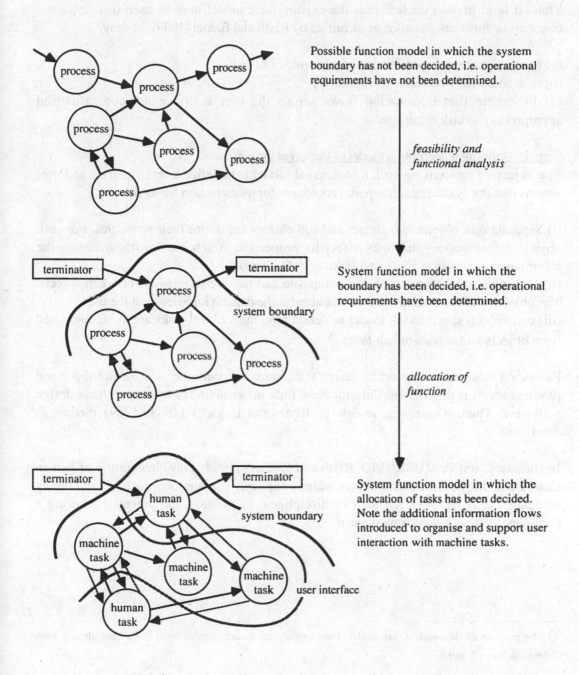

Possible function model in which the system boundary has not been decided, i.e. operational requirements have not been determined.

feasibility and functional analysis

System function model in which the boundary has been decided, i.e. operational requirements have been determined.

allocation of function

System function model in which the allocation of tasks has been decided. Note the additional information flows introduced to organise and support user interaction with machine tasks.

(b) How individual KRG sentences may be organised into task structures and user roles.

Thus, it is at present unclear how the existing task model may be used to resolve the concerns of function allocation as identified by Blyth and Hakiel (1989); namely:

(a) to ensure coherent specification of jobs, roles and tasks;
(b) to account for workloads appropriately;
(c) to ensure that information flows across the user interface are contextualised appropriately to task requirements.

Step 5: Defining a conceptual model of the target system
The objective for deriving such a conceptual model is to define a set of objects and user actions that the system must support. Procedures for its derivation are as follows:

(i) Separate task objects into classes and sub-classes and define their properties. For each object, define actions that may affect its properties. A scheme for documenting the information is shown in Blyth and Hakiel (1988, 1989).
(ii) Describe on a network diagram, composite and taxonomic relations between objects. The objective of the description is to characterise the domain knowledge of the user.
(iii) construct a specific task model to define how higher level tasks are to be composed from objects and actions of sub-tasks.[25]

Following this step, user interface design at the semantic, syntactic, lexical, alphabetic and physical levels is undertaken. Unfortunately, little information is available on these design activities. Thus, a complete review of Blyth and Hakiel's (1988, 1989) method is precluded.

In summary, unlike MUSE*/JSD, Blyth and Hakiel's (1988, 1989) integration of human factors with the SASD method did not address explicitly the inter-dependencies and timing of design activities between the two disciplines. In addition, the potential of using a common notation was not investigated.

---

[25] The purpose of the specific task model is not entirely clear, since higher level tasks have already been defined in Steps 3 and 4.

7.4.2. Integration of Human Factors with the Structured Systems Analysis and Design Method (SSADM)

This project, undertaken by HUSAT (Loughborough), aims to extend the version of SSADM adopted by the Department of Health and Social Security (DHSS).[26] The objective was to integrate human factors with SSADM and PROMPT (Project Resource Organisation Management Technique).

HUSAT's human factors method assumes a participative design approach and is to be used by designers with little or no training in the discipline.[27] Four areas of human factors design were targeted by the client for incorporation into SSADM; namely user analysis, job design, task allocation (job stream charts) and prototyping. Thus, the project involved integrating activities and procedures of specific areas of human factors design with SSADM (see Figure 7-8).

Since the scope of human factors design addressed by the method is incomplete and disparate, it is unclear how its contribution to system development should be realised. For instance, it is difficult to see how high-level descriptions of task allocation and job design prescribed by the method (see Figure 7-8, right-hand part), may be decomposed to support dialogue design/user interface specification. Further clarification is not possible since few reports on the project have been published and the method is not available to the public.

Specifically, brief reports on only two of the areas of human factors design addressed have been published; namely user analysis and task allocation. Consequently, a complete review of the method is precluded. Instead, a review of the two design concerns reported by Damodaran et al. (1988) and Ip et al. (1990) follows.

User analysis involves three groups of design activities, namely user classification; job and task characterisation; and work role analysis. The design checklists, questionnaires, observations sheets and description summary forms that support user analysis are shown in Figure 7-9. Unfortunately, details of the checklists and forms have not been reported.

---

[26] The present review is based on a seminar presentation (Damodaran, 1988) and two conference papers (Damodaran et al. 1988; Ip et al. 1990).

[27] Thus, the method includes reference manuals on selected areas of human factors design. Since the manuals are not generally available, further discussion is not possible.

Figure 7-8:   Integration of Human Factors with SSADM (Damodaran et al. 1988)

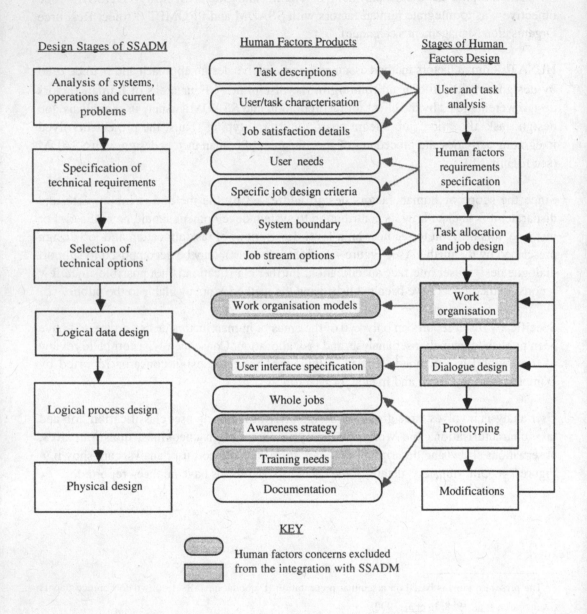

Design Stages of SSADM   Human Factors Products   Stages of Human Factors Design

Analysis of systems, operations and current problems

Task descriptions

User/task characterisation

Job satisfaction details

User and task analysis

Specification of technical requirements

User needs

Specific job design criteria

Human factors requirements specification

Selection of technical options

System boundary

Job stream options

Task allocation and job design

Logical data design

Work organisation models

Work organisation

User interface specification

Dialogue design

Logical process design

Whole jobs

Awareness strategy

Training needs

Prototyping

Physical design

Documentation

Modifications

KEY

Human factors concerns excluded from the integration with SSADM

Figure 7-9: Checklists, Questionnaires, Observation Sheets and Summary Forms that Support User Analysis (Damodaran et al. 1988)

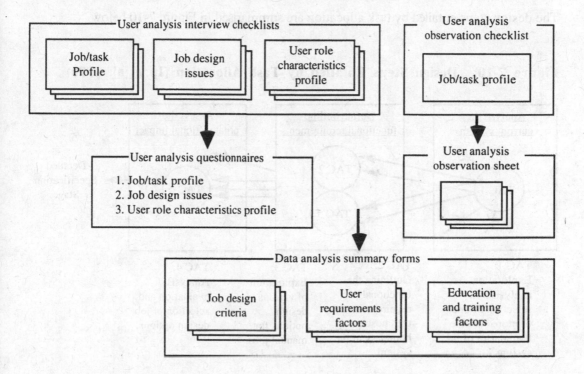

The second area of human factors design reported to be incorporated into SSADM, involves the allocation of tasks. In particular, job stream charts were developed to support the following concerns of requirements specification:

(a) Defining the boundary of the computer system. The definition entails an exploration of alternative allocations of tasks between the human and machine, and the implications for users' jobs.

(b) Defining the functional requirements of design alternatives considered in (a) above. In this way, an appropriate allocation of tasks may be identified and the boundary of the computer system defined. These design decisions precede the Logical Design Stage of SSADM.

(c) Communication of design alternatives to various groups of users. In particular, alternative job roles are discussed with users and their feedback incorporated into the design. The integration and evaluation of on-line and manual job designs are thus facilitated. User requirements of promising designs may then be specified to constrain the development of an automated system.

The design steps entailed by task allocation are summarised in Figure 7-10 below.

Figure 7-10:   Design Steps Entailed by Task Allocation (Ip et al. 1990)

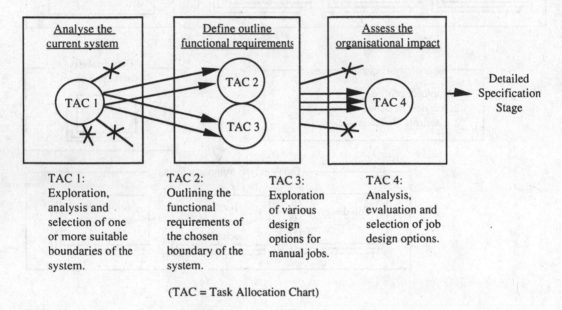

TAC 1:
Exploration, analysis and selection of one or more suitable boundaries of the system.

TAC 2:
Outlining the functional requirements of the chosen boundary of the system.

TAC 3:
Exploration of various design options for manual jobs.

TAC 4:
Analysis, evaluation and selection of job design options.

(TAC = Task Allocation Chart)

The task allocation charts used to describe alternative job designs are shown in Figure 7-11. The notation was chosen over data flow and entity life history diagrams, since it was considered to be better for eliciting user feedback. In particular, task allocation charts:

(a) provide visual representations of the procedures for each task function;
(b) can be used to link screen format designs to a textual description of the functions.

The charts were thus found to be particularly useful for highlighting relationships between users' jobs and dialogue and screen designs. However, several problems with the notation were also reported by Ip et al (1990), namely:

(a) The construction of task allocation charts is cumbersome. Specifically, the drawings were found to be time-consuming and labour intensive. In addition, an inordinately large volume of paper is required to produce a set of charts for each level of task description, e.g. job and work organisation levels.

(b) Designers could not identify the relationship between chart descriptions and the design outputs of SSADM. In retrospect, Ip et al. (1990) reported that the charts may be linked to events associated with one or more entities of SSADM. For instance, particular user task events could be related to items in the Events Catalogue of SSADM.

In summary, unlike MUSE*/JSD, HUSAT's integration of human factors with SSADM did not address explicitly the inter-dependencies and timing of design activities between the two disciplines. In addition, the scope of human factors design addressed is incomplete. Consequently, it remains unclear how human factors design stages and activities are located within SSADM. In this respect, there is little evidence from the information available, to suggest that a structured human factors method was developed prior to its integration with SSADM. Instead, it appears that HUSAT's brief was to assign a limited set of disparate human factors techniques against the framework of SSADM. In the absence of detailed publications, a more comprehensive review of the integration of human factors with SSADM is not possible.

Figure 7-11:   Task Allocation Charts (Ip et al. 1990)

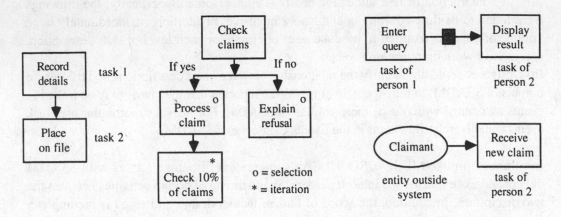

Job design option 1

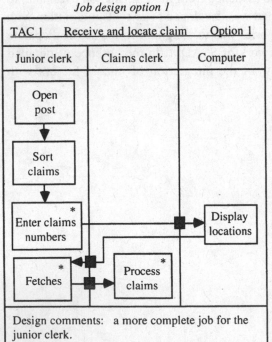

Job design option 2

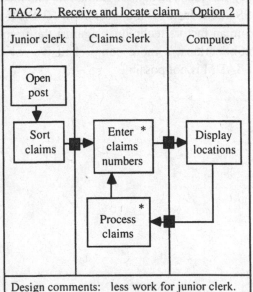

7.4.3. Integration of Human Factors with the Jackson System Development (JSD) Method

Two other attempts at integrating human factors with the Jackson System Development (JSD) method have been reported by Carver et al. (1987) and Sutcliffe (1988a and b). Their contributions are reviewed in turn.

Sutcliffe's work (1988a) is concerned with the recruitment of existing human factors techniques to extend the scope of the JSD method. In particular, techniques for task analysis and the specification of user-computer dialogue were recruited and located appropriately against the design stages of the JSD method.

In respect of task analysis, three enhancements were proposed to facilitate its integration with the JSD method. Firstly, it was suggested that the initial task description derived should be subjected to complexity analysis. It was argued that such an analysis could support the following:

(a) allocation of tasks into on-line, off-line and automated components. Appropriate computer functions and displays may then be designed to support the on-line tasks;

(b) design analysis and modification, e.g. an unacceptably complex task may indicate the need for further decomposition into smaller and simpler sub-tasks;

(c) user-task match, i.e. appropriate matching of user skills to complex tasks;

(d) job design, e.g. specifying appropriate variations in task complexity for a particular work duration.

To this end, Sutcliffe (1988a) investigated the applicability of the Cognitive Complexity Theory (CCT). Since CCT as it stands was considered too complicated for application by designers, a simplified version was developed and tested in a trial involving students. The results were inconclusive, since the benefits of a complexity analysis may not be realised for the following reasons:

(a) the complexity metrics may be too difficult to interpret and apply despite the use of a simplified version of CCT;

(b) the complexity assessments derived may not be accurate. In particular, the assumption that 'complexity units' assigned subjectively may be summated to determine the overall complexity of a task remains to be demonstrated;

(c) it may be difficult to ascertain the design implications of a particular assessment. Specifically, the interpretation of assessment results depends largely on expert judgement.

Secondly, Sutcliffe suggested that the outputs of task analysis should be intersected explicitly with the JSD model. In particular, user task activities may be linked to the JSD model by extending the scope of JSD interactive functions. A similar suggestion was made by Carver et al. (1987), see later.

Thirdly, it was suggested that the JSD structured diagram notation should be used for task description. By using a common language, potential problems in design communication may be avoided. A similar suggestion was also made by Carver et al. (1987), see later. When using the structured diagram notation for task description, Sutcliffe (1988a) observed that the occurrences of a selection construct correspond generally to logical break-points in the execution of a task. In other words, selections may be regarded as indicators of task closures, which should then be accommodated appropriately during display design. Unfortunately, an illustration of how task closures should be addressed was not provided.

Sutcliffe's (1988a) extension of the JSD method also includes four proposals on how the user-computer dialogue may be specified, namely the following:

(a) Actions of JSD entities should map onto actions on user interface objects since the JSD model is essentially an object and event model. For instance, in a library system, actions carried forward from the JSD model to the user interface may include 'Acquire' and 'Archive' actions on the entity 'Book'. This suggestion may be compared with Carver et al. (1987), who reported that JSD entity actions do not necessarily show a one-to-one relationship with actions of user interface objects.

(b) The design of the user-computer dialogue should be based on the functional supports required by the user's task. Unfortunately, a comprehensive illustration of how dialogue design may be constrained in this way was not provided.

(c) JSD filter processes constitute a framework for user interface design (Sutcliffe, 1988b). In particular, it was suggested that specifications of the user-computer dialogue may be derived by extending the JSD input sub-system. It was argued that the latter specifications relate user inputs and associated errors to the context established by a JSD model. For instance, dialogue control requirements for error recovery, prompts and feedback messages may be described as another simple filter process. Although such descriptions would be consistent with the JSD method, components of the user's interactive task would be scattered across various filter processes. Since a segmentation of the user's interactive task would destroy its coherence, Sutcliffe (1988b) suggested that inputs of filter processes should be grouped into a set of inputs consistent with a user's view. Unfortunately, an example of this grouping of inputs was not provided to illustrate his suggestion. Such an example may be found in Walsh et al. (1989), where a similar proposal was made. Specifically, it was proposed that the timing of filter process inputs should be specified in a separate JSD structured diagram, to provide a coherent user-centered view of the interactive

task. The elicitation of user feedback is thus facilitated.
(d) JSD structured diagram notation should be used to describe user interface objects, e.g. to relate object actions and roles.

In conclusion, Sutcliffe's work did not include an independent account of the existing scope and process of human factors design. The limited set of human factors methods examined were those targeted directly for incorporation into the JSD method. Thus, a reasonably complete structured human factors method was not developed. Consequently, his proposals are restricted solely to the JSD method. Notwithstanding these limitations, a more comprehensive illustration of his proposals is also needed.

A second group of workers, namely Carver et al. (1987), also reported an attempt at integrating human factors with the JSD method. Their attempt was motivated by observations derived from earlier system development projects, namely:

(a) inadequately specified systems were extremely difficult to modify;
(b) significant benefits would accrue from earlier and closer collaboration between human factors designers and software engineers. The problems observed in (a) may thus be avoided.

They concluded from the observations that the JSD method could be enhanced as follows:

(a) its usability may be improved by making existing procedures more explicit;
(b) its scope should be extended to include the specification of the user-computer interface;
(c) its user interface specifications should ideally be documented in machine readable form.

To improve existing procedures of the JSD method, the following proposals were made:

(i) The identification of entities and actions by extracting nouns and verbs from interview transcripts should be modified. Carver et al. (1987) noted that the derivation of separate lists of nouns and verbs resulted in the loss of contextual information, e.g. particular noun-verb relationships. To address the problem, they proposed that verbs, subjects and objects should be collated with respect to a list of events.
(ii) An explicit requirements statement should be made prior to the modelling stage of the JSD method. Specifically, information elicited from interviews and existing documentation should be collated to identify user needs; hardware constraints; and the facilities to be supported by the system.

In respect of extensions of the existing scope of the JSD method, Carver et al. (1987)

considered briefly the inclusion of project selection, cost and benefit analysis, project planning and management, and user interface specification. Owing to resource constraints, methodological extensions relating to user interface specification only were addressed. Two extensions were suggested:

(i) JSD specifications derived at the modelling stage, should map explicitly onto human-computer interactions. In particular, since the input sub-system interposes between the real world and the JSD model, its specifications may be used as a basis for user interface design. Thus, the design may be conceptualised as comprising the specification of a further set of interpositions, performed by intermediaries of the system; namely entities of the computer display and the user (see Figure 7-12). Interactive facilities that support the processes and connections with the display entities may then be specified at the information function stage. On-line interactions with the facilities are thus linked to specific actions of the JSD model (the link may not be one-to-one). Displays may then be designed to support the interactions appropriately.

Figure 7-12:   JSD Specifications Extended to Include the Human-Computer Interface

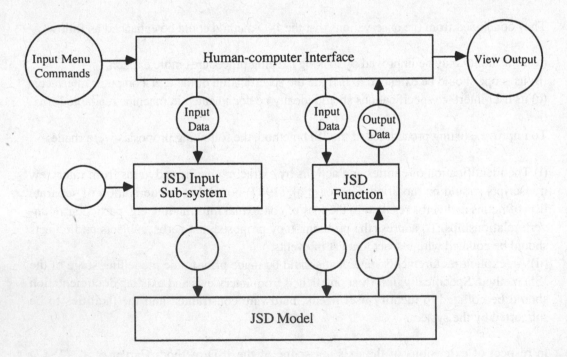

(ii) Task and goal analysis should be recruited to the JSD method to clarify the purpose of the computer system and the functional support it should provide to the user.

To address the concerns of user interface design, Carver and Cameron (1987) suggested the following steps for the extended JSD method:

(1) derive the JSD model as per the original method;
(2) specify functions in the network phase. A basic set of inputs (one for each action and enquiry) is thus defined;
(3) associate the inputs with users' tasks;
(4) define the interactions required for each input and express them as a set of actions on the user interface;
(5) introduce further functions to support the required interactions and users' task;
(6) specify off-line events to complete the description of the users' task.

To document user interface specifications in a machine readable form, Carver et al. (1987) had to address the inadequacies of an earlier version of the JSD structured diagram notation. Specifically, it was observed that the notation could not describe events that are ordered unpredictably; e.g. multiple events that occur haphazardly; and multiple tasks with no pattern of control between the ongoing streams. These inadequacies were resolved later by extending the constructs of the JSD notation to include concurrency and backtracking. With these extensions, Carver et al. (1987) reported that the notation is a powerful language that could be used to support the specification of tasks and the user-computer dialogue. In addition, the human factors specifications would be facilitated by computer-based tools that had already been developed to support the notation, e.g. Program Development Facility (PDF). It was also reported that MacDraw™ and FileVision™ may be recruited to support a complete documentation of the user interface specifications in machine readable form.

To summarise, the work of Carver et al. (1987) is essentially a feasibility study aimed at determining the basic requirements for a comprehensive integration of human factors with the JSD method. In particular, they identified important intersections between JSD and human factors design, and the potential of using JSD structured diagrams as a common notation to facilitate inter-disciplinary design communications. However, aside from identifying high-level design steps, the development of a structured human factors method was not addressed.

The above account completes a review of the integration of human factors with structured software engineering methods. In the concluding chapter, the methods developed by the authors (namely MUSE and MUSE*/JSD) are assessed. Potential areas for future research and development may then be identified and reviewed.

PART FIVE:

SYNOPSIS

8
Assessment and Future Development of MUSE and MUSE*/JSD

The old order changeth, yielding place to new.....
> Lord Tennyson, 1809–1892

Knowledge advances by steps, and not by leaps.
> Lord Macaulay, 1828, **Edinburgh Review**

The following concerns are addressed in this concluding chapter:

(a) An assessment of the development of MUSE and MUSE*/JSD. For instance, have appropriate case-studies and tests been used to support the development and demonstration of the methods?
(b) An assessment of the methodological characteristics of MUSE and MUSE*/JSD. For instance, is their scope of human factors design appropriate? Are requirements identified in Chapters One and Two satisfied by MUSE and MUSE*/JSD, and have they any limitations?
(d) A review of potential developments of MUSE and MUSE*/JSD. For instance, how could the methods be enhanced with respect to (a), (b) and (c) above? What computer-based tools could be developed to support the methods; and should declarative human factors knowledge be collated and integrated with them to facilitate method application at each stage of system development?

These concerns are discussed in turn in the sub-sections that follow.

8.1. An Overview and Assessment of Method Development Activities of MUSE and MUSE*/JSD

Generally, activities for developing the methods were implemented as planned, e.g. literature surveys; specification and test of method conceptions; case-study selection, planning and familiarisation; etc. An assessment of how key concerns of method development were addressed is discussed below:

(1) Case-study selection. It was clear that the number of case-studies undertaken specifically to develop and test the methods would be limited by the resources available.[1] Thus, considerable care was devoted to the planning and selection of appropriate case-studies for developing and testing the methods. For instance, the implications of selecting particular case-studies for the latter purpose were considered carefully so as to support the interpretation and generalisation of test results across various classes of systems and design scenarios. Thus, appropriate capabilities are ensured in the method being developed. Specifically, the following criteria were applied during case-study selection:

(a) size and complexity of case-study systems (increments should be made from small to large systems, from well-defined to ill-defined systems);
(b) domain of application of case-study systems (a range of domains should be addressed, e.g. a Recreation Booking System and Digital Network Security Management System);
(c) design scenarios presented by case-study systems (both variant and new/novel design scenarios should be addressed, e.g. by varying the system development context and the familiarity of the designer with the domain of application);[2]
(d) user interface styles required by case-study systems (both WIMP/GUI and command-line interfaces should be addressed).

Appropriate case-study systems that satisfy the above criteria were thus selected to support each stage of method development. For instance, to facilitate the management of complexity, small and well-defined case-study systems were used during the early stages of method development. The reader is referred to Lim et al. (1990a and b) and Lim (1992) for a more detailed account of the relationship between case-study selection and the plan and strategies used to support method development;

(2) Case-study tests. Generally, the objective of the tests was to demonstrate the capability of the method for supporting human factors contribution throughout the system

---

[1] In addition, it is assumed here that a method should be developed initially by using a 'dedicated' set of case-studies. In this way, methodological concerns may be addressed more intensively. Following the derivation of an acceptable version, the method may then evolve progressively in the long term, through successive applications in system development projects.

[2] A consistent definition of what constitutes 'novel design' was not found in the literature. Thus, novel design was interpreted loosely to involve an ill-defined domain, and/or an entirely new product, and/or the development of any product that is unfamiliar to the designer.

development cycle. It should be noted that the objective excluded field tests, which validate the efficacy of the method for ensuring superior system designs[3] (see Chapter Seven for an account of the measures taken to address these concerns). It suffices to say here that the measures were implemented satisfactorily during method development. Thus, future work should include field studies to assess the acceptability and efficacy of the method with respect to the following:

(a) social implications of introducing the method (if any), e.g. potential impact on the work relationships and practices of individual designers and a design team (for both software engineers and human factors designers);
(b) the costs and benefits (both short and long term) of method application. In particular, cost-benefit data for 'real world' projects should be collated and analysed.

The results of such studies would support appropriate enhancements of the method to improve its uptake.

With the exception of field studies, case-study tests applied during method development may be categorised generally into two classes of assessment, namely:

(a) Functionality assessment. This class of assessment is concerned with determining the pertinence of the design support provided by a particular method. The assessment entails an examination of how well the designer's task (e.g. design management, reasoning, documentation, etc.) is supported by the design scope, process and notation defined at each stage of the method. For an integrated structured software engineering and human factors method (e.g. MUSE*/JSD), the assessment would include an examination of the design inter-dependencies specified by the method. Specifically, the design inter-dependencies should be assessed on how appropriate and complete they are for supporting collaborative design.
(b) Usability assessment. This class of assessment is concerned with determining the cost of applying a particular method. An extended assessment may include opportunity costs to account for benefits foregone by adopting a particular method over an alternative design approach, e.g. in choosing structured methods over rapid prototyping. Thus, usability assessment provides a gauge of the user's perception of the cost-benefit ratio or utility of a method. For instance, the benefits of using a method may be compared with the effort required to learn the method (i.e. its learnability), and with the need to change current work practices (i.e. its acceptability). The assessment may also indicate a method's capacity for

---

[3] It is commonly acknowledged that a method alone cannot guarantee the derivation of a superior design.

accommodating the requirements of different users, design scenarios and project characteristics, i.e. an indication of its flexibility and tailorability.

Since these characteristics are important determinants of the uptake of a method, they were considered a basic part of method development. However, in view of the limited resources available and the absence of a structured human factors method, functionality assessment was given greater priority during the development of MUSE and MUSE*/JSD. Specifically, greater effort and attention had to be directed at specifying and testing the 'functionality' of a design method using case-studies; while 'usability' concerns were accommodated largely by specifying alternative expressions of the method. For instance, to accommodate:

(a) learnability and acceptability concerns – existing methods were recruited and incorporated into MUSE to maximise a positive transfer of learning and the JSD method (i.e. the chosen structured software engineering method) was maintained largely unchanged in its integration with MUSE;
(b) tailorability and flexibility concerns – a flexible range and level of extant system analysis was built into MUSE; more than one level of description of MUSE was specified to facilitate various degrees of method application.

Unfortunately, extensive usability assessments were precluded during method development, since the resources required to organise and train designers in the use of the methods were not available. However, informal observations on the learnability of MUSE were generally positive (see Sub-section 8.2).

In summary, the development activities of MUSE and MUSE*/JSD were completed as planned. Assessments of the functionality and usability of the methods were positive. However, it is expected that the methods could be improved further by conducting field studies and more extensive case-study tests on the design inter-dependencies. These studies and tests have been proposed for inclusion in European research initiatives (ESSI and ESPRIT).

8.2. An Assessment of MUSE and MUSE*/JSD

In Part Three, a structured human factors method, namely MUSE, was described in detail as follows:

(a) its stage-wise design scope was described in terms of a set of products;
(b) its stage-wise design process was described in terms of a set of procedures, rules of thumb and design inter-dependencies;

(c) its stage-wise design notation was described in terms of a set of documentation schemes.

On the basis of these explicitly defined methodological characteristics, MUSE was integrated with the JSD method (a structured software engineering method) to derive an inter-disciplinary method, termed MUSE*/JSD. Case-study assessments of MUSE and MUSE*/JSD[4] indicated that the requirements of method development and integration were generally satisfied. In particular, the case-studies were used to support the following assessments:

(I) The adequacy of MUSE as a solution to existing problems of human factors contribution to system development; e.g. the 'too-little-too-late' problem of human factors input, encroachment of resources for human factors design due either to poor project planning or its exclusion from the design agenda, etc. (see Chapters One and Two). Specifically, the objective was to assess the limitations of the method and the extent to which it alleviated the problems of human factors input.

(II) The potential of MUSE relative to other human factors methods. The objective was to compare the design support provided by MUSE (as a structured human factors method) and other existing (non-structured) human factors methods.

(III) The potential of MUSE*/JSD relative to other integrated methods. Specifically, its effectiveness in supporting inter-disciplinary design collaboration was addressed, and the appropriateness of its integration was compared with other integrated methods; e.g. those proposed by Blyth and Hakiel (1989), etc.

(IV) The adequacy of the methodological characteristics of MUSE and MUSE*/JSD relative to the requirements of a structured and an integrated method respectively. Specifically, the methods were assessed to determine how appropriate and well defined their stage-wise design scope, process and notation were. Such assessments map onto the functionality and usability assessments of a method.

It should be noted that the above assessments may intersect one another, i.e. they are not mutually exclusive. For instance, the assessments in (III) above may involve a composite of the assessments in (I), (II) and (IV). To clarify these relationships further, a detailed account of each of the assessments follows.

---

[4] Case-study assessments were directed only at the MUSE* component of the integrated method (its design inter-dependencies in particular), since the JSD method remains essentially unchanged.

8.2.1   Adequacy of MUSE as a Solution to Existing Problems of Human Factors Contribution to System Development

In this respect, the results of case-study assessments were generally positive. In particular, its structured and comprehensive coverage of system design supports a more explicit and complete account of human factors contributions throughout the system development cycle. Since the methodological characteristics of MUSE are well defined, the identification of appropriate design inter-dependencies between human factors and software engineering design was facilitated. Thus, by adhering to the design inter-dependencies, human factors contributions could be made timely and contextually relevant to software engineering concerns at each stage of system development. Thus, a greater uptake of human factors contributions may be expected.

In addition to the above case-study assessments undertaken during method development, the utility of MUSE was also exemplified in a human factors evaluation of a commercial system developed by a third party using a rapid prototyping approach. Specifically, post hoc observations revealed that important problems with the user interface design could have been avoided by the application of MUSE (see Lim, 1991). The assertions were supported by a demonstration of how and when the design problems would have been identified and addressed, had MUSE been applied. Nevertheless, it should be emphasised that the evidence is only circumstantial, since controlled studies were not conducted. Thus, such studies and field trials should be included in future work on the method. Other limitations of MUSE are discussed at the end of this sub-section.

8.2.2   Potential of MUSE Relative to Other Human Factors Methods

In this respect, it was observed in Chapters One and Two that existing human factors methods provide only a narrow and implicit coverage of the system development cycle. In contrast, MUSE provides an explicit account of system development concerns spanning user requirements to display design (see Chapters Three to Six). Specifically, the well-defined design scope, process and notation of MUSE represents a significant enhancement of the system development support provided by existing human factors methods. In addition, since MUSE provides a comprehensive coverage of the system development cycle, problems associated with the identification and application of an appropriate set of individual human factors methods are avoided.[5] Further benefits that accrue from the structured characteristics of MUSE have been indicated in (I) above, where its integration

---

[5] Owing to the uncontrolled proliferation of disparate human factors methods of narrow design scope, the recruitment of an appropriate set of methods to support the system development cycle has now become a major problem (see Lim and Long, 1992).

with the JSD method is discussed.

8.2.3 Potential of MUSE*/JSD Relative to Other Integrated Methods

For these assessments, MUSE*/JSD was compared with the reported integration of human factors with other structured software engineering methods (see Chapter Seven). Since all the integrated methods have been developed recently, and are used largely by the organisation that developed the method, a survey of users across the methods would not be possible. Thus, as an interim assessment, the integrated methods reviewed in Chapter Seven were compared and rated subjectively by the present authors with respect to the following:

(a) The design scope, process, procedures and notation of the different integrated methods. Essentially, the subjective assessment involves rating the explicitness and completeness of the design support provided by the human factors component of the integrated method. This inference follows since the structured software engineering components of the integrated methods remain largely unchanged.
(b) The support for inter-disciplinary design collaboration provided by the different integrated methods. In particular, the integrated methods were assessed on the extent of their exploitation of a common design notation and on whether design inter-dependencies have been specified.

Since the above assessment supports only a very crude comparison of the integrated methods, the ratings assigned to (a) and (b) were not weighted in any way; i.e. concerns represented by (a) and (b) were assumed to be equally important. The results of the subjective assessment indicated MUSE*/JSD to be better developed than other reported integration of human factors with structured software engineering methods. The outcome may be expected for the following reasons:

(1) The development of MUSE*/JSD benefited from earlier work on methodological integration. Thus, lessons from preceding work were assimilated to avoid similar pitfalls, e.g. the need to define explicit human factors inputs and products for each design stage.
(2) Unlike MUSE*/JSD, some of the other attempts at methodological integration were not concerned with the development of a structured human factors method. Instead, disparate human factors concerns were simply located against particular design stages of the structured software engineering method.
(3) Some of the other attempts at methodological integration were 'incidental'. In other words, the integrated method was developed indirectly either by inferences drawn from previous experience, or as a minor part of a commercial system development project. Since the resources would be rather limited in such instances, the development and integration of

a comprehensive structured human factors method would be precluded. In contrast, seven person-years were allocated specifically for the development of MUSE and MUSE*/JSD.

(4) Some of the other attempts at methodological integration recruited early outputs from the development of MUSE and MUSE*/JSD. Since then, the recruited outputs have been developed further or superseded.

(5) Unlike MUSE*/JSD, most of the other attempts at methodological integration did not include the specification of inter-dependencies between human factors and software engineering design. These specifications may have been precluded, since an acceptably structured human factors method was not developed in most cases. An assessment of the design inter-dependencies specified by MUSE*/JSD, is reported later in this sub-section.

8.2.4 Adequacy of MUSE as a Structured Human Factors Method, and MUSE*/JSD as an Integrated Method

For these assessments, the functionality and usability of MUSE and MUSE*/JSD were examined. An account of these assessments follows.

<u>(I) Functionality Assessment of MUSE and MUSE*/JSD</u>

To support functionality assessments, various case-studies were undertaken to affirm the satisfaction of basic requirements of a structured and integrated method. These requirements may be considered to comprise the following:

(a) A reasonably complete coverage of the scope of system development. In particular, the scope of human factors design addressed by the products of MUSE was assessed.

(b) An appropriately operationalised process of human factors design. Specifically, the design process of MUSE was examined at two levels of description. Firstly, its design stages were assessed to determine whether design activities have been grouped coherently, ordered logically, organised manageably and specified completely. Secondly, the design procedures of MUSE were assessed on their explicitness and completeness for supporting human factors specification by the targeted user of the method.

(c) An adequately powerful set of design notations. Specifically, the objective was to ascertain how well the requirements for comprehensive and unambiguous human factors descriptions were supported by the design notations and documentation schemes of the method. To a lesser extent, the notations were assessed on their appropriateness for facilitating design communication among human factors designers, software engineers and end-users.[6]

---

[6] The results of such assessments have already been reported to be positive (see Chapter Seven, Sub-section 7.3.2).

(d) An appropriately defined set of design inter-dependencies. Essentially, MUSE*/JSD was examined during case-study tests to determine whether intersections in system design concerns addressed by the disciplines have been identified correctly and completely. On determining the latter to be true, design inter-dependencies specified by MUSE*/JSD were then assessed to ascertain their adequacy for supporting effective inter-disciplinary design collaboration. In particular, human factors and software engineering design specifications should converge (efficiently) without incurring unnecessary design iterations.

It may be inferred from the above that concerns (a) to (c) address the development of MUSE as a structured human factors method; while concern (d) addresses the development and subsequent integration of MUSE with the JSD method. The results for the two groups of assessments were generally positive. These are discussed in greater detail below.

Functionality Assessment of MUSE

During the early stages in the development of MUSE, it was observed that the scope of human factors design to be addressed was rather wide. Since the scope that could be addressed during method development was limited by the resources available, a set of 'key' human factors concerns was identified by accounting for the following:

(i) The current state of design knowledge with respect to a particular human factors concern. Specifically, design concerns that were already well established and supported were assigned a low or zero priority, e.g. late human factors evaluation.

(ii) The completeness and coherence of a selected set of concerns with respect to the logical flow of human factors design. Owing to resource limitations, it was not possible to address in equal detail each of the design concerns in the selected set. Thus, some of the design concerns to be addressed at particular stages in MUSE could only be indicated (breadth-wise support); while other design concerns had been detailed explicitly (in-depth support).

(iii) The resources required to address a particular design concern. To avoid jeopardising other requirements of method development, design concerns that require extensive resources were not addressed in detail.

(iv) The impact of accounting for a particular design concern on existing problems of human factors contribution, i.e. the solution potential of a design concern. Since human factors contributions at early stages of system development were most important and yet addressed poorly (see Chapter One), requirements analysis and specification; task analysis and specification; and user interface specification, were considered to be particularly relevant.

(v) The impact of accounting for a particular design concern on the quality of the developed system. This consideration was rather contentious since design improvements could not be attributed unequivocally to the accommodation of particular human factors concerns. Thus, the consideration was only used indirectly to support (i), (ii) and (iv) above.

(vi) The human factors design support required by the structured software engineering method chosen for integration. In particular, human factors concerns that were considered relevant to the JSD method were already included in the design scope addressed by MUSE (see Chapter Seven).

Having established the above context, assessments of the scope, process and notation of MUSE may now be reviewed.

First, an in-depth address of user requirements analysis and specification was precluded since extensive resources would be involved. Instead, its component concerns, namely user requirements elicitation, analysis and specification, were addressed as follows:

(i) Existing 'off-the-shelf' techniques for requirements elicitation were recruited to the method since they were already well developed. To support the recruitment of an appropriate set of techniques, the following pre-requisites were addressed:

(a) location of requirements elicitation in relation to other design stages of MUSE (see (ii) below);
(b) subject matter, scope and products of requirements elicitation (see (iii) below).

(ii) Requirements analysis was incorporated with task analysis since their design concerns overlap to a large extent. Thus, a number of existing techniques for task analysis were recruited and incorporated in the first two stages of MUSE; i.e. the Extant Systems Analysis Stage and Generalised Task Model Stage. However, the method would benefit from a wider survey of knowledge engineering literature since more advanced requirements analysis techniques may be uncovered for recruitment, e.g. repertory grid and cluster analyses.

(iii) Basic products of requirements specification were defined in MUSE, namely statement of user needs, domain of design discourse and performance specification tables (see Chapter Five). Although case-study tests indicated the products to be generally helpful in supporting design specification, the notations used for the description of the domain of design discourse and system performance could be enhanced. Thus, alternative notations should be investigated in follow-up work on the method.

To summarise, resource limitations precluded an in-depth account of requirements analysis and specification. Instead, a breadth-wise perspective was adopted during the development of MUSE, to support the recruitment of existing techniques to the method.

Second, system development concerns relating to task and user interface design were addressed completely during the development of MUSE. Notable methodological developments in these areas of human factors design comprise the following:

(i) The development of a structured technique for task analysis. The technique, termed extant systems analysis, was incorporated into the first phase of MUSE (see Chapter Four). It should be emphasised that the technique, together with the Generalised and Composite Task Model Stages of MUSE, could support both novel and variant design since task synthesis is addressed by the latter stages. The extant systems analysis technique improves on existing techniques as follows:

(a) It facilitates wider consideration of design alternatives by supporting the analysis of a class of *extant* systems. The latter emphasis may be contrasted with the common practice of analysing the *current or existing* system only. By encouraging wider investigations, premature design commitments (leading to 'blinkered' design) may be avoided.
(b) Its design stages, procedures, inputs and products are defined explicitly. By supporting appropriate application of the technique in this way, a better and more compete analysis and specification of user tasks may thus be expected.
(c) Its design scope is defined explicitly. Thus, wider concerns of human factors design (such as transfer of learning, projected training programmes, and definition of system performance and semantics) may be located against specific stages of the method. The design concerns may then be addressed appropriately with respect to their timing and relevance to the system development context.

(ii) A complete and explicit exemplification of the contribution of task analysis to user interface specification. In particular, user interface specification is operationalised in MUSE as follows: extant system analysis $\longrightarrow$ derivation of system and user task models $\longrightarrow$ derivation of an interaction task model $\longrightarrow$ user interface design. A more complete scope of human factors support for system development was thus advanced in MUSE.
(iii) An explicit definition of human factors specifications of a user interface design. In particular, the specifications were defined as comprising an interaction task model and a set of interface models and display design descriptions.

To conclude, a structured method, MUSE, was developed to support early and continuous human factors contribution to system development. Thus, the scope of human factors design supported by the method was extended. The support is expressed in terms of a comprehensive set of human factors products, procedures and notations at each stage of system development (spanning requirements specification to user interface design).

Functionality Assessment of MUSE*/JSD

These assessments were concerned with determining the appropriateness of human factors and software engineering integration specified in MUSE*/JSD. Two aspects of MUSE*/JSD may be assessed, namely:

(a) The timing and inter-dependencies between human factors and software engineering design specified in the integrated method. The purpose of the assessments was to ascertain how well the methodological characteristics of MUSE*/JSD would support the co-ordination of inter-disciplinary design contributions to system development. In particular, intersecting design concerns and inter-dependencies should be identified adequately to permit the specification of appropriate contact points between the disciplines. Design information and assumptions (including criteria, rationale and constraints) common to both disciplines may then be established and counter-checked at appropriate stages of system development. A convergent design may thus be managed more effectively in the two design streams of the integrated method.

(b) The integration and implementation of design specifications of MUSE and the JSD method. In particular, explicit relationships may be established between human factors and software engineering specifications to facilitate their integration and final implementation.

The results of assessments for the above concerns are discussed below.

Timing and inter-disciplinary design dependencies of MUSE*/JSD: The method was assessed as follows:

(i) A 'real-time' test of the co-ordination of human factors and software engineering design supported by MUSE*/JSD. The objective of the test was to assess the effectiveness of the support for design collaboration between the disciplines provided by the method.

(ii) A post hoc comparison of expected and actual intersections between design descriptions derived by the application of MUSE and the JSD method. The objective of the test was to assess the appropriateness of the inter-dependencies (specified by the method) for supporting design collaboration between the disciplines.

Generally, the results of the assessments may be considered only provisionally positive,[7] since the 'real-time' test was not implemented satisfactorily. In particular, resource constraints precluded a strict adherence to the obligatory contact points specified by

---

[7] Note that these limitations refer only to the integrated method (i.e. MUSE*/JSD) and *not* to MUSE.

MUSE*/JSD.[8] For instance, design meetings at these contact points could not be realised as planned. Specifically, the meetings were delayed, and common information was not shared at the design stages required by the integrated method. Thus, human factors and software engineering design streams were not synchronised. As a result of the failure to adhere to the inter-dependencies, additional design iterations were required to rectify inconsistencies in design contributions from the individual disciplines.

In other words, though the case-study tests indicated the inter-dependencies to be appropriate for supporting design collaboration between the disciplines, the effectiveness of the support provided could not be inferred. Consequently, further case-study tests should be conducted to investigate the following:

(i) The effectiveness of the Functions List in ensuring design convergence. To this end, the 'real-time' tests above should be repeated. By determining its effectiveness, appropriate enhancements of the Functions List may then be proposed. For instance, its scope may be extended, or further design inter-dependencies may be specified to ensure that a consistent design is derived efficiently in component streams of MUSE*/JSD (see (ii) and (iii) below).

(ii) The possibility of specifying lower level design inter-dependencies between MUSE and the JSD method. In particular, the extent to which human factors products may be influenced by JSD specifications derived at the Functions Stage (e.g. data stream merges; time grain markers; etc.), has not been addressed completely. Future investigations should determine whether additional inter-dependencies should be specified to support efficient design collaboration.

(iii) The extent to which human factors and software engineering design streams of MUSE*/JSD may be performed in parallel. Presently, the design stages of the integrated method have been operationalised rather conservatively to ensure efficient derivation of a consistent design (see Chapter Seven, Sub-section 7.3.6). In particular, by specifying a largely sequential performance of method stages, inter-disciplinary design contributions would be more likely to converge without the need for additional design iterations. However, a price is paid for such a conservative application of the integrated method. For instance, sequential application may disrupt design continuity in each of the streams of

---

[8] It may be argued that the unplanned case-study failures at inter-disciplinary design co-ordination may be a better simulation of the pressures of real system development projects. In accepting the argument, one may be forced to conclude that only high-level design inter-dependencies should be specified by a method. However, a price has to be paid for a less specific configuration of the method; namely more design iterations may be needed (see later account on a conservative application of the method).

MUSE*/JSD. Thus, the resource savings that may be accrued by a conservative application of the method, may be eroded by slower 'pick-up' (due to re-orientation needs) at each 'stop-and-start' cycle. Alternatively, to avoid leaving design resources (both human factors and software engineering) 'idle' at particular stages of system development, a greater number of system development projects may need to be inter-leaved to meet productivity levels. The result may be unacceptably stressful for the designer and a lower quality of the systems designed. Thus, it may be important to establish the necessity of a sequential application of the method.

Integration and Implementation of Design Specifications of MUSE and the JSD method: Following the derivation of human factors specifications of the user interface, design discussions are required to clarify how human factors and JSD design contributions should be intersected. At this stage, the inter-disciplinary design contributions are also checked for consistency. To derive an overall specification of the target system, the individual contributions are integrated explicitly by JSD analysts. The specifications may then be implemented as per the original JSD method.

To support the above design discussions, high-level intersections were established explicitly between the specifications of MUSE and the JSD method. In this respect, the following rules of thumb proposed by Carver and Cameron (1987) and Carver et al. (1987), were found to be useful:

(1) active user interface objects should be linked communicatively with the JSD model and function processes;
(2) user interface message and display objects should be linked communicatively with JSD information functions;
(3) an input to a JSD function process may require one or more user inputs at the user interface, i.e. the relationship may be one-to-one or one-to-many;
(4) an action of the JSD model may correspond to one or more on-line task actions performed by the user, i.e. the relationship may be one-to-one or one-to-many.

(Note that the scope of rules (1) and (3) may overlap rules (2) and (4) respectively.)

On the basis of these rules, the following high-level intersections were inferred between the specifications of MUSE and the JSD method:

(i) rules (1) and (2) indicate potential intersections between implicit JSD specifications[9] of a user interface and the human factors products derived at the Interface Model and Display Design Stages of MUSE;
(ii) rules (3) and (4) indicate potential intersections between the JSD model and function processes, and the Target Interaction Task Model (ITM(y) – a product of MUSE).[10]

Unfortunately, these inferences concerning MUSE*/JSD could not be substantiated,[11] since the case-study did not include the integration and implementation of inter-disciplinary design specifications.

As regards the implementation of integrated specifications, little could be inferred from the present work. This outcome is expected since the work was concerned mainly with the development of a method to support design specification (see Chapters Three, Six and Seven). In other words, an assessment of the implementation of MUSE*/JSD specifications was excluded from the remit of the work. Nevertheless, by examining the present concerns of JSD implementation, it may be anticipated that human factors support in this respect would be concerned largely with the specification of transient response times of the target system. For instance, unacceptably long response times would either require an alternative JSD implementation, or the provision of additional feedback to the user. It should be noted, however, that wider human factors support for design implementation can not be precluded.

In conclusion, future case-studies and functional development of MUSE*/JSD should include the following:

(a) An account of the intersections between MUSE and JSD design specifications and the processes entailed by their integration. By understanding these concerns better, further requirements for supporting inter-disciplinary design collaboration may be defined. A more complete and explicit set of procedures may then be specified to enhance the present

---

[9] The word 'implicit' is emphasised here because the official version of the JSD method does not include user interface design.

[10] The rules also indicate similar intersections with the Target System Task Model (STM(y)). However, this product of MUSE is not included in the human factors specifications of a user interface design; i.e. it is an intermediate design product.

[11] See also Footnote 7.

version of MUSE*/JSD.

(b) An extension of MUSE to include more specific human factors support for JSD implementation. Such an extension would involve an account of the integration of MUSE and JSD specifications and the 'knock-on' implications (if any) of the integration for JSD implementation.

(c) An account of the implications of late design modifications. By examining the consequential effects of such modifications on earlier MUSE*/JSD specifications, the method may be developed further to provide better support for the management of late design modifications. In facilitating a wider consideration of preceding design information, it may be expected that more appropriate design modifications would be identified.

The above review completes an exposition of the functionality assessments applied to MUSE and MUSE*/JSD.

(II) Usability Assessment of MUSE and MUSE*/JSD
Since the development of MUSE and MUSE*/JSD was already a substantial undertaking, resources could not be set aside specifically for assessing the usability of the methods. However, the following opportunities for informal assessments were exploited:

(a) The recruitment of a new member to the method development team a year before the end of the project. An informal assessment of the learnability of the method was thus afforded, since the member was expected to assimilate the methods after a short period of training. In other words, the role of a 'method user' was assumed implicitly by the new member. As the level and rate of method uptake were achieved reasonably, it was concluded that the learnability of the methods was acceptable.

(b) The conduct of industrial and tertiary training courses on the method. These courses conducted following the project, were targeted at qualified designers (tutorial attendees at several conferences) and students (undergraduates and postgraduates at a number of universities). The backgrounds of the 'method trainees' included software engineering, computer science and human factors/ergonomics. As before, the overall response to the applicability and learnability of the methods was good.

Although these responses indicate that usability would not be a problem, more extensive studies should be conducted to substantiate the conclusion. The studies could also assess the costs and benefits of method application. In this respect, an increase in the resources required for design analysis and documentation may be expected (as is the case for all structured analysis and design methods).[12] However, the overall result need not be an increase in the *total* resource cost. For instance, a higher expenditure of resources on design analysis and documentation may be off-set by subsequent savings due to greater efficiency in design planning, management, specification and maintenance (general arguments supporting structured analysis and design methods). Such concerns can only be addressed if quantitative data are collected over a longer term.

In summary, field studies should be conducted to assess further the following usability concerns of MUSE and MUSE*/JSD:

(1) The 'real world' performance of the methods. Specifically, the methods should be assessed to determine how well inter-disciplinary collaboration is supported in 'real' design situations. Questions to be answered would include:

(a) how well the methods would support interactions among members of the design team;
(b) how much disruption to current design practices would result from the introduction of the methods;
(c) to what extent is design creativity constrained by the methods?

(2) The cost and benefit of applying the methods. In particular, both qualitative and quantitative data should be gathered from case-study applications of the methods. Questions to be answered would include:

(a) the impact of the methods on the resources and management of system development;
(b) the extent to which the methods would facilitate the derivation of superior system designs;
(c) the problems commonly faced by users of the methods.

The methods may then be enhanced by appropriate modifications and extensions and their uptake improved. The above review completes an account of the assessment of MUSE and MUSE*/JSD. In the next sub-section, further developments to extend and support the methods are discussed.

---

[12] The resource costs for design documentation may be reduced by appropriate computer-based tools.

8.3. Further Developments to Extend and Support MUSE and MUSE*/JSD

Two concerns are addressed in this sub-section, namely:

(a) The extension of the design support provided by MUSE to include substantive human factors knowledge. Specifically, the structured framework of MUSE may be exploited to identify and locate substantive human factors knowledge (e.g. design guidelines), against appropriate stages of system development.

(b) The development of computer-based tools to support the application of MUSE and MUSE*/JSD. Following the extensions indicated in (a) above, more advanced tools may also be developed to support the delivery of both procedural and substantive human factors knowledge.

The potential of these developments is discussed further below.

8.3.1. Incorporation of Substantive Human Factors Knowledge into MUSE

Figure 8-1 shows that, at present, the design support provided by MUSE is largely procedural. Consequently, it was emphasised in earlier chapters that the method is targeted at designers who are trained appropriately in human factors. To widen the user base of the method (e.g. to include software engineers with some knowledge of human factors), its design support would have to be extended to include substantive human factors knowledge. To achieve this objective, the following requirements would have to be satisfied:

(1) A set of established 'topics' of human factors design would have to be located appropriately against specific stages of MUSE. Such a set would include: organisational design; socio-technical design; job design; training design; personnel selection; workstation design; environment and workplace design. Having set the design 'topics' against the system development context defined by MUSE, 'modular repositories' of substantive human factors knowledge may then be collated (see (3) below). Thus, the application of substantive knowledge at appropriate stages of system development, is facilitated.

(2) Design procedures of MUSE would have to be specified to a lower level of description. The procedural human factors knowledge supported by MUSE, may thus be enhanced appropriately to accommodate a wider range of method users.

(3) A comprehensive set of human factors design concepts, techniques and reference materials, would have to be collated and presented appropriately. Information sources for part of a prospective set are listed below:

(a) basic concepts and techniques of human factors design – requirements analysis and specification techniques (see Life, 1991; Checkland, 1981); socio-technical design

Figure 8-1: Locating MUSE against a Range of Human Factors Support for System Development

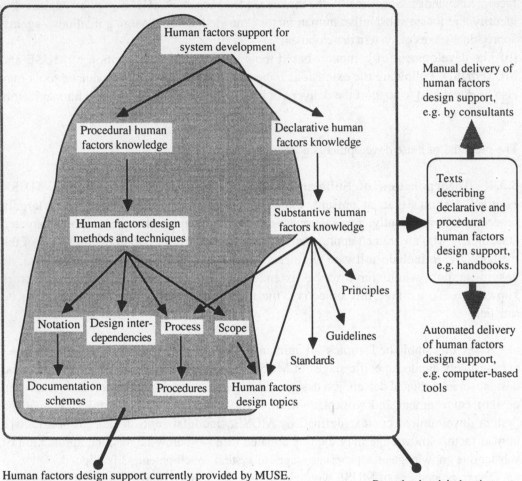

Human factors design support currently provided by MUSE.
Main characteristics of the method are as follows:
(a) The human factors support is provided collaboratively according to MUSE*/JSD. The latter is an integrated method comprising separate human factors and software engineering design streams, and their stage-wise scope, process and notation are co-ordinated by a set of design inter-dependencies. Human factors contributions are thus timed and set appropriately against the system development context.
(b) The human factors support provided is largely procedural.
(c) The intended user of the method is a human factors designer.

Procedural and declarative human factors design support should both be provided, if the user base of the method is extended to include designers not trained specifically in human factors.

techniques (e.g. ETHICS[13] developed by Mumford and Weir, 1979); organisational and participative design techniques (see Eason, 1988; Eason and Cullen, 1988); late evaluation techniques (see Long and Whitefield, 1986);

(b) reference materials on human factors design – human factors design handbooks, guidelines, standards and principles, e.g. Smith and Mosier (1984); Helander (1988).

The substantive human factors knowledge supported by MUSE may thus be enhanced appropriately to accommodate a wider range of method users.

To summarise, the procedural human factors knowledge supported now by MUSE would have to be enhanced, if a wider method user base is to be accommodated. In addition, its design support would have to be extended to include substantive human factors knowledge.

8.3.2. Development of Computer-based Tools to Support MUSE and MUSE*/JSD

Generally, three types of computer-based tools may be developed to support the application of MUSE and MUSE*/JSD,[14] namely CSCW-type tools (**C**omputer **S**upported **C**o-operative **W**ork); IPSE-type tools (**I**ntegrated **P**roject **S**upport **E**nvironment); and CASE-type tools (**C**omputer **A**ided **S**oftware **E**ngineering). The potential development of computer-based support for each of the methods is discussed below.

Computer-based Tools to Support MUSE
In the case of MUSE, it would be useful to develop computer-based tools that provide IPSE- and CASE-type support. Specifically, the following computer support may be considered:

(1) IPSE-type support of the design management tasks defined by MUSE. For instance, computer-based tools may be developed to support project planning and the tracking of design deliverables against planned schedules. In addition, compliance with the design process required by the method may be facilitated by building appropriate inter-locks *across* the *design stages* of *MUSE* that are supported by the tool. Specifically,

---

[13] ETHICS is the acronym for 'Effective Technical and Human Implementation of Computer Systems'.

[14] IPSE and CASE tools that support the JSD method are already available, e.g. MacPDF (Macintosh-based Program Development Facility); PDF™ (Program Development Facility) and SpeedBuilder™. For this reason, the JSD method is excluded from the present account on the development of computer-based tools.

computer functions that support the documentation of display designs may be disabled by the tool until a Target Composite Task Model (CTM(y)) has been specified. To this end, a simple design may be to implement a 'signing-off' scheme for the designer to indicate the satisfactory completion of each product of MUSE. The tool may then counter-check the input by searching through entry fields designated for the documentation of these products. If all entry fields have been completed, the tool may then release the inter-locks and enable the documentation of products to be derived at later design stages of the method. The derivation of an appropriate conceptual design prior to interaction level specification may be encouraged in this way.

(2) CASE-type support of the design specification tasks defined by MUSE. For instance, computer-based tools may be developed to support the following:

(a) text and graphics editing to facilitate design documentation;
(b) consistency checking to ensure the appropriate application of notation constructs; and the consistent propagation of structured diagram descriptions of products derived *across* design stages of the method;
(c) design simulation to facilitate the investigation and comparison of alternative solutions, e.g. MicroSaint Human Operator Simulator (MS HOS)™, HARDMAN III™ Manpower and Personnel Integration (MANPRINT) toolset (see Dahl et al. 1991a, b), etc.;
(d) design prototyping and animation to facilitate the demonstration of promising solutions to users, and thus elicit their feedback for further analysis and design.

Computer-based Tools to Support MUSE*/JSD

To facilitate the management of inter-disciplinary design collaboration required by MUSE*/JSD, computer-based tools that provide CSCW- and IPSE-type support may be developed. Specifically, the following computer support may be considered:

(1) CSCW-type support of the information exchanges between software engineers and human factors designers, as required by MUSE*/JSD. For instance, computer-based tools may be developed to despatch the required information automatically, to the designers involved at each design inter-dependency of the method. By despatching the information as soon as it is available, inter-disciplinary design collaboration may be supported more effectively and efficiently.

(2) IPSE-type support of the management of inter-disciplinary design tasks defined by MUSE*/JSD. For instance, computer-based tools may be developed to support overall project planning and the co-ordination of inter-disciplinary design. In addition, compliance with the design process required by the method may be facilitated by building appropriate inter-locks *across* the *design stages* of *JSD* and *MUSE*. Specifically, computer functions that support the documentation of JSD Model specifications (software

engineering design stream) may be disabled by the tool until products of the Composite Task Model Stage (human factors design stream) have been specified. Other design inter-dependencies may also be supported similarly by the tool.

In conclusion, it can not be over-emphasised that the methods, namely MUSE and MUSE*/JSD, have been developed sufficiently to support the specification of computer-based tools.[15] Pending further extensions of MUSE as described in Sub-section 8.3.1, computer-based tools may also be developed later to support the appropriate application of substantive human factors knowledge (see Perlman, 1988).

8.4.   Concluding Summary

It was observed in Chapters One and Two that the 'too-little-too-late' problem of human factors contribution to system development can only be solved by satisfying the following requirements:

(a) Human factors input should commence at the early stages of system development, and then maintained throughout the design cycle. In particular, early involvement is required to ensure a more complete conception of the human-computer system, while continuous human factors input ensures an appropriate and accurate translation of user requirements.

(b) The scope, process and notation of human factors design should be specified explicitly and extended to support the entire system development cycle. To this end, human factors design should also be decomposed at a lower level of description, to define an adequate set of design products, procedures and documentation schemes. Current conceptions of human factors design (which are largely implicit and incomplete) may thus be enhanced. Following the derivation of an explicit and complete conception, human factors design may then be related more specifically to the concerns and processes of software engineering design.

(c) Human factors design needs should be represented explicitly on the agenda for system development. In this way, resources may be allocated appropriately to support the requirements of human factors analysis and design. By ensuring explicit allocation of resources during the project planning stage, encroachments on human factors design resources may be avoided.

A solution that satisfies these requirements, is the development of a structured human factors method. Such a method, named MUSE, has been developed as described in

---

[15] The development of CASE-type tools to support the automatic generation of code from human factors descriptions may only be considered following more rigorous specification of the notational rules of MUSE.

Chapters Two to Six. Since the scope, process and notation of MUSE are defined explicitly, its integration with similarly structured software engineering methods is facilitated. The scope, granularity and timing of human factors contributions may thus be set appropriately against the system development context, as defined by the chosen structured software engineering method. Such an integrated method has also been developed in respect of MUSE and the JSD method, namely MUSE*/JSD.

Both MUSE and MUSE*/JSD have been developed via an iteration of method specification-and-test cycles, involving a number of case-study systems and design scenarios. Generally, the development of the methods involved the following:

(a) Iterative development of a reasonably complete and comprehensive structured human factors method, namely MUSE.
(b) Specification of explicit design inter-dependencies between MUSE and the chosen structured software engineering method. As described in Chapter Seven, methodological integration was instantiated for the JSD method. By operationalising inter-disciplinary design concerns appropriately in the integrated method, timely and contextually relevant human factors input may then be facilitated throughout the system development cycle. Consequently, a more effective and efficient uptake of human factors contributions may be expected.

To conclude, the foundation established by the present work would support two directions for follow-up research. Firstly, the method has been developed sufficiently to support field tests/trials involving 'real world' applications of the method.[16] Such tests are particularly important since comprehensive assessments of the methods could not be accommodated completely by the resources allocated for their development. Thus, to confirm the positive results of current assessments, limitations of the present case-study tests should be rectified as follows:

(a) More extensive usability assessments of the methods should be conducted, since they were precluded by the limited project resources available. Specifically, functionality assessments took precedence over usability assessments during the development of the methods. Consequently, usability assessments that address the appropriate expression of the methods, could only be conducted indirectly following the derivation of satisfactory

---

[16] Follow-up projects may also consider testing the method on larger and more complex case-study systems, to assess the effects of system scale-up on the efficacy of its support for design specification; the appropriateness of its design inter-dependencies; etc.

versions of the methods. The imbalance in assessments should be rectified. To this end, the methods should be assessed on the following: flexibility, utility, acceptability, learnability, compatibility with the chosen structured software engineering method and compatibility with other established human factors design methods and practices.

(b) Functionality assessments of the methods should be extended to include a more representative population of method users. Although extensive functionality assessments of the methods were conducted during the development of the methods, the method users involved were confined largely to the developers of the methods (and to a lesser extent, to 'in-house' designers and design teams). Consequently, future functionality assessments should focus on method users comprising designers and design teams from other organisations.

(c) Objective assessments of the methods should be conducted, since they were also precluded by the limited project resources available. Specifically, subjective assessments took precedence over objective assessments during the development of the methods. Nevertheless, it is expected that objective assessments may be feasible only in the longer term, since sufficient data for analysis have to be accumulated from repeated applications of the methods. At which time, the efficacy of the methods may be assessed with respect to the following:

(i) quality of project management;
(ii) quality of design documentation;
(iii) quality of the final design artefact;
(iv) number and seriousness of design errors committed during system development;
(v) stage at which design errors are detected and rectified during system development;
(vi) project turn-around time;
(vii) overall project resource requirements.

It is envisaged that the assessments could prompt further enhancements of the methods.[17]

Secondly, the explicitly defined design scope, process and notation of MUSE could be used as a framework to support the development and recruitment of complementary forms of human factors input. As indicated in this chapter, the methodological characteristics of MUSE constitute a reasonably complete and explicit definition of the context of system development. The human factors design support required at each stage of system

---

[17] As with any design method, MUSE and MUSE*/JSD are expected to 'evolve' with repeated applications in the field. For instance, SSADM and JSD have both undergone several updates and versions as part of their maturation process.

development may thus be specified. On this basis, complementary forms of human factors contributions may be developed and recruited as follows:

(a) The design support presently provided by MUSE may be extended to include established modules of substantive human factors knowledge (see earlier part of this chapter). To this end, specific reference materials may be collated and located against particular design stages of MUSE.
(b) The procedural design support presently provided by MUSE may be extended to include declarative human factors support for system development, e.g. design principles, guidelines and standards. Existing forms of declarative human factors support may thus be recruited and located appropriately against particular design stages of MUSE.
(c) The methodological design support provided presently by MUSE and MUSE*/JSD may be enhanced by the various types of computer-based tools described earlier. Thus, the delivery of the above procedural, substantive and declarative supports for system development may be made more effectively. Taking the precedence set by existing structured software engineering methods such as SSADM and JSD, the development of computer-based tools should follow naturally from the development of similarly structured methods such as MUSE and MUSE*/JSD.

The work described in this book would support and benefit from follow-up projects that address these concerns.

References

Akscyn, R. M., and McCracken, D. L., (1984), ZOG and the USS CARL VINCENT: Lessons in System Development. In: B. Shackel (ed.), *Proceedings of the First IFIP Conference on Human-Computer Interaction (Interact '84)*, Vol. 2, pp. 303–308, London, Elsevier Science Publishers, North-Holland.

Alexander, H., (1987), Executable Specifications as an Aid to Dialogue Design. In: H. J. Bullinger and B. Shackel (eds.), *Proceedings of the Second IFIP Conference on Human-Computer Interaction (Interact '87)*, pp. 739–744, London, Elsevier Science Publishers, North-Holland.

Alvey Human Interface Committee Report, (1987), Human Interface Issues in the IT'86 Programme, pp. 15, 27, 32, 33 and 34, July 1987.

Alvey Man-Machine Interface Workshop, (1984), User Interface Design and Design Methods, Coventry, pp. 20, 27, 28, 37, 41 and 89, February 1984.

Alvey Man-Machine Interface Project 143, (1988), User Skill Task Match Methodology, Final Report, April 1988.

Anderson, J. M., (1988), The Integration of HCI Principles in Structured System Design Principles. In: *Proceedings of Milcomp'88, Military Computers, Graphics and Software*, September 1988, London.

Annett, J. and Duncan, K. D., (1967), Task Analysis and Training Design. *Occupational Psychology*, 41, pp. 211–221.

Benyon, D. and Skidmore, S., (1987), Towards a Tool Kit for the Systems Analyst, *The Computer Journal*, Vol. 30, No. 1, 1987, pp. 2–7, Cambridge University Press.

Berns, T. A. R., (1984), The Integration of Ergonomics into Design, *Behaviour and Information Technology*, Vol. 3, pp. 277–284, London: Taylor and Francis.

Birchenough, A. and Cameron, J. R., (1989), JSD and Object-Oriented Design, In: J. R. Cameron, *JSP and JSD: The Jackson Approach to Software Development*, Second Edition, pp. 293–304, IEEE Computer Society Press.

Blyth, R. C. and Hakiel, S. R., (1988), A Methodology for Man-Machine Interface Design, Internal Plessey Research Report 72/88/R467C, Roke Manor.

Blyth, R. C. and Hakiel, S. R., (1989), A User Interface Design Methodology and the Implication for Structured Systems Design Methods. In: *Proceedings of the IEE Third International Conference on Command, Control, Communications and Management Information Systems*, Bournemouth, UK, 2–4 May.

Boar, B. H., (1984), Application Prototyping: A Requirements Definition Strategy for the 80's, New York: John Wiley and Sons Inc., 1984.

Böhm, B. W., (1976), Software Engineering, *IEEE Transactions on Computing*, December 1976, pp. 1226–1241.

Böhm, B. W., (1981), *Software Engineering Economics*, Prentice-Hall, Englewood Cliffs, New Jersey, 1981.

Böhm, B. W., (1984), Software Life-Cycle Factors, In: C. R. Vick and C. V. Ramamoorthy (eds.), *Handbook of Software Engineering*, New York: van Nostrand Reinhold Co., 1984.

Boldyreff, C., (1986), Using Jackson Structured Programming to Describe Syntax, *Computing Notebook Software*, March 26 1986.

Bott, M. F., (1988), Systems Analysis and Design Methods and Integrated Development Environments: The State of the Art and the Future. In: E. D. Megaw (ed.), *Contemporary Ergonomics 1988, 'Ergonomics Giving Quality to Life', Proceedings of the Ergonomics Society 1988 Annual Conference*, pp. 164–170, London: Taylor and Francis.

Bury, K. F., (1984), The Iterative Development of Usable Computer Interfaces. In: B. Shackel (ed.), *Proceedings of the First IFIP Conference on Human-Computer Interaction (Interact '84)*, Vol. 2, pp. 343–348, London, Elsevier Science Publishers, North-Holland.

Butler, K., Bennett, J., Polson, P., and Karat, J., (1989), Report on the Workshop on Analytical Models, *SIGCHI Bulletin*, Vol. 20, No. 4, April 1989, pp. 63–77.

Buxton, W., Lamb, M. R., Sherman, D. and Smith, K. C., (1983), Towards a Comprehensive UIMS, *Computer Graphics*, Vol. 17, No. 3, July 1983, pp. 35–42.

Cameron, J. R., (1987), Mapping JSD Network Specifications into ADA, *ADA User*, Vol. 8, Supplement, pp. 591–599, ADA Language U.K. Ltd.

Cameron, J. R., (1989), *JSP and JSD: The Jackson Approach to Software Development*, Second Edition, IEEE Computer Society Press.

Carroll, J. M. and Campbell, R. L., (1986), Softening Up Hard Science: Reply to Newell and Card, *Human Computer Interaction*, 1986, Vol. 2, No. 3, pp. 227–250, Lawrence Erlbaum Associates, Publishers, Hillsdale, New Jersey.

Carver, M. K., (1988), Practical Experience of Specifying the Human-Computer Interface Using JSD. In: E. D. Megaw (ed.), *Contemporary Ergonomics, Proceedings of the Ergonomics Society's 1988 Annual Conference*, Manchester, pp. 177–182, London: Taylor and Francis.

Carver, M. K. and Cameron, J., (1987), The Jackson System Development Method: A Framework for the Specification of the Human-Computer Interface. Unpublished Internal Report of Michael Jackson Limited, 1987.

Carver, M. K., Clenshaw, D. C., Myles, D. J. L. and P. J. Barber, (1987), Final Report on the Use of JSD in the Design of an ADP System to Provide Support to the Corps All Sources Cell, Internal RARDE Report.

CCTA (Draft) Report, (1988), User System Interaction Strategy Scoping Study. CCTA Office Systems Branch, June 1988.

Chapanis, A. and Budurka, W. J., (1990), Specifying Human-Computer Interface Requirements, *Behaviour and Information Technology*, Vol. 9, No. 6, pp. 479–492, London: Taylor and Francis.

Checkland, P., (1981), *Systems Thinking and Systems Practice,* Chichester, John Wiley Publishers.

Chikofsky, E. J. and Cross II, J. H., (1990), Reverse Engineering and Design Recovery: A Taxonomy, *IEEE Software,* Vol. 7, No. 7, pp. 13–17, January 1990, IEEE Computer Society Press.

Clark, I. A., and Howard, S., (1988), Façading a Medical Application for Usability and Utility. In: Proceedings of the APL Conference, University of Kent, September 1988.

Clegg, C., Ravden, S., Corbett, M. and Johnson, G., (1989), Allocating Functions in Computer Integrated Manufacturing: A Review and a New Method, *Behaviour and Information Technology,* 1989, Vol. 8, No. 3, pp. 175–190, London: Taylor and Francis.

Crinnion, J., (1989), A Role for Prototyping in Information Systems Design Methodology, *Design Studies,* Vol. 10, No. 3, July 1989, pp. 144–150, Butterworth Scientific Ltd, London.

Dahl, S., Laughery, K. R. and Hood, L., (1991a), Integrating Task Network and Anthropometric Models, In ed. E. Lovesey, *Proceedings of the Ergonomics Society's 1991 Annual Conference,* pp. 151–156, London: Taylor and Francis.

Dahl, S., Laughery, K. R. and Hood, L., (1991b), HARDMAN III MANPRINT Tools, *Special Workshop at the Ergonomics Society's 1991 Annual Conference,* Southampton, April 1991.

Damodaran, L., (1988), DIADEM, Ergonomics Society Workshop on SSADM and Task Analysis, May 1988.

Damodaran, L., Ip, K. and Beck, M., (1988), Integrating Human Factors Principles into Structured Design Methodology: A Case-Study in the UK Civil Service. In: H. J. Bullinger et al (eds.), *Information Technology for Organisational Systems,* Elsevier Science Publishers, pp. 235–241, North Holland.

Diaper, D., (1989a), *Task Analysis for Human-Computer Interaction,* Ellis Horwood Books in Information Technology, John Wiley and Sons.

Diaper, D., (1989b), *Knowledge Elicitation: Principles, Techniques and Applications,* Ellis Horwood Books in Expert Systems, John Wiley and Sons.

Dowell, J., and Long, J. B., (1989), Towards a Conception for an Engineering Discipline of Human Factors. In: P. Barber and J. Laws (eds.), *Ergonomics (Special Issue)* on 'Methodological Issues in Cognitive Ergonomics', Vol. 32, No. 11, pp. 1513–1536, London: Taylor and Francis.

Drury, C. G., (1983), Task Analysis Methods in Industry, In: *Applied Ergonomics,* 14, 1, pp. 19–28.

Duncan, K., (1974), Analysis Techniques in Training Design, In Edwards, B. and Lees, F. P., *The Human Operator in Process Control,* London: Taylor and Francis.

Eason, K. D., (1987), Methods of Planning the Electronic Workplace, *Behaviour and Information Technology,* Vol. 6, No. 3, pp. 229–238, London: Taylor and Francis.

Eason, K. D., (1988), *Information Technology and Organizational Change*, London: Taylor and Francis.

Eason, K. D. and Cullen, J., (1988), Human Factors Contributions in the Context of I.T. System Design and Implementation. In: H. J. Bullinger et al. (eds.), *Information Technology for Organisational Systems*, pp. 811–816, Elsevier Science Publishers, North-Holland.

Esgate, A., Whitefield, A. and Life, A., (1990), Developing Usability Integration Principles for the Design of IBCN Systems, In: G. van der Veer et al. (eds.), *Proceedings of the Fifth European Conference on Cognitive Ergonomics*, Urbino (Italy), September 1990, pp. 359–374, Golem Press.

ESPRIT 385, (1989), In: E. D. Megaw (ed.), *Contemporary Ergonomics, Proceedings of the Ergonomics Society's 1989 Annual Conference*, Reading, pp. 82–131, London: Taylor and Francis.

ESPRIT 385, (1990), In: D. Diaper et al (eds.), *Proceedings of the Third IFIP Conference on Human-Computer Interaction (Interact '90)*, pp. 371–382, Cambridge, Elsevier Science Publishers, North-Holland.

Essink, L. J. B., (1988), A Conceptual Framework for Information Systems Development Methodologies. In: H. J. Bullinger et al. (eds.), *Information Technology for Organisational Systems,* pp. 354–362, Elsevier Science Publishers, North-Holland.

Fähnrich, K., Fauser, A. and Heller, N., (1984), The Extent of Introduction of Electronic Machinery in the Office. Consolidated Report, Dublin: European Foundation for the Improvement of Living and Working Conditions, 1984.

Finkelstein, A. and Potts, C., (1985), Evaluation of Existing Requirements Extraction Strategies, FOREST Report R1.

Fitter, M. and Green, T. R. G., (1979), When Do Diagrams Make Good Computer Languages? *International Journal of Man-Machine Studies*, Vol. 11, pp. 235–261, 1979, Academic Press Inc., London.

Fitzgerald, G., (1988), Information Systems Development for Changing Environments: Flexibility Analysis. In: H. J. Bullinger et al. (eds.), *Information Technology for Organisational Systems,* pp. 587–592, Elsevier Science Publishers, North-Holland.

Fox, J. M., (1982), *Software and its Development.* Englewood Cliffs, New Jersey: Prentice-Hall Inc., 1982.

Frohlich, D. M. and Luff, P., (1989), Some Lessons From an Exercise in Specification, *Human-Computer Interaction,* 1989, Vol. 4, pp. 121–147, Lawrence Erlbaum Associates, Publishers, Hillsdale, New Jersey.

Galliers, R. D., (1984), An Approach to Information Needs Analysis. In: B. Shackel (ed.), *Proceedings of the First IFIP Conference on Human-Computer Interaction (Interact '84),* Vol. 1, pp. 409–418, London, Elsevier Science Publishers, North-Holland.

Gillett, P. E. and Northam, D. J., (1990), Matching Warships and Sailors. In: *Proceedings of the Symposium on Human Factors in Warships and Naval Systems,* Westminster, November 1990, pp. 84–98.

Gould, J. D., (1988), How to Design Usable Systems. In: M. Helander (ed.), *Handbook of Human Computer Interaction,* pp. 757–790, Elsevier Science Publishers, North Holland, 1988.

Gould, J. D., and Lewis, C., (1983), Designing for Usability – Key Principles and What Designers Think. In: *Proceedings of CHI'83 Human Factors in Computing Systems,* Boston, December 1983, pp. 50–53, ACM, New York.

Grandjean, E., (1984), Forward, Ergodesign '84, *Behaviour and Information Technology,* Vol. 3, pp. 261–262, London: Taylor and Francis.

Grandjean, E., (1988), *Fitting the Task to the Man: An Ergonomic Approach,* 4th edition. London: Taylor and Francis.

Grønbák, K., (1989), Rapid Prototyping with Fourth Generation Systems – An Empirical Study, *Office: Technology and People,* 5:2, 1989, pp. 105–125, Elsevier Science Publishers Ltd, England.

Grudin, J., (1991), Systematic Sources of Sub-optimal Interface Design in Large Product Development Organisations, *Human Computer Interaction,* Vol. 6, No. 2, pp. 147–196.

Grudin, J., Ehrlich, S. F. and Shriner, R., (1987), Positioning Human Factors in the User Interface Development Chain. In: *CHI + GI 1987,* pp. 125–131, ACM Press.

Hakiel, S. R. and Blyth, R. C., (1990a), Keeping the Human in Context, In: E. Lovesey (ed.), *Contemporary Ergonomics 1990, 'Ergonomics Setting Standards for the '90s', Proceedings of the Ergonomics Society's 1990 Annual Conference,* Leeds, 3–6 April, pp. 123–128, Taylor and Francis.

Hakiel, S. R. and Blyth, R. C., (1990b), Keeping the Human in Context, *Contemporary Ergonomics 1990, 'Ergonomics Setting Standards for the '90s',* Presentation OHPs, Leeds, 3–6 April.

Hares, J., (1987), Methods for a Longer Life, *Computer News/Databases,* pp. 18 and 6 August, 1987.

Hartson, H. R. and Hix, D., (1988), Human-Computer Interface Development: Concepts and Systems for its Management. In: *Proceedings of Tutorial Sessions, CHI '88,* New York: ACM Press.

Hartson, H. R. and Hix, D., (1989), Towards Empirically Derived Methodologies and Tools for Human-Computer Interface Development, *International Journal of Man-Machine Studies,* Vol. 31, pp. 477–494, Academic Press.

Haubner, P. J., (1990), Ergonomics in Industrial Product Design, *Ergonomics,* 1990, Vol. 33, No. 4, 477–485, London: Taylor and Francis.

Hekmatpour, S. and Ince, D. C., (1987), Evolutionary Prototyping and the Human Computer Interface, In: H. J. Bullinger and B. Shackel (eds.), *Proceedings of the Second IFIP Conference on Human-Computer Interaction (Interact '87),* pp. 479–484, London, Elsevier Science Publishers, North-Holland.

Helander, M., (1988), *Handbook of Human Computer Interaction*, Elsevier Science Publishers, North Holland.

Hewett, J. and Durham, T., (1987), *Computer-Aided Software Engineering: Commercial Strategies*, Ovum Ltd.

Hirsch, R. S., (1984), VDTs and the Human Factors Community: Tipping the Iceberg, *Human Factors Society Bulletin*, Vol. 27, No. 6, pp. 1–3.

Hirschheim, R., (1985), *Office Automation: A Social and Organisational Perspective*. Chichester: Wiley, 1985.

Ip, W. K., Damodaran, L., Olphert, C. W. and Maguire, M. C., (1990), The Use of Task Allocation Charts in System Design: A Critical Appraisal. In: D. Diaper et al. (eds.), *Proceedings of the Third IFIP Conference on Human-Computer Interaction (INTERACT '90)*, pp. 289–294, Elsevier Science Publishers, North-Holland.

Jackson, M. A., (1983), *System Development*, Englewood Cliffs New Jersey: Prentice-Hall International.

Johnson, P., Diaper, D. and Long, J. B., (1984), Tasks, Skill and Knowledge; Task Analysis for Knowledge Based Descriptions. In: B. Shackel (ed.), *Proceedings of the First IFIP Conference on Human-Computer Interaction (Interact '84)*, Vol. 1, pp. 23–28, London, Elsevier Science Publishers, North-Holland.

Johnson, P. and Johnson, H., (1987), Generification: A Process of Identifying Generic Properties of Tasks within a given Domain. Queen Mary College Report to ICL, No. 2, 1987.

Johnson, P., Johnson, H. and Russell, F., (1988), Collecting and Generalising Knowledge Descriptions from Task Analysis Data, ICL Technical Journal.

Jones, J. C., (1973), *Design Methods: Seeds of Human Futures*, Wiley Inter-Science, pp. 123–133, John Wiley and Sons Ltd., London.

Keller, R., (1987), *Expert System Technology*, Yourdon Press, Englewood Cliffs, New Jersey, 1987.

Kieras, D. and Polson, P. G., (1985), An Approach to the Formal Analysis of User Complexity, In: *International Journal of Man-Machine Studies*, Vol. 22, pp. 365–394, Academic Press Inc., London.

Klein, G. A. and Brezovic, (1986), Design Engineers and the Design Process: Decision Strategies and Human Factors Literature. In: *Proceedings of the Human Factors Society, 30th Annual Meeting*, 1986, pp. 771–775.

Klein, L. and Newman, W., (1987), Quality Assurance Aspects of IT'86. In: Alvey Human Interface Club, Report of Open Meeting, Strand, London, 13 October 1987, pp. 41–66.

Kloster, G. V. and Tischer, K., (1984), Man-Machine Interface Design Process. In: B. Shackel (ed.), *Proceedings of the First IFIP Conference on Human-Computer Interaction (Interact '84)*, Vol. 2, pp. 236–241, London, Elsevier Science Publishers, North-Holland.

Life, A., (1991), A Structured Analysis and Design Method for User Requirements Specification, Ergonomics Unit, University College London, JCI Research Proposal.

Lim, K. Y., (1986), Display Structure and Memory Location Task Performance. MSc (Ergonomics) Dissertation, University of London.

Lim, K. Y., (1988a), On Reasoning about User Interface Design using Extended JSD in Conjunction with an Extant Systems System Analysis Approach, RARDE Project Internal Working Document Number 19.

Lim, K. Y., (1988b), Some Considerations on Notational Requirements for Task and Interface Information Capture: Towards the Conception of a JSD* Notation, RARDE Project Internal Working Document Number 23.

Lim, K. Y., (1991), An Energy Management System for the Home: Human Factors Evaluation of the SmallTalk Prototype, London HCI Centre Report, LHC/9013/REP1, January 1991.

Lim, K. Y., (1992), Integrating Human Factors with Structured Analysis and Design Methods, Doctoral Thesis, University of London.

Lim, K. Y. and Long, J. B., (1992), A Method for (Recruiting) Methods: Facilitating Human Factors Input to System Design. In: Brooks, R. (ed.), *Proceedings of the ACM Annual Conference on Human Factors in Computing Systems (CHI'92)*, Monterey (USA), May 3–7, 1992, ACM.

Lim, K. Y. and Long, J. B., (1993a), Structured Notations for Human Factors Specification of Interactive Systems. In: *Proceedings of HCI International 1993 Conference*, Orlando, Florida (USA), August 1993, Elsevier Science.

Lim, K. Y. and Long, J. B., (1993b), Structured Notations for Human Factors Specification. In: Lovesey, E. J. (ed.), *Contemporary Ergonomics, Proceedings of the Ergonomics Society's 1993 Conference*, Edinburgh (UK), April 1993, Taylor and Francis.

Lim, K. Y., Long, J. B. and Silcock, N., (1990a), Motivation, Research Management and a Conception for Structured Integration of Human Factors with System Development Methods: An Illustration Using the Jackson System Development Method. In: van der Veer, G et al. (eds.), *Proceedings of the Fifth European Conference on Cognitive Ergonomics*, Urbino (Italy), September 3–6, 1990, pp. 359–374, Golem Press.

Lim, K. Y., Long, J. B. and Silcock, N., (1990b), Requirements, Research and Strategy for Integrating Human Factors with Structured Analysis and Design Methods: The Case of the Jackson System Development Method. In: Lovesey, E.J. (ed.), *Contemporary Ergonomics, Proceedings of the Ergonomics Society's 1990 Conference*, Leeds, April 1990, 32–38, Taylor and Francis.

Lim, K. Y., Long, J. B. and Silcock, N., (1992), Integrating Human Factors with the Jackson System Development Method: An Illustrated Overview, In: Barber, P. and Laws, J. (eds.), *Ergonomics Special Issue on Methodological Issues in Cognitive Ergonomics III*, Vol 33(12), London: Taylor and Francis.

Long, J. A. and Neale, I. M., (1989), Validating and Testing in KBS – A Case-Study. In: *Proceedings of the Second International Conference on Industrial and Engineering Applications of Artificial Intelligence and Expert Systems,* Tennessee, U.S.A., June 1989.

Long, J. B. and Dowell, J., (1989), Conceptions of the Discipline of HCI: Craft, Applied Science, and Engineering. In: A. Sutcliffe and L. Macaulay (eds.), *People and Computers V, Proceedings of the Fifth Conference of the British Computer Society Human-Computer Interaction Specialist Group,* Nottingham, September 1989, pp. 9–34, Cambridge University Press.

Long, J. B. and Whitefield, A. D., (1986), Evaluating Interactive Systems, *HCI'86 Tutorial,* York, September 1986.

Lucas, H. C., (1975), *Why Information Systems Fail,* Columbia University Press, New York, 1975.

Lundell, J. and Notess, M., (1991), Human Factors in Software Development: Models, Techniques, and Outcomes, In: P. Robertson, G. M. Olson, and J. S. Olson (eds.), *Proceedings of the CHI'91 Conference,* New Orleans, May 1991, pp. 145–152, ACM Press, New York.

Maddison, R. N., (1983), Information System Methodologies, In: P. A. Samet (ed.), *BCS Monographs in Informatics,* Wiley Heyden.

Maguire, M., (1982), An Evaluation of Published Recommendations on the Design of Man-Computer Dialogues, *International Journal of Man-Machine Studies,* Vol. 16, No. 3, pp. 237–261, Academic Press Inc., London.

Malin, J. T., Schreckenghost, D. L. and Thronesbery, C. G., (1991), Design for Interaction between Humans and Intelligent Systems during Real-Time Fault Management. In: *Proceedings of the Fifth Annual Space Operations, Applications, and Research Symposium,* (NASA Johnson Space Center, Houston, Texas, July 9–11.

Mantei, M., (1986), Techniques for Incorporating Human Factors in the Software Life-Cycle. In: *Proceedings of STA-III Conference: Structured Techniques in the Eighties: Practice and Prospect,* Chicago, June 1986.

Mantei, M., and Teorey, T. J., (1988), Cost/Benefit Analysis for Incorporating Human Factors in the Software Life-Cycle, Computing Practices, *Communications of the ACM,* Vol. 31, No. 4, pp. 428–439, April 1988.

Marshall, C. R., (1984), System ABC: A Case-Study in the Design and Evaluation of a Human-Computer Dialog. In: B. Shackel (ed.), *Proceedings of the First IFIP Conference on Human-Computer Interaction (Interact '84),* Vol. 1, pp. 419–423, London, Elsevier Science Publishers, North-Holland.

McClleland, I., (1990), Marketing Ergonomics to Industrial Engineers, *Ergonomics,* 1990, Vol. 33, No. 4, pp. 391–398, London: Taylor and Francis.

McKenzie, J., (1988), Guidelines and Principles of Interface Design. In: N. Heaton and M. Sinclair (eds.), *State of the Art Report 15:8,* 'Designing End-User Interfaces', pp. 73–84, England: Pergamon Infotech Limited.

McNeile, A. T., (1986), Jackson System Development. In: T. W. Olle et al. (eds.), *Information Systems Design Methodologies: Improving the Practice*, pp. 225–246, Elsevier Science Publishers, North Holland.

Meister, D., (1984), A Catalogue of Ergonomic Design Methods. In: *Proceedings of the International Conference on Occupational Ergonomics*, pp. 17–25.

Moraal, J. and Kragt, H., (1990), Macro-Ergonomic Design: The Need for Empirical Research Evidence, *Ergonomics,* 1990, Vol. 33, No. 5, pp. 605–612, London: Taylor and Francis.

Morrison, W., (1988), Communicating with Users during Systems Development, *Information and Software Technology,* June 1988, Vol. 30, No. 5, pp. 295–298, Butterworth Scientific Ltd, London.

Multi-User Computing, (1989), Automated Tools Become a Reality, pp. 20–26 and 29, January 1989.

Mumford, E. and Weir, M., (1979), *Computer Systems in Work Design – the ETHICS (Effective Technical and Human Implementation of Computer Systems) Method,* Associated Business Press London.

Norman, D. A., (1986), Cognitive Engineering, In: Norman, D. A. and Draper, S. W. (eds.), *User Centered System Design: New Perspectives on Human Computer Interaction,* pp. 31–61, Lawrence Erlbaum Associates Publishers, Hillsdale, New Jersey.

Norman, M. A., (1988), Developments in Computing and the User Interface – Emerging Issues in End-User Interface Design. In: N. Heaton and M. Sinclair (eds.), *State of the Art Report 15:8,* 'Designing End-User Interfaces', pp. 85–96, England: Pergamon Infotech Limited.

Norris, M. T., (1985), The Application of Formal Methods in Systems Design, *British Telecom Technology Journal,* Vol. 3, No. 4, October 1985, pp. 53–59.

O'Niel, D., (1980), The Management of Software Engineering Part II: Software Engineering Program, *IBM Systems J.,* Vol. 19, No. 4, pp. 421–431.

Olson, J., (1991), Human-Computer Interface Design: Success Cases, Emerging Methods and Real World Context (Boulder, Colorado, July 23–26), Discussion handout on existing human factors methods.

Payne, S. J. and Green, T. R. G., (1986), TAG: A Model of the Mental Representation of Task Languages, *Human Computer Interaction,* 1986, Vol. 2, pp. 93–133, Lawrence Erlbaum Associates, Publishers, Hillsdale, New Jersey.

Perlman, G., (1987), An Overview of SAM: A HyperText Interface to Smith and Mosier's Guidelines for Designing User Interface Software. Tyngsboro, MA: Wang Institute, Wang Institute Technical Report TR-87-09, 1987.

Perlman, G., (1988), Software Tools for User Interface Development. In: M. Helander (ed.), *Handbook of Human Computer Interaction,* pp. 819–834, Elsevier Science Publishers, North Holland, 1988.

Pikaar, R. N., Lenior, T. M. J. and Rijnsdorp, J. E., (1990), Implementation of Ergonomics in Design Practice: Outline of an Approach and some Discussion Points, *Ergonomics,* 1990, Vol. 33, No. 5, 583–587, London: Taylor and Francis.

Price, H. E., (1985), The Allocation of Functions in Systems, *Human Factors,* Vol. 27, No. 1, pp. 33–45, Human Factors Society Inc., Santa Monica, U.S.A.

Ragoczei, S. and Hirst, G., (1990), The Meaning Triangle as a Tool for the Acquisition of Abstract, Conceptual Knowledge, *International Journal of Man-Machine Studies,* Vol. 33, pp. 505–520, Academic Press Ltd.

Reisner, P., (1977), Use of Psychological Experimentation as an Aid to the Development of a Query Language, In: *IEEE Trans. in Software Engineering,* SE-3, pp. 218–229.

Renold, A., (1989), Jackson System Development for Real Time Systems, In: J. R. Cameron, *JSP and JSD: The Jackson Approach to Software Development,* Second Edition, pp. 235–278, IEEE Computer Society Press.

Rogers, J. G. and Pegden, C. D., (1977), Formatting and Organisation of a Human Engineering Standard, *Human Factors,* Vol. 19, No. 1, pp. 55–61.

Rosson, M. B., (1987), Real World Design, *SIGCHI Bulletin,* Vol. 19, No. 2, October 1987, pp. 61–62.

Rouse, W. B. and Boff, K. R., (eds., 1987), *System Design: Behavioural Perspectives on Designers, Tools and Organisations,* Elsevier Science North Holland.

Rubinstein, R. and Hersh, H., (1984), *The Human Factor: Designing Computer Systems for People,* Digital Press, Bedford, Massachusetts, 1984.

Shackel, B., (1985), Ergonomics in Information Technology in Europe – A Review, *Behaviour and Information Technology,* Vol. 4, No. 4, pp. 263–287, London: Taylor and Francis.

Shackel, B., (1986a), Ergonomics in Design for Usability. In: M. D. Harrison and A. F. Monk (eds.), *People and Computers: Designing for Usability,* pp. 44–64, 1986, Cambridge University Press.

Shackel, B., (1986b), IBM Makes Usability as Important as Functionality, *The Computer Journal,* Vol. 29, pp. 475–476.

Shuttleworth, M., (1987), The Role of Application Developers, Graphics Systems Centre, ICL Office Systems, Human Computer Co-Operation, HCC/1/15 (Issue 1), March 1987.

Smith, S. L., (1986), Standards versus Guidelines for Designing User Interface Software, *Behaviour and Information Technology,* 1986, Vol. 5, No 1, pp. 47–61.

Smith, S. L., and Mosier, J. M., (1984), Design Guidelines for User-System Interface Software, Hanscom Airforce Base MA, USAF Electronic Systems Division, NTIS No. AD A154 907, Tech Rep ESD-TR-84-190, 1984.

Sridhar, K. T. and Hoare, C. A. R., (1985), JSD Expressed in CSP, *Technical Monograph PRG-51*, Oxford University Computing Laboratory; Also in: J. R. Cameron, *JSP and JSD: The Jackson Approach to Software Development*, Second Edition, pp. 334–363, IEEE Computer Society Press.

Stevens, G. C., (1983), User-Friendly Computer Systems ? A Critical Examination of the Concept, *Behaviour and Information Technology*, Vol. 2, pp. 3–16, London: Taylor and Francis.

Sutcliffe, A., (1988a), Some Experiences in Integrating Specification of Human Computer Interaction within a Structured System Development Method. In: D. M. Jones and R. Winder (eds.), *Proceedings of the Fourth Conference of the BCS HCI SIG Conference*, Cambridge, pp. 145–160, Cambridge University Press.

Sutcliffe, A., (1988b), *Jackson System Development*, Prentice-Hall, London.

Sutcliffe, A., (1989), Task Analysis, Systems Analysis and Design: Symbiosis or Synthesis?, *Interacting With Computers*, Vol. 1, No. 1, April 1989, pp. 6–12, Butterworth Scientific Ltd, London.

Sutcliffe, A., and Wang, I., (1991), Integrating Human-Computer Interaction with Jackson System Development, *The Computer Journal*, Vol. 34, No. 2, April 1991, pp. 132–142, Cambridge University Press.

Thimbleby, H., (1987), Delaying Commitment, Internal Report of the Department of Computing Science, University of York.

Thimbleby, H., (1990), *User Interface Design*, ACM Press New York: Addison-Wesley Publishers.

Underwood, M. J., (1987), Alvey Human Interface Club Response to the IT'86 (Bide) Report: Organisation. In: Alvey Human Interface Club, Report of Open Meeting, Strand, London, 13 October 1987, pp. 15–28.

Waddington, R. and Johnson, P. (1989), A Family of Task Models for Interface Design, In: *Proceedings of HCI'89 Conference*, Cambridge University Press.

Walsh, P., (1987a), Using JSD as a Description Language, RARDE Project Internal Working Document Number 5.

Walsh, P., (1987b), Task Analysis Methods in HCI Design, RARDE Project Internal Working Document Number 13.

Walsh, P. and Lim, K. Y., (1987), Structured Methods and the Design of Interactive Software, Internal Working Document Number 3.

Walsh, P., Lim, K. Y., Long, J. B. and Carver, M. K., (1989), JSD and the Design of User Interface Software. In: Barber, P. and Laws, J. (eds.), *Ergonomics* (Special Issue on Methodological Issues in Cognitive Ergonomics), Vol 32, No 11, November 1989, pp. 1483–1498, London: Taylor and Francis.

Whiteside, J., Jones, S., Levy, P. S., and Wixon, D., (1985), User Performance with Command, Menu and Iconic Interfaces. In: Borman and Curtis (eds.), *Human Factors in Computing Systems II*, 1985, pp. 185–191, North Holland.

Williams, J. R., (1989), Menu Design Guidelines, ISO/WD 9241-XX (Working Draft -2), March 1989.

Wilson, J. and Rosenberg, D., (1988), Rapid Prototyping for User Interface Design. In: M. Helander (ed.), *Handbook of Human Computer Interaction*, pp. 859–876, Elsevier Science Publishers, North Holland, 1988.

Wilson, M., Barnard, P. J. and MacLean, A., (1986), Task Analysis in Human Computer Interaction, Report HF 122, IBM Hursley Human Factors.

Wilson, M., Duce, D. and Simpson, D., (1989), Life-Cycle in Software and Knowledge Engineering: A Comparative Review, *The Knowledge Engineering Review*, Vol. 4, No. 3, pp. 189–204, Cambridge University Press.

Zave, P., (1984), The Operational versus the Conventional Approach to Software Development, Reports and Articles, *Communications of the ACM*, February 1984, Vol. 27, No 2, pp. 104–118, ACM Press New York.

Glossary

Abstraction: See Chapter 2, Sub-section 2.2.

Automated task: A task performed entirely by a device.

Decomposition: See Chapter 2, Sub-section 2.2.

Design phase: A group of design *stages* that addresses a common aspect of system development. For instance, the Design Specification Phase of the method is concerned primarily with human factors specification of a user interface design.

Design stage: A group of design *activities* concerned with transforming input(s) from a preceding stage(s) into products characteristic of that stage.

Device independent: A term used to describe a task that is not specific to a particular device. For instance, an Extant Task Description (TD(ext)) is a device *dependent* description. In contrast, an Extant Generalised Task Model (GTM(ext)) is a predominantly device-*independent* description, since it is derived by removing device-specific details from an Extant Task Description (TD(ext)). The purpose of deriving a device-independent description is to uncover the logic underlying functional features of a specific design. The knowledge gained may then be generalised and applied across separate design instances. In this way, appropriate design features of a particular extant system may be identified and recruited to the design of a new or target system. However, a description that is completely device-independent may not be desirable in all cases, e.g. in instances where the preservation of low-level design details is desirable.

Domain objects: Objects associated with the domain of application.

Extant System or EXT: A general term for a class of systems comprising the Extant Current System, the Extant Partial System and the Extant Related System.

Extant Composite System or X: A 'hypothetical' extant system synthesised analytically from a number of partial and/or complete extant systems. The composite description is derived to support later reasoning about the system to be designed.

Extant Related System: An existing system that shares the same domain of application as the system to be designed. The term is used to differentiate existing systems used by other organisations, from the Extant Current System used by the client organisation.

Extant Current System: The existing system destined to be replaced by the system to be designed, i.e. an existing system used currently by the client organisation.

Extant Partial System: Parts of an existing system that may be relevant to the system to be designed. For instance, its sub-tasks (and associated design features) may be similar to those anticipated for the system to be designed. In other words, the domains of the systems intersect partially.

Generification: See Chapter 2, Sub-section 2.2.

Inter-dependencies: Design stage at which human factors and software engineering concerns intersect. Thus, at each inter-dependent point, design information of common interest is shared, agreed, and then adhered to throughout succeeding stages of system development. Since the shared information is mutually binding, unavoidable violations in one design stream must be communicated to the other. Furthermore, design iterations across the stages governed by the particular inter-dependent point, should be undertaken appropriately. In this way, inter-disciplinary specifications derived in separate human factors and software engineering design streams would converge more efficiently.

MUSE: A structured human factors method.
MUSE*: The structured human factors method adapted for integration with the Jackson System Development (JSD) method.
MUSE*/JSD: An integrated and structured multi-disciplinary method comprising MUSE (a structured human factors method) and JSD (a structured software engineering method).

Off-line task: User's tasks that do not involve a computer.
On-line task: User's tasks that involve interacting with a computer.

Screen objects: A set of user interface objects displayed on a screen. The set includes information display objects and interactive objects that may be manipulated by a user.
Synthesis: See Chapter 2, Sub-section 2.2.
System: A particular configuration of human and computer entities interacting to perform tasks within a specific environment. Work may or may not be achieved in the process.

Target System: The system to be designed.
Task: Activities performed by system entities to achieve work goals.

Work: Work is achieved if desired changes in attributes state(s) of domain objects have been brought about by the tasks performed by system entities.

Annexes

Annexes A and B are provided here for the sake of completeness.

Annex A completes the set of human factors descriptions that may be derived for the case-study described in Chapter Four. The extant system descriptions shown are applicable only if the system to be developed is very similar to an existing system. In addition, note that the procedures described here are simplified versions of the sets presented in Chapters Four to Six.

Annex B provides the reader with an advance view of possible enhancements of the design descriptions and notations of MUSE. The case-study descriptions presented are for illustration only.

Annex A: Case-study Illustration of Secondary Activities and Products of the Extant Systems Analysis (ESA) Stage (Network Security Management System)

This account completes an illustration of the Extant Systems Analysis (ESA) Stage, for the case-study used in Chapters Three to Six; namely the Network Security Management System. Specifically, secondary human factors activities and products applicable in a variant design scenario are described. Note that the extent to which such activities and products are addressed depends largely on how similar the domain characteristics and implementation technology are between the extant and target systems. Consequently, illustrations of design products are provided only when their derivation was considered appropriate during the case-study.

(I) Extant System Task Model (STM(ext)) and Extant User Task Model (UTM(ext))

To characterise the on-line task of the extant system in terms of the human-computer interaction required, a human factors description termed an Extant System Task Model (STM(ext)), is derived. Since the Extant System Task Model is intended to be a conceptual level description, the form of the interaction need not be specified. Such details are addressed by other design products of the Extant Systems Analysis Stage (see later).

A complementary description of relevant off-line tasks of the extant system is also derived at this stage. The description, termed an Extant User Task Model (UTM(ext)), is collated to support target system design at later stages of the method.

The procedures for deriving the Extant System Task Model (STM(ext)) and Extant User

Task Model (UTM(ext)) are summarised below.

Procedures for deriving Extant System and User Task Models (STM(ext) and UTM(ext))

1. With reference to the structure of the Extant Generalised Task Model (GTM(ext)), identify on-line and off-line tasks for the extant system concerned. If a more detailed description is desired, consult the Extant Task Description (TD(ext)) again for a lower level description. Repeat the information elicitation cycle if necessary.

2(a) To derive an Extant System Task Model (STM(ext)), note existing user actions and computer responses for each on-line task. Thus, H: (Human) and C: (Computer) actions are identified. An Extant System Task Model (STM(ext)) is then derived by incorporating the actions into appropriate sub-nodes of the Extant Generalised Task Model (GTM(ext)).

2(b) To derive an Extant User Task Model (UTM(ext)), construct a structured diagram description of all the off-line tasks for the extant system; i.e. the tasks are described using a single diagram.

3. Augment the structured diagram descriptions of the Extant System and User Task Models (STM(ext) and UTM(ext)) by recording additional information textually in accompanying tables.

Rules of Thumb for deriving Extant System and User Task Models (STM(ext) and UTM(ext))

1. If it is uninformative to decompose on-line tasks into separate H: (Human) and C: (Computer) leaves, an Extant System Task Model (STM(ext)) may be left at a higher level of description by using combined H-C: (Human-Computer) sub-nodes.

2. Whenever possible, the structure of the Extant Generalised Task Model (GTM(ext)) should be carried forward to the Extant System and User Task Models (STM(ext) and UTM(ext)). Reference across the models is thus facilitated by providing a more coherent view of the task.

3. For the same reason as in (2) above, important off-line tasks should be noted in the Extant System Task Model (STM(ext)). In particular, off-line tasks that may influence the user interface design of the extant and target systems, should be represented explicitly to prompt appropriate consideration by the designer.

(II) Extant Interaction Task Model (ITM(ext))

An Extant Interaction Task Model is a device-level description of the interactions performed by the user on the existing computer system. It is derived by extending H: (Human) leaves of an Extant System Task Model (STM(ext)), following appropriate observation of the user.

The procedures for deriving an Extant Interaction Task Model are summarised overleaf.

Procedures for deriving an Extant Interaction Task Model, ITM(ext)

1. With reference to each H: (Human) leaf in an Extant System Task Model (STM(ext)), observe how user inputs are made using the user interface of the extant system. Consult the Extant Task Description (TD(ext)) for more detailed information as appropriate. Repeat the information elicitation cycle if necessary.

2. On the basis of the observations and notes made in (1) above, derive an Extant Interaction Task Model (ITM(ext)) by extending the Extant System Task Model (STM(ext)). Specifically, user-computer interactions observed earlier are incorporated into appropriate H: (Human) leaves of the Extant System Task Model (STM(ext)).

3. Document the Extant Interaction Task Model (ITM(ext)) using structured diagrams, and note user problems and additional information textually in a supporting table.

(III) Extant Interface Models (IM(ext))

Extant Interface Models describe the appearance and behaviour of user interface objects of the existing computer system. The models are derived following human factors observations of the existing user interface design. C: (Computer) leaves of the Extant System Task Model (STM(ext)) are then extended to describe the behaviours of the objects.

The procedures for deriving Extant Interface Models are summarised below.

Procedures for deriving Extant Interface Models, IM(ext)

1. Identify systematically user interface objects of the existing computer system. Do this for each C: (Computer) leaf of the Extant System Task Model (STM(ext)). In addition, note the responses of screen objects to user inputs described in the Extant Interaction Task Model (ITM(ext)).

2. Document the appearance and behaviour of screen objects using pictures and structured diagrams respectively.

Rule of thumb for deriving Extant Interface Models, IM(ext)

User interface objects associated with the adopted user interface environment need not be described in any detail, since they should be familiar to members of the design team.

(IV) Display Design Descriptions of the Extant Computer System

The set of display design descriptions that may be derived for an extant system comprises the following:

(a) An Extant Dialogue and Inter-Task Screen Actuation Description (DITaSAD(ext)). The structured diagram description specifies the context for actuating computer displays (including dialogue and error message screens).

(b) Extant Pictorial Screen Layouts (PSL(ext)). The layouts describe static characteristics of computer displays, such as screen composition, screen layout and grouping of screen objects. The pictorial description is augmented textually by a supporting table termed an Extant Dictionary of Screen Objects (DSO(ext)).

(c) An Extant Dialogue and Error Message Table (DET(ext)). The table is an index that describes textually the contents of computer messages referenced in the Extant Dialogue and Inter-Task Screen Actuation Description (DITaSAD(ext)).

The procedures for deriving Extant Display Design descriptions are summarised overleaf.

Procedures for deriving Display Design Descriptions of the extant computer system

With reference to the extant system descriptions derived earlier, namely the Extant Interaction Task Model (ITM(ext)) and Extant Interface Models (IM(ext)), note existing screen designs and actuations for important task steps performed by the user. In particular, note the characteristics of existing display designs that may be relevant to the target system. Generate the set of Extant Display Design descriptions as follows:

1. Note the relationship between important screen actuations and user actions described by the Extant Interaction Task Model (ITM(ext)). Action leaves of the latter model that are bounded between the screen actuations may be ignored. Assign unique identifiers to the screen displays to facilitate reference across the Extant Interaction Task Model (ITM(ext)), Extant Interface Models (IM(ext)) and the Extant Display Design descriptions to be generated. Referring to the notes, construct a structured diagram to describe how the behaviour of the computer is related to task executions of the user. Conditions that should be satisfied for each screen actuation should be indicated in the structured diagram and expanded textually in an accompanying table. The description derived is termed an Extant Dialogue and Inter-Task Screen Actuation Description (DITaSAD(ext)).

2. Note potential user errors and associated computer messages for the screen displays referenced in (1) above. In addition, note the contents of computer dialogue and information messages that support the user's task. Assign a unique identifier to each message, and index them according to the format of an Extant Dialogue and Error Message Table (DET(ext)).

3. Note the design characteristics of screen displays (including dialogue and error messages) referenced in (1) above, e.g. screen composition; screen layout; and object groupings. Document the information pictorially. The resulting description is termed an Extant Pictorial Screen Layout (PSL(ext)). To support the description, note the design characteristics of object constituents of the screens; e.g. how screen displays are actuated by particular objects, salient behaviours of objects, potential user problems with each screen display, and the design rationale underlying existing designs. The information is then tabulated textually according to the format of an Extant Dictionary of Screen Objects (DSO(ext)).

(V) Extant Statement of User Needs (SUN(ext))

An Extant Statement of User Needs (SUN(ext)) is essentially a summary of human factors observations made during the analysis of extant systems. Only information that is relevant to target system design, is recorded in the statement. Such information may include the following:

(a) problems experienced by users with existing designs;
(b) rationale, requirements and constraints of existing designs;
(c) potential solutions to problems observed in (a) above;

(d) needs of users that are either unsupported or supported poorly by existing designs.

The information on extant systems is carried forward to the Statement of User Needs Stage, where it is synthesised with new requirements of the target system. The extended set of user needs and requirements is then used as a basis for designing the target system.

The procedures for deriving an Extant Statement of User Needs are summarised below.

Procedures for deriving an Extant Statement of User Needs, SUN(ext)

1. With reference to key requirements of the target system, list the general design concerns and user needs to be investigated by extant systems analysis. Note that the list may be incremented or modified later, to accommodate additional design concerns identified following initial observations of the users of extant system(s).

2. For each item on the list, note information that is potentially relevant to the design of the target system; e.g. the design rationale, design constraints, and user problems of extant systems.

3. Record suggestions by users concerning how current problems may be avoided or solved. The suggestions should be interpreted with respect to the requirements of the target system.

4. Collate the information into appropriate categories. List them in order of priority so that they may be addressed appropriately during the design of the target system.

Case-Study Illustrations of an Extant Statement of User Needs (SUN(ext))
Figures A-1 and A-2 show case-study illustrations of an Extant Statement of User Needs derived for two extant systems; namely the system used at University College London Computer Centre (UCLCC) and the MacPassword™ (MPASS) application. An account of how the statements contributed to the design of a target system follows.

The statement collated from interviews conducted at University College London Computer Centre indicated that the computer should signal failed log-on events to the network manager in two ways. Firstly, if the network management workstation is attended, then occurrences of the events may be signalled either at a fixed time, or immediately in critical situations. In the latter instance, the computer may interrupt the network manager who may be engaged in other on-line tasks. Secondly, for failed log-on events that occur when the management workstation is unattended, the computer should record details of the event and alert the network manager on next log-on. In both cases, the user needs statements indicated that information pertinent to the failed log-on event should be summarised in the security alert display. Thus, managerial decisions on an appropriate response are supported. An example of the information that may be included (as suggested by the user needs statement for the MacPassword™ application), is the log-on password and time. The information (recorded automatically by the computer) may help to differentiate failed log-on events due to password mis-types, from 'real' attempts at hacking.

These suggestions derived from extant systems analysis were thus considered and incorporated appropriately during the design of the target system.

Figure A-1: Extract from the Extant Statement of User Needs for University College London Computer Centre (SUN(UCLCC))

1. The network manager should be alerted immediately to failed log-on events that involve sensitive databases. The alert should capture sufficiently the attention of the network manager (consider both visual and auditory alarms). Should the security breach occur when the network management workstation is unattended, the manager should be alerted to the event on next log-on.

2. Communication requirements between the network manager and users (and between the manager and the staff of external networks) should be supported adequately. In particular, facilities for synchronous and asynchronous communication should be provided, e.g. telephone and electronic-mail facilities respectively.

3. Information processing functions should accompany security alerts so that pertinent information on the event may be retrieved by the network manager. Thus, appropriate information may be collated to support decisions on the correct response to a security violation. To this end, the computer should provide functions to support basic database searches and the collation of various reports concerning network usage; e.g. a report of atypical log-ons (which may be defined by the network manager as usage outside normal working hours); log of previous security violations (which may include a breakdown of failed log-on and illegal log-on events); etc.

4. The permitted number of successive failed log-ons should be limited to ensure a secure network. When the limit is reached, the network management workstation should be 'locked out' temporarily; i.e. further log-ons are ignored by the computer for a specified period.

........etc.

Figure A-2: Extract from the Extant Statement of User Needs for the MacPassword™ Application (SUN(MPASS))

1. The owner of the computer was required to search event logs for evidence of security breaches. To support the task, basic search functions were provided to facilitate the identification of unusual usage events that have been recorded by the computer together with other information.

2. Password logs were useful for distinguishing between various causes of security alerts. Thus, passwords used in failed log-ons were recorded.

3. Obligatory password changes were enforced at regular intervals. Parameters that control computer access were easy to configure and implement.

5. Secondary measures to prevent access to the event logs by the hacker were omitted by the existing design. Such measures (e.g. a second password to access the logs) should be considered since event logs were the only record of usage activity. Thus, it will be more difficult for the hacker to remove traces of illegal access; e.g. by destroying or modifying entries in the event logs.

.........etc.

(VI) Extant Domain of Design Discourse (DoDD(ext))

The Extant Domain of Design Discourse describes the semantics of the extant system domain. The description supports target system design as follows:

(a) its establishes a basis for recruiting design features of extant systems;
(b) it supports the derivation of a Target Domain of Design Discourse (DoDD(y)).

Generally, a complete Extant Domain of Design Discourse is derived for an Extant *Current* System or an Extant *Related* System only if the systems are expected to be very similar to the *Target* System. Nevertheless, an Extant *Partial* System would be excluded in most cases. This condition follows because the domains of various types of extant systems, would intersect to different extents with the domain of the target system (by definition). In particular, the extent of intersection with the target system decreases in the following order: Extant Current System > Extant Related System >> Extant Partial System. Thus, the domain information derived from Extant Partial Systems would be too fragmented to contribute significantly to the conceptual design of the target system. Consequently, a complete characterisation of the domains of Extant Partial Systems is usually unnecessary.

The procedures for deriving an Extant Domain of Design Discourse are summarised below.

Procedures for deriving an Extant Domain of Design Discourse, DoDD(ext)

1. Identify general design concepts and real world objects manipulated by the extant system(s).

2. From the set identified in (1) above, select a subset of design concepts and objects considered to be relevant to the target system. Describe the semantics and entity relationships for the selected subset.

3. Record the information as a semantic net and assign unique identifiers to all object relations. For readability, the identifiers should be assigned serially from left to right, and from top to bottom (where possible). Note additional information textually, for all object relations in an accompanying table.

Rules of thumb for deriving an Extant Domain of Design Discourse, DoDD(ext)

1. The Extant Domain of Design Discourse should be sufficiently detailed to support the construction of task scenarios for the extant system. Discussions and analyses of extant designs may thus be facilitated.

2. The Extant Domain of Design Discourse should exclude device-dependent information. Instead, the information should focus on the semantics of the extant system domain.

Case-Study Illustrations of an Extant Domain of Design Discourse (DoDD(ext))
Figures A-3 and A-5 show the domain descriptions derived for the case-study. In particular, Extant Domain of Design Discourse descriptions were derived for two extant systems, namely the system used at University College London Computer Centre (UCLCC) and the MacPassword™ (MPASS) application. Additional information is recorded textually in tables that accompany the descriptions (see Figures A-4 and A-6).

On the basis of key characteristics of the target system, relevant subsets of the Extant Domain of Design Discourse for the extant systems (i.e. DoDD(UCLCC) and DoDD(MPASS)) were selected and synthesised. The composite description is then carried forward to the Statement of User Needs Stage, to support the derivation of a Target Domain of Design Discourse (DoDD(y)).

Figure A-3:   Domain of Design Discourse Description for University College London Computer Centre (DoDD(UCLCC))

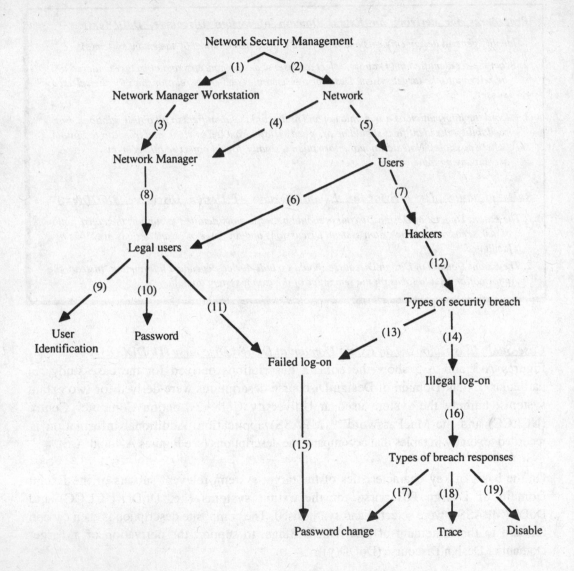

Figure A-4:   Table Supporting the Domain of Design Discourse Description for University College London Computer Centre (DoDD(UCLCC)) – Page 1

Node	Description	No.	Relations
Network Security Management	The network manager is responsible for enforcing legal access and usage of the network and network management workstation.	(1)	The task of ensuring workstation security is minor, since remote access is impossible without prior arrangement with the computer centre.
		(2)	The main task of the network manager is to ensure the security of the network.
NMW	The Network Management Workstation (NMW) is the computer used by the manager to control the network.	(3)	The network manager is normally the only user of the workstation.
Network	The network comprises a number of host machines and terminals.	(4)	Using the management workstation, the network manager can access and control the network remotely.
		(5)	The network is open to a range of users who may log-on locally or remotely via other terminals, networks and dialling lines.
Users	Users access the network to use its services.	(6)	Only authorised users can access the network legally.
		(7)	A hacker is an unauthorised user of the network.
Legal users	Legal users are authorised users of the network.	(8)	The network manager is a legal user of the network and network management workstation.
		(9)	A legal user possesses a unique user identification.
		(10)	A legal user is issued with a confidential password.
		(11)	Legal users may unintentionally commit failed log-ons, e.g. by mis-typing a password.
Hackers	Hackers are unauthorised users of the network.	(12)	Hackers commit security breaches.
Types of security breach	There are two types of security breach.	(13)	Failed log-on.
		(14)	Illegal log-on.

Figure A-4:   Table Supporting the Domain of Design Discourse Description for University College London Computer Centre (DoDD(UCLCC)) – Page 2

Node	Description	No.	Relations
Failed log-on	Failed log-ons occur when an incorrect user identification or password is input. In both cases, network access is denied.	(15)	In response to a failed log-on by a legal user, the network manager may enforce a password change, so as to encourage the selection of a more suitable password, e.g. one that is remembered easily.
Illegal log-on	An illegal log-on occurs when a hacker is successful in accessing the network.	(16)	Appropriate actions must be taken in response to an illegal log-on.
Types of breach responses	One or more actions may be taken in response to a security breach.	(17)	The user's password may be changed.
		(18)	Attempts may be made to trace the hacker.
		(19)	The user identification may be disabled until the user can be contacted to ascertain the cause of a security breach.

Figure A-5:   Domain of Design Discourse Description for the MacPassword™ Application (DoDD(MPASS))

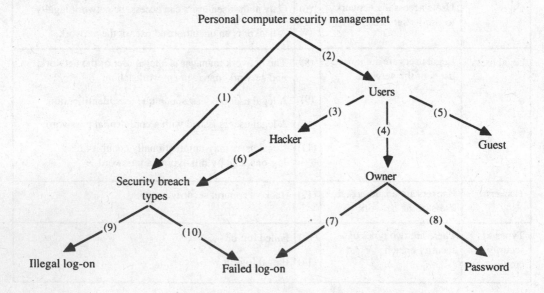

Figure A-6: Table Supporting the Domain of Design Discourse Description for the MacPassword™ Application (DoDD(MPASS))

Node	Description	No.	Relations
Personal computer security management	The owner of the personal computer is responsible for managing its security.	(1)	Security management involved searching through logs of usage information.
		(2)	The objective is to ensure that personal files are accessed only by the owner.
Users	There are three categories of users.	(3)	A hacker is an unauthorised user who attempts to access the computer.
		(4)	The owner is an authorised user, responsible for ensuring the security of the computer.
		(5)	A guest is an authorised user who may access particular files at the owner's discretion. A password is not required to access the files.
Hacker	A hacker is an illegal user of the computer.	(6)	A hacker may be responsible for two types of security breach, namely illegal log-ons (9); and failed log-ons (10).
Owner	The owner is responsible for securing the computer, and for the detection and action on any security breach.	(7)	A failed log-on may be attributed to a password mis-type by the owner.
		(8)	The owner uses a password to access the computer system.
Types of security breach	There are two types of security breach.	(9)	An illegal log-on is a successful attempt by a hacker at accessing the computer.
		(10)	A failed log-on is an unsuccessful attempt by either a hacker or the owner, at accessing the computer.

Annex B: Case-Study Illustration of Potential Extensions of the Design Descriptions and Notations of MUSE

Figures B-1 to B-5 show case-study examples of a preliminary attempt at extending the existing design notations and descriptions of MUSE. Specifically, the extensions comprise a simple organisation hierarchy, an information network description and a function flow description of performance. The objective of the extension is to enhance the support provided by the method for conceptual design specification. Since the proposed design notations and descriptions have not been subjected to comprehensive case-study tests, their promise and use are presently speculative. However, they are described here for the sake of completeness.

Figure B-1 shows a variant of the semantic net notation; namely a simple hierarchy. It is used here to describe the basic hierarchy of a work organisation, such as a job chart. The description defines basic contextual information that supports the specification of the work system and its sub-systems. For instance, basic relationships between job roles and information flows among entities of the work organisation are established by the hierarchy. For the case-study, a basic requirement of the organisation hierarchy was to free the managers (as much as possible) from repeated interruptions by network users. To prevent users contacting the managers directly, a problem referral scheme was operated. Thus, the network user was required to contact a network operator, who would solve the problem if possible. If not, the problem was referred to the network manager for solution or onward transmission (as appropriate). The solution was then communicated to the user directly, by the manager concerned (see Figure B-3 later).

Figure B-2 shows a simple network diagram.[1] The notation may be used to describe the content, direction and types of information flows between system (and sub-system) entities (informal/implicit information flows may also be included if appropriate). In this respect, two types of information flows are shown in Figure B-2; namely obligatory updates of new information (denoted by a circle, e.g. c1 and c2), and information requests (denoted by a diamond, e.g. r1 and r2). Note that system entities are denoted by rectangles and the flow of information corresponds to the direction of the linking arrow. The information exchanged is expanded in a supporting table.

---

[1] This notation is a modified version of the network diagrams used in the Jackson System Development method.

Figure B-1: Simple Organisation Hierarchy for University College London Computer Centre (UCLCC)

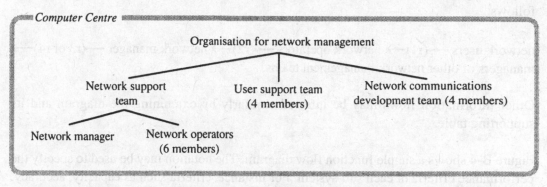

Staff Member	Basic Responsibilities
Network manager	Refer user problems to managers of other teams; solve user problems; plan, control and manage network (on- and off-site).
Network operators	Refer user problems to network manager; solve user problems; operate and control network (on- and off-site).
User support team	Solve user problems with software applications; introduce and develop new applications (on- and off-site).
Network communications development team	Solve user problems with specialised network communications; introduce and develop new systems (on- and off-site).

Figure B-2: A Simple Network Diagram of Information Flows

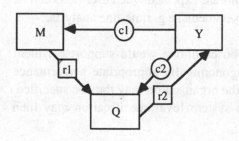

(1) Y is obliged to send reports c1 and c2 to M and Q respectively.
(2) Q may request information r1 from M, while Y may request information r2 from Q.

Information ID	Sender	Receiver	Content Summary
c1	Y	M	etc.
r1	etc.	etc.	etc.

A more detailed case-study illustration of information flows between entities of the network management organisation is shown in Figure B-3. For an example of how an information network may be described, consider the problem referral scheme considered earlier. In this respect, Figure B-3 shows that problems reported by network users may be forwarded as follows:

network users ——(r1)——> network operators ——(r2)——> network manager ——(r3 or r4)——> managers of other network management teams.

Other information flows may be inferred similarly by examining the diagram and its supporting table.

Figure B-4 shows a simple function flow diagram. The notation may be used to specify the performance criteria of each sub-system. For instance, criteria such as capacity, accuracy, range, response time, etc., may be specified for a particular set of function modules (performed by one or more sub-systems, e.g. an operator-computer worksystem). By comparing function flow descriptions of alternative specifications for a set of organisational goals, a design that incurs an acceptable level of worksystem costs (which include user costs) may then be selected. Note that function flow diagrams may also be used to facilitate high-level assessments of the safety and reliability of a system. For instance, alternative function flow diagrams (representing different paths for achieving organisational goals at comparable performance levels) may be constructed to support the computation and comparison of failure probabilities. Similar assessments at a lower level of specification may then be supported by structured diagrams.

A more detailed illustration of performance specification is shown in Figure B-5, for the network management case-study. In deriving the specifications, high-level requirements for staffing would have been considered. The projected staffing requirements constitute initial design assumptions that may be modified or defined more specifically, at later stages of system development. In other words, design iterations are expected when user tasks can be specified in sufficient detail to support workload assessments, e.g. time-line analysis.

It is anticipated that the design descriptions proposed above would support pertinent consideration of different conceptual designs. Ergonomically appropriate performance requirements that are consistent with the goals of the organisation may thus be specified. Having established these design constraints, sub-system level specification may then proceed according to MUSE.

Figure B-3: Information Network Description for University College London Computer Centre (UCLCC)

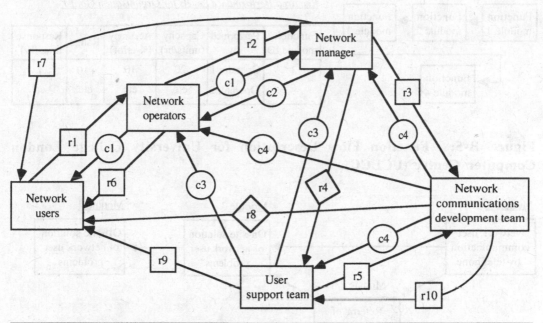

Info. ID	Sender	Receiver	Content Summary
c1	Network operators	Network users and manager	Information bulletin; updates on network faults and services.
c2	Network manager	Network operators	Changes in network status.
c3	User support team	Network operators and manager	Newly available applications and support services.
c4	Network communications development team	Network manager, operators and user support team	Newly developed applications and external network connections.
r1	Network users	Network operators	Queries concerning network status and problems with the network (Receiver replies to sender via r6).
r2	Network operators	Network manager	Advanced network problems encountered by users (Receiver replies to user directly via r7).
r3	Network manager	Network communications development team	Specialised comms. problems encountered by users (Receiver replies to user directly via r8).
r4	Network manager	User support team	Problems with software applications encountered by users (Receiver replies to user directly via r9).
r5	User support team	Network communications development team	Details on newly developed systems (Receiver replies to sender via r10).

Figure B-4:   A Simple Function Flow Description of System Performance

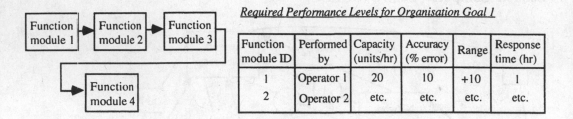

Required Performance Levels for Organisation Goal 1

Function module ID	Performed by	Capacity (units/hr)	Accuracy (% error)	Range	Response time (hr)
1	Operator 1	20	10	+10	1
2	Operator 2	etc.	etc.	etc.	etc.

Figure B-5:   Function Flow Description for University College London Computer Centre (UCLCC)

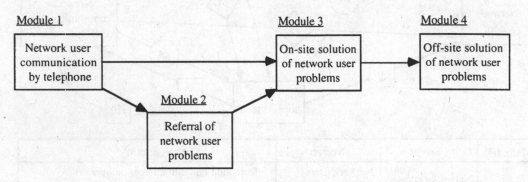

Function module ID	Performed by	User calls per day	Success rate (%)	Range (user calls per day)	Response time (hr)
Module 1	Network users	72	Indeterminate	0 to 144	–
Module 2	Network manager and operators	72	100	0 to 144	immediate
Module 3	Network operators	24	70	0 to 34	1
	Network manager	8	90	0 to 12	2
	Network communications development team	3	90	0 to 4	2
	User support team	8	90	0 to 12	2
Module 4	Network operators	8	80	0 to 10	3
	Network manager	4	90	0 to 6	4
	Network communications development team	1	90	0 to 2	6
	User support team	4	90	0 to 6	4

Bibliography

(a) List of Publications

1994

[1] Lim, K. Y. and Long, J. B., 1994, *MUSE:* A Structured Human Factors *M*ethod
for *US*ability *E*ngineering. In: Kidd, P. T. (ed.), *Proceedings of Fourth
International Conference on Human Aspects of Advanced Manufacturing & Hybrid
Automation,* Manchester (UK), July 1994, IOS Press.

[2] Lim, K. Y. and Long, J. B., 1994, Integration of a Structured Human Factors
Method with the Jackson System Development Method. To appear in: *Proceedings of
the Conference on 'Inter-Disciplinary Approaches to System Analysis and Design',*
European Association for Cognitive Ergonomics (EACE), 1994, Schaerding, Austria.

[3] Lim, K. Y. and Long, J. B., 1994, Structured Notations to Support Human Factors
Specification of Interactive Systems. To appear in: *Proceedings of BCS HCI'94
Conference,* August 1994, Glasgow, UK.

[4] Long, J. B. and Lim, K. Y., 1994, (Informal) MUSE Reduces Long Queues (at
ATM). In: *Proceedings of CHI'94 Conference (Research Symposium), Human
Factors in Computing Systems,* April 1994, Boston, USA.

[5] Palanque, Ph. A., Long, J. B., Tarby, J. C., Barthet, M. F. and Lim, K. Y., 1994,
Conception d'applications ergonomiques: une methodé pour informaticiens et une
methodé pour ergonomes. To appear in: *Ergonomie et Informatique Avancee (Ergo-
IA),* October 1994, Biarritz, France.

1993

[6] Lim, K. Y. and Long, J. B., 1993, Structured Notations for Human Factors
Specification of Interactive Systems. In: *Proceedings of HCI International 1993
Conference,* Orlando, Florida (USA), August 1993, Elsevier Science.

[7] Lim, K. Y. and Long, J. B., 1993, Instantiation of Task Analysis in a Structured
Method for User Interface Design. To appear in: Wearn, Y. (ed.), *Task Analysis in
HCI Workshop,* European Association for Cognitive Ergonomics (EACE) and USA
National Centre for Geographic Information and Analysis (NCGIA), Schärding
(Austria), June 9–11, 1992.

[8] Lim, K. Y. and Long, J. B., 1993, Task Analysis for System Design: Current Problems, Requirements and Solutions for Improving the Applicability of Task Analysis to System Design. To appear in: Wearn, Y. (ed.), *Task Analysis in HCI Workshop,* European Association for Cognitive Ergonomics (EACE) and USA National Centre for Geographic Information and Analysis (NCGIA), Schärding (Austria), June 9–11, 1992.

[9] Lim, K. Y. and Long, J. B., 1993, Structured Notations for Human Factors Specification. In: Lovesey, E. J. (ed.), *Contemporary Ergonomics, Proceedings of the Ergonomics Society's 1993 Conference,* Edinburgh (UK), April 1993, London: Taylor and Francis.

1992

[10] Lim, K. Y. and Long, J. B., 1992, A Method for (Recruiting) Methods: Facilitating Human Factors Input to System Design. In: Brooks, R. (ed.), *Proceedings of the ACM Annual Conference on Human Factors in Computing Systems (CHI'92),* Monterey (USA), May 3–7, 1992, ACM.

[11] Lim, K. Y. and Long, J. B., 1992, Computer-Based Tools for a Structured Human Factors Method. In: Mattila, M. (ed.), *Proceedings of the International Conference on Computer-Aided Ergonomics and Safety (CAES'92),* Tampere (Finland), May 18–20, 1992, Elsevier Science Holland.

[12] Lim, K. Y. and Long, J. B., 1992, Pitfalls of Rapid Prototyping: Observations on a Commercial System Development Project. In: Lovesey, E. J. (ed.), *Contemporary Ergonomics, Proceedings of the Ergonomics Society's 1992 Conference,* Aston (UK), April 7–10, 1992, London: Taylor and Francis.

[13] Lim, K. Y. and Long, J. B., 1992, Rapid Prototyping, Structured Methods and the Incorporation of Human Factors in System Design. In: MacLean, A. (ed.), *The St. Petersburg International Workshop on Human Computer Interaction,* Int. Centre of Scientific and Technical Information (Moscow), ACM SIGCHI (USA) and HFS (USA), August 4–7, 1992, St. Petersburg).

[14] Lim, K. Y. and Long, J. B., 1992, Integrating Ergonomics with System Development. In: Sabourin, M. (ed.), *Abstracts of the XXV International Congress of Psychology,* Brussels, 19–24 July 1992, *International Journal of Psychology,* Vol. 27, Issues 3 and 4, June/August 1992.

[15] Lim, K. Y., Long, J. B. and Silcock, N., 1992, Integrating Human Factors with System Development: An Overview of a Structured Human Factors Method. In: Hitchins, D. K. (ed.), *Proceedings of the International Conference on Information-Decision-Action Systems in Complex Organisations (IDASCO'92),* Oxford (UK), April 6–8, 1992, IEE.

[16] Lim, K. Y., Long, J. B. and Silcock, N., 1992, Integrating Human Factors with the Jackson System Development Method: An Illustrated Overview. In: Barber, P. and Laws, J. (eds.), *Ergonomics* (Special Issue on Cognitive Ergonomics III), 1992, 33(12), London: Taylor and Francis.

1991

[17] Lim, K. Y., Silcock, N. and Long, J. B., 1991, Case-Study Illustration of a Structured Method for User Interface Design. In: Lovesey, E.J. (ed.), *Contemporary Ergonomics, Proceedings of the Ergonomics Society's 1991 Conference,* Southampton, April 1991, London: Taylor and Francis.

[18] Silcock, N., Lim, K. Y. and Long, J. B., 1991, A Structured Method for User Interface Design. In: Queinnec, Y. and Daneillou, F. (eds.), *Proceedings of the 11th Congress of the International Ergonomics Association's 1991 Conference,* Paris, July 1991, pp. 67–68, London: Taylor and Francis.

1990

[19] Lim, K. Y., Long, J. B. and Silcock, N., 1990, Motivation, Research Management and a Conception for Structured Integration of Human Factors with System Development Methods: An Illustration Using the Jackson System Development Method. In: van der Veer, G et al. (eds.), *Proceedings of the Fifth European Conference on Cognitive Ergonomics,* Urbino (Italy), September 3–6, 1990, pp. 359–374, Golem Press.

[20] Lim, K. Y., Long, J. B. and Silcock, N., 1990, Integrating Human Factors with Structured Analysis and Design Methods: An Enhanced Conception of the Extended Jackson System Development Method. In: Diaper, D. et al (eds.), *Proceedings of the Third IFIP Conference on HCI (Interact '90),* pp. 225–230, Elsevier Science Publishers, North Holland.

[21] Lim, K. Y., Long, J. B. and Silcock, N., 1990, Requirements, Research and Strategy for Integrating Human Factors with Structured Analysis and Design Methods: The Case of the Jackson System Development Method. In: Lovesey, E.J. (ed.), *Contemporary Ergonomics, Proceedings of the Ergonomics Society's 1990 Conference,* Leeds, April 1990, pp. 32–38, London: Taylor and Francis.

[22] Silcock, N., Lim, K. Y. and Long, J. B., 1990, Requirements and Suggestions for a Structured Analysis and Design (Human Factors) Method to Support the Integration of Human Factors with System Development. In: Lovesey, E.J. (ed.), *Contemporary Ergonomics, Proceedings of the Ergonomics Society's 1990 Conference,* Leeds, April 1990, pp. 425–430, London: Taylor and Francis.

1989

[23] Walsh, P., Lim, K. Y., Long, J. B. and Carver, M. K., 1989, JSD and the Design
of User Interface Software. In: Barber, P. and Laws, J. (eds.), *Ergonomics* (Special
Issue on Methodological Issues in Cognitive Ergonomics), Vol 32(11), November
1989, pp. 1483–1498, London: Taylor and Francis.

1988

[24] Walsh, P., Lim, K. Y., Long, J. B. and Carver, M. K., 1988, Integrating Human
Factors with System Development. In: Heaton, N. and Sinclair, M. (eds.) Designing
End-User Interfaces. *Pergamon Infotech State of the Art Reports 15:8,* 1988, pp.
111–120, Pergamon Infotech Limited England, Oxford.

(b) List of Internal Reports

[WD 1]   Lim, K. Y., Integrating Human Factors into System Development – The
Project Proposal.

[WD 2]   Walsh, P. and Lim, K. Y., Elaboration of Aims in the Project Planning
Document [WD 1].

[WD 3]   Walsh, P. and Lim, K. Y., Structured Methods and the Design of Interactive
Software.

[WD 4]   Lim, K. Y. and Walsh, P., Formal Methods of Software Development.

[WD 5]   Walsh, P., Using JSD as a Description Language.

[WD 6]   Walsh, P., Specification of Direct Manipulation Interfaces (incomplete report).

[WD 7]   Walsh, P., Description of the MacDraw User Interface using Action Effect
Rules.

[WD 8]   Walsh, P., On Building JSD Models from Informal User Requirements
Specifications.

[WD 9]   Lim, K. Y., An Assessment of the MacDraw Application Package.

[WD 10] Walsh, P., Applying JSD to the Specification of Human Factors Design
Issues.

[WD 11] Lim, K. Y., An Anatomy of a Software Methodology.

[WD 12] Lim, K. Y., On Terminology and Design Perspectives.

[WD 13] Walsh, P., Task Analysis Methods in HCI Design.

[WD 14]   Long, J. B., Some Tentative Initial Thoughts Towards a Possible Framework for Modelling Systematic Methods of System Development.

[WD 15]   Lim, K. Y., Task Strategies, Metaphors and the Integration of Interface Design into JSD.

[WD 16]   Walsh, P., Proposed Plan of Action for Network Manager Case-Study.

[WD 17]   Lim, K. Y., Essential Considerations for Interfacing Task Analysis and Task Modelling with JSD Modelling.

[WD 18]   Lim, K. Y., On Reasoning about the Project and DDN Case-Study Proposals.

[WD 19]   Lim, K. Y., On Reasoning about User Interface Design using Extended JSD in Conjunction with an Extant Systems Analysis Approach.

[WD 20]   Walsh, P., The Analysis of Task Objects Method (ATOM): A Method of Representing User Activities for User Interface Design.

[WD 21]   Walsh, P. and Lim, K. Y., Functional Specification for the Network Manager Workstation.

[WD 22]   Lim, K. Y., Rationalization of the Project Developments Based on the JSD* Models Described in WD 19 and Infotech Paper 1.

[WD 23]   Lim, K. Y., Some Considerations on Notational Requirements for Task and Interface Information Capture: Towards the Conception of a JSD* Notation.

[WD 24]   Lim, K. Y., Reply To D&L's Human Computer Interaction Engineering (HCIE) Conception – An Explication of the Corresponding Definitions of Human Factors (HF) Terms adopted by the RARDE Project and KYL's PhD Work.

[WD 25]   Lim, K. Y., Explication of KYL's Conception of the Research Activities Required for the Derivation and Specification of the JSD* Method.

[WD 26]   Lim, K. Y., A Perspective on HCI Model Classes and their Life-Cycle w.r.t. the System Design Process: Providing a Rational Basis for the Current Conception of JSD*.

[WD 27]   Lim, K. Y., Case-Study Illustrations of a Conception of Structured Interface Design Within JSD*.

[WD 28]   Lim, K. Y., Towards a JSD* Method – A Review of the Research Scope, Requirements and Constraints; and the Proceduralisation of the JSD* User Interface Design Process.

[WD 29]   Lim, K. Y., A Preliminary Conception of the Stage-Wise Process of User Interface Design within JSD*: A Case-Study Instantiation using the University College London Recreation Facility Booking System (UCL RFBS).

[WD 30]   Coles, S. and Lim, K. Y., Towards a Task Analysis Method for Interface Design within JSD*: The Usefulness of Generification Procedures.

[WD 31]   Silcock, N. and Lim, K. Y., Towards a Task Analysis Method for JSD*: An Analytical and Procedural Review of Task Analysis for Knowledge Descriptions and Knowledge Analysis of Tasks.

[WD 32]   Silcock, N., Towards a Task Analysis Method for JSD*: An Analytical and Procedural Review of 'Hierarchical Task Analysis'; 'Hierarchical Planning' and 'GOMS'.

[WD 33]   Lim, K. Y., An Overview of the First Pass Version of the JSD*(HF) Method.

[WD 34]   Silcock, N. and Lim, K. Y., A First Pass Version of the Proceduralised JSD*(HF) Method.

[WD 35]   Lim, K. Y., An Appraisal of the Requirements of the Digital Data Network Network Management Case-Study Test – Perspectives Corresponding to Client Simulation and Research Constraints.

[WD 36]   Silcock, N. and Lim, K. Y., Event Tables for the DDN Case-Study.

[WD 37A] Lim, K. Y., JSD*(HF) Deliverables Corresponding to the First Conjunction with the JSD*(SE) Design Stream – Outputs of the CTM and SUN Stages for the Trouble-Shooting Module of the DDN NMS Case-Study.

[WD 37B] Silcock, N. and Lim, K. Y., JSD*(HF) Deliverables Corresponding to the First Conjunction with the JSD*(SE) Design Stream – Outputs of the CTM and SUN Stages for the Security Module of the DDN NMS Case-Study.

[WD 38A] Lim, K. Y., The DDN NMS Case-Study – Documenting Outputs of the ESA and GTM Stages for the Trouble-Shooting Module and Associated Refinements Suggested for the JSD*(HF) Method.

[WD 38B] Silcock, N., The DDN NMS Case-Study – Documenting Outputs of the ESA and GTM Stages for the Security Module and Associated Refinements Suggested for the JSD*(HF) Method.

[WD 39A] Lim, K. Y., The DDN NMS Case-Study – Documenting Outputs of the CTM and Post-CTM Stages for the Trouble-Shooting Module and Associated Refinements Suggested for the JSD*(HF) Method.

[WD 39B] Silcock, N. and Lim, K. Y., The DDN NMS Case-Study – Documenting Outputs of the CTM and Post-CTM Stages for the Security Module and Associated Refinements Suggested for the JSD*(HF) Method.

[WD 40A] Lim, K. Y., JSD*(HF) Specifications of the User Interface for the DDN NMS Case-Study (Trouble-Shooting Module).

Subject Index

Printed in the United States
By Bookmasters